Melbou

Melbourne, the "world's most liveable city" has many unique views, some readily identifiable, while other aspects are less prominent but a favourite for many.

Melbourne's **D**elights represents a "through the lens" photographic essay by people from various walks of life... respected political leaders, media personalities and sporting and corporate achievers. It brings together a diverse range of community leaders to present Melbourne as they see it. For some, this was their first attempt at serious photography.

The contributors to **M**elbourne's **D**elights share another vision - to demonstrate their support for the research and service programs of the Muscular Dystrophy Association.

Muscular Dystrophy Association

Melbourne's Delights

Contents

Web
www.MelbournesDelights.org

Email
Ask@MelbournesDelights.org

Foreword

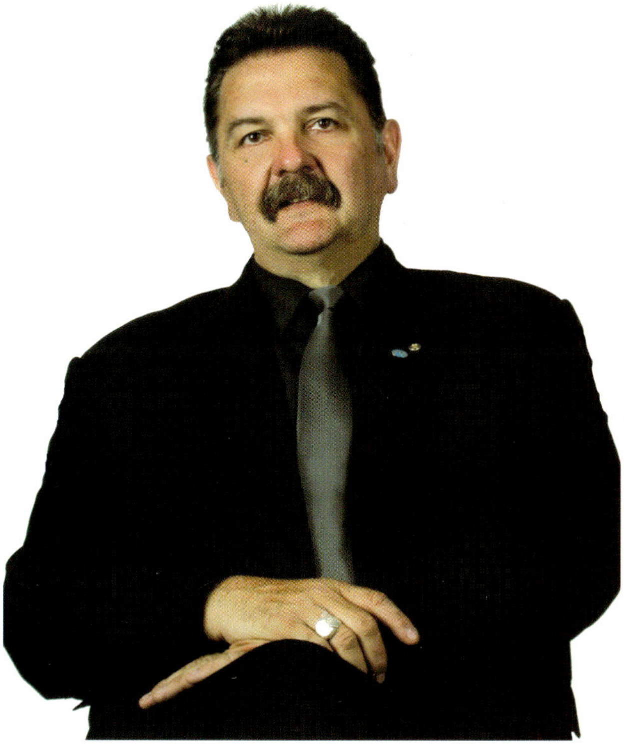

Melbourne's **D**elights was born from an original idea several years ago, the catalyst being my interest in photography.

This interest has spanned many years with several published photos, however photography took a back seat shortly after my youngest son Ryan, was diagnosed to be affected by Duchenne Muscular Dystrophy.

My family, like many others who live with Muscular Dystrophy have learnt to make the most of opportunities as they present themselves and while they are possible. Ryan loves Melbourne and enjoys sampling its variety, particularly its many coffee establishments.

In creating **M**elbourne's **D**elights, I saw the opportunity to showcase this amazing city in which we live, and in the process, rekindle my love of photography. More importantly, **M**elbourne's **D**elights presented the opportunity to raise awareness of Muscular Dystrophy within the larger community through the involvement of the diverse group of people who have lent their talents to creating this beautiful collection of images.

The contributors to **M**elbourne's **D**elights have, through their involvement, demonstrated their support for the research and service programs provided by the Muscular Dystrophy Association.

Melbourne's **D**elights provided me with the opportunity to see Melbourne from a different perspective - through the eyes of many of our community leaders. The diversity and ever-changing nature of Melbourne's scenery is perhaps its greatest charm, and it is this diversity that has been captured by the "celebrity photographers" in **M**elbourne's **D**elights. It is a photographic celebration that will endure and continue to remind us of the city's beauty.

Boris M Struk

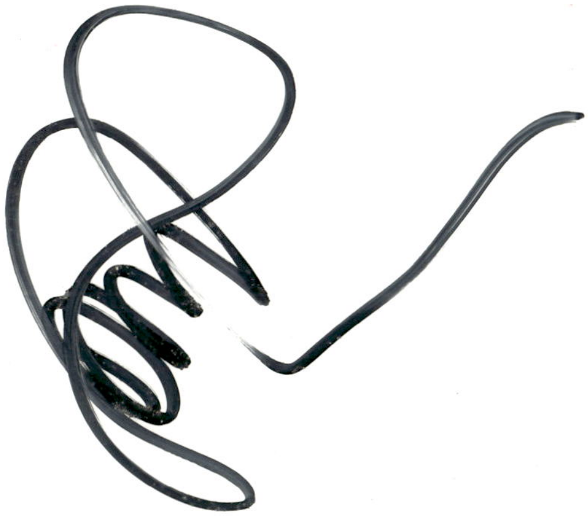

John Bertrand

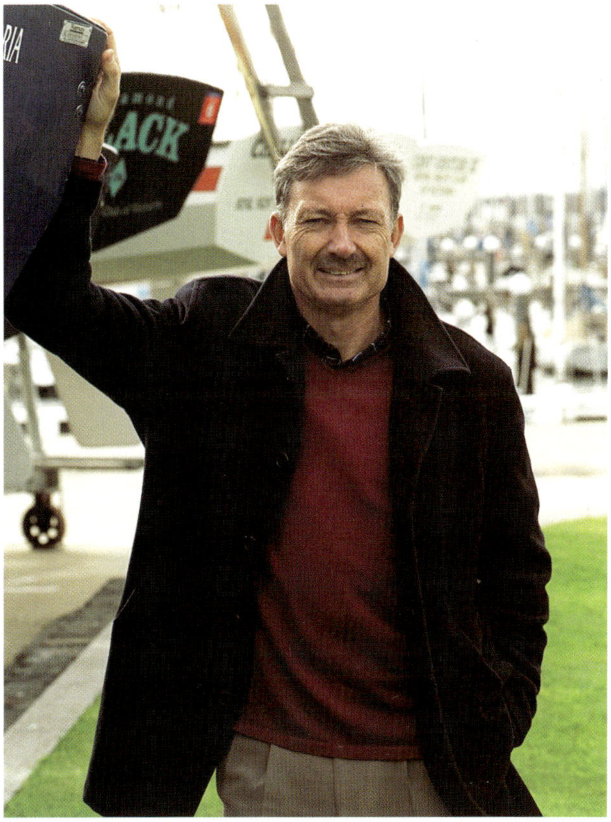

John Bertrand AM, would have you believe that his main claim to fame is that he is a proud Australian.

To his fellow Australians he is much more.

He is the Australian who skippered the winged keel *Australia 2* to victory against Dennis Connor's *Liberty* to win the 1983 America's Cup, breaking 132 years of American domination and, in the process, breaking the longest-running record in the history of modern sport. The comeback from 3-1 down and the final race victory, billed as the *race of the century*, was perhaps the greatest upset in modern sports history.

Ask any Australian where he or she was the day that it happened, and they will remember.

The *Australia 2* team victory was voted by Australia's Sports Hall of Fame as *the greatest team performance in 200 years of Australian sport.*

A World Champion and Olympic medallist, John represented Australia in five America's Cups and two Olympic Games. In over 25 years of America's Cup campaigning, he was involved in all areas of activity…from skipper of *Australia 2* to Chairman of *OneAustralia*.

Australia conferred a Member of the Order of Australia (AM) on John in 1985. His biography 'Born to Win" published in 1985, was at the time the largest-selling biography in Australian publishing history.

Together with Herb Elliot and Dawn Fraser, John was a member of the 2000 Australian Olympic team, acting as a mentor to the team athletes during the Sydney Olympic Games.

John is both a businessman and philanthropist. He is co-owner and Chairman of the television production and distribution company World Wide Entertainment which exports television shows to 120 countries worldwide.

He is Chairman of the Alannah and Madeline Foundation which provides crisis care for children who suffer violent crime. He is also a Director of the Australia Day Committee.

John holds a Degree in Mechanical Engineering from Monash University and a Master of Science Degree from MIT in Boston.

He is a life member of both the America's Cup Hall of Fame and Australia's Sports Hall of Fame.

Williamstown - "Melbourne traditionally has turned it's back on the sea. But with all the new developments of Webb Dock and Port Melbourne, more and more people are now understanding and appreciating the beauty and tranquility of the sea.

I chose this view of Melbourne since it represents another very important aspect of our city....over looking Port Phillip Bay from Williamstown, a view more people are discovering".

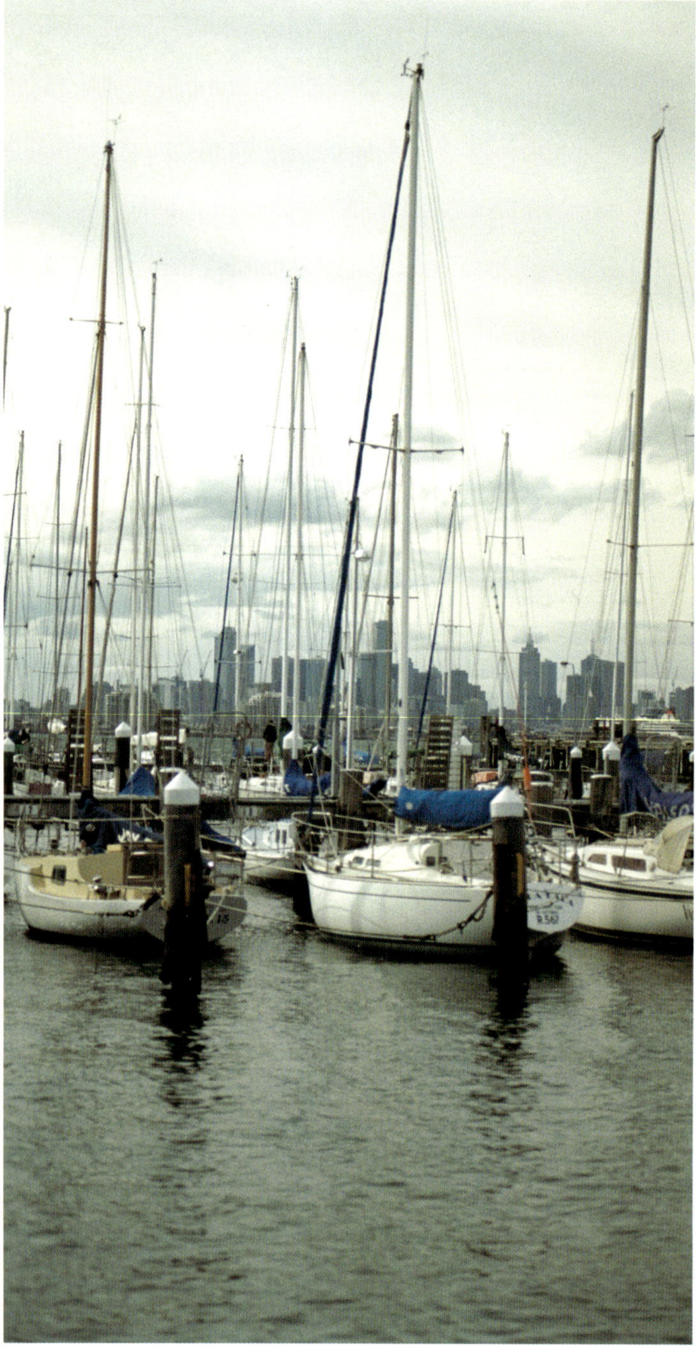

Yachts on the Bay

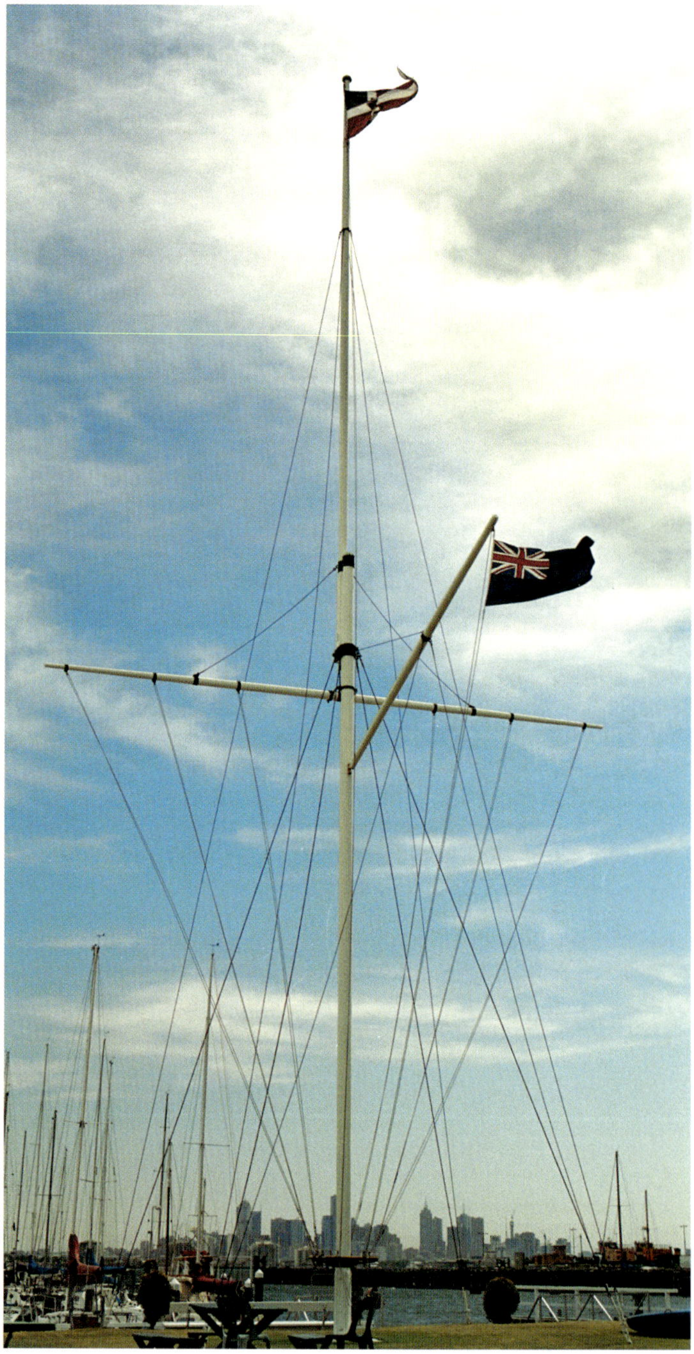

Royal Victoria Yacht Club flag pole

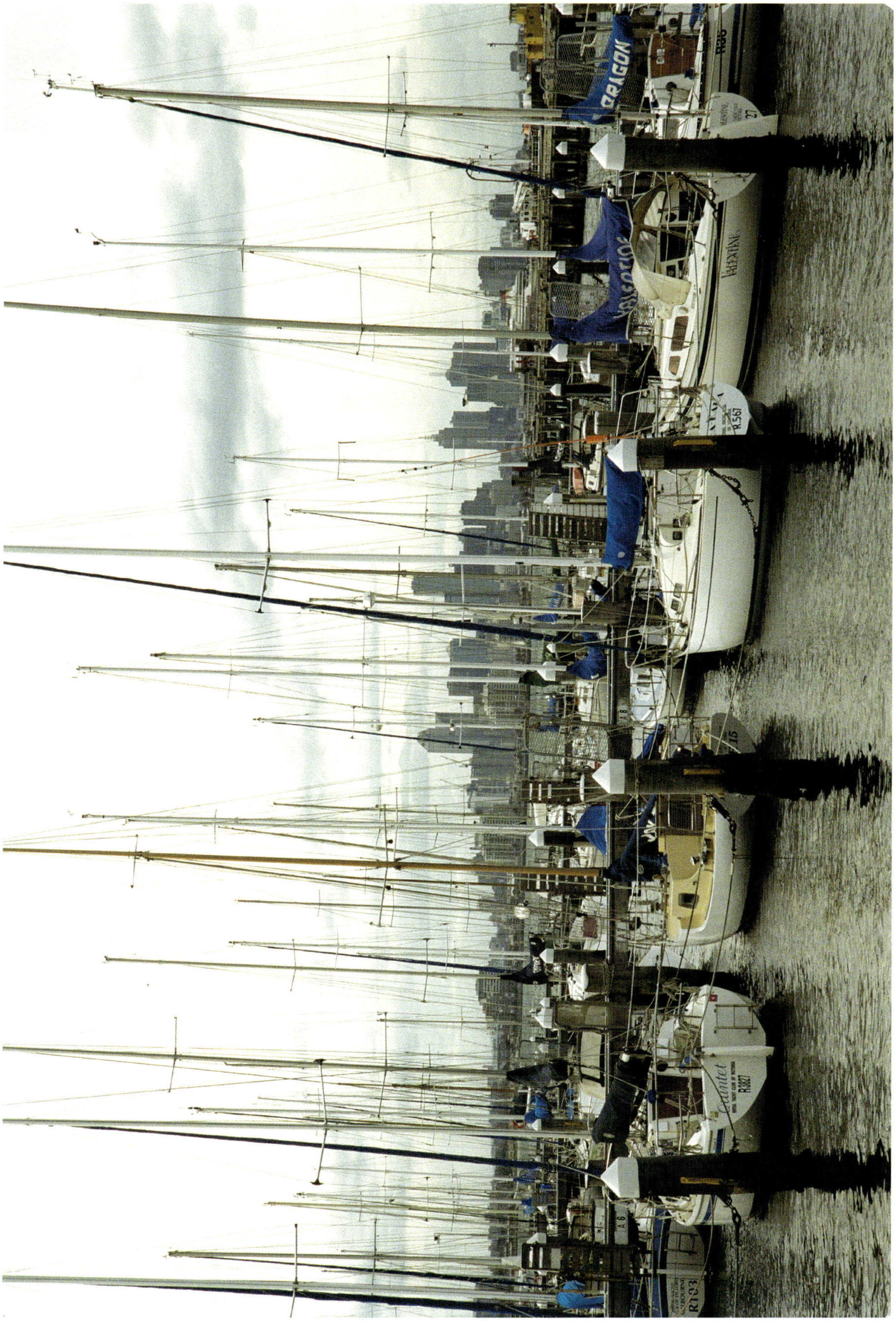

Santo Cilauro

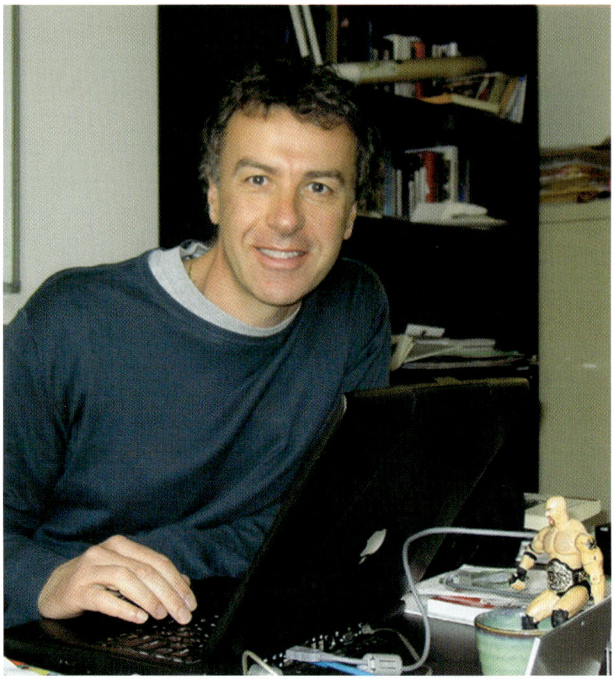

Santo Cilauro, regularly seen as a presenter on *The Panel*.

He is a writer, director and producer of film and television with the Working Dog team. Credits include *The Dish, The Castle, All Aussie Adventures*, *Frontline, The Campaign, A River Somewhere, Funky Squad* and *The Late Show*. Santo's latest venture, with his longtime partners Tom Gleisner and Rob Sitch, is an hilarious comedy/travel book: *Molvania – A Land Untouched By Modern Dentistry* published in Australia by Hardie Grant Books.

The Old Shot Tower, Alexandra Parade, Collingwood - I love the shot tower (I hope it IS a shot tower – that's what our only Australian neighbour told us it was – Italians used to call it "the chimney" despite the fact no smoke ever came out of it). It is the very first building I can ever remember. I was born in a house that was directly across the road from it and moved to a house where it was visible from both the front and back yards.

I have vivid memories of how every September (in those days Collingwood would make it to the finals each year), the top would be adorned in black and white flags and balloons. Unfortunately, throughout the 70s and early 80s, they never won a premiership – and the mornings after they lost, the decorations would suddenly and mysteriously disappear. I have never to this day seen anyone going in or out of the tower. I don't know whether it's still being used. In fact, I'm not sure it was EVER used. It is and always has been "just there".

(By the way, I think a shot tower is a tall building where, inside, they drop molten lead from the top. By the time it gets to the bottom it's perfectly round – and this is how they make the buckshot or ball for ammunition.)

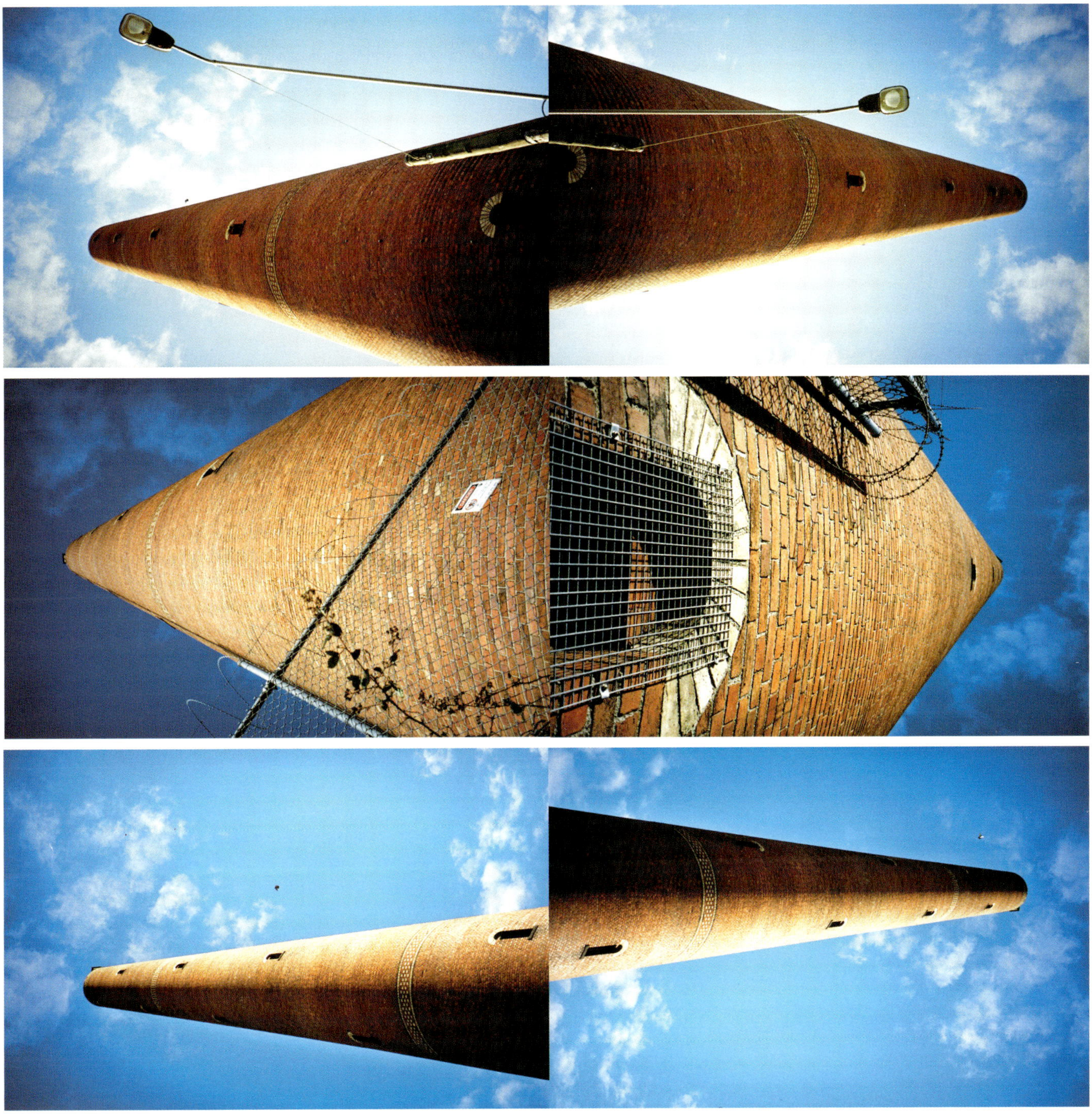

The Old Shot Tower, Alexandra Parade, Collingwood

Ron Clarke

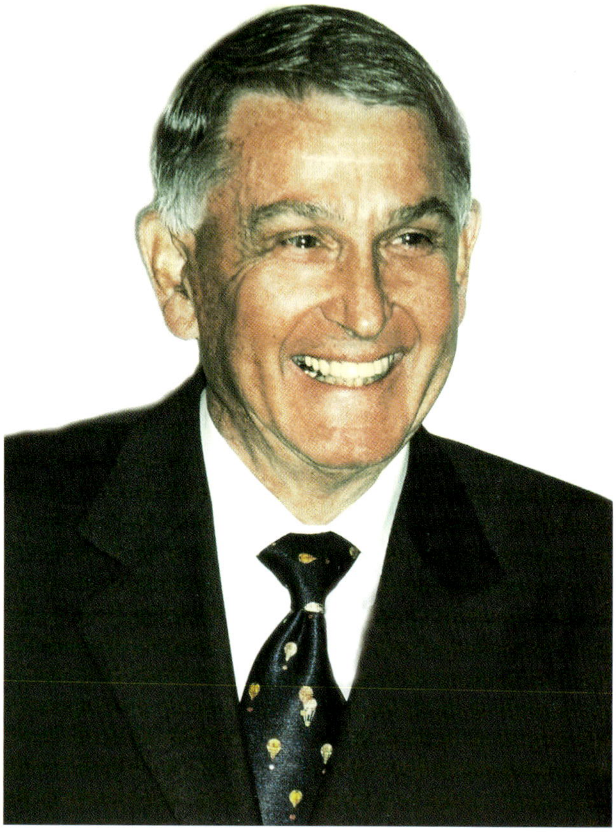

Ron Clarke MBE

Ron Clarke's sporting prowess is legendary. During the period 1965 to 1972 he was the holder of every world record between the track distances of two and ten miles. His sporting achievements sometimes over shadowed the significant impact that he has also made within the community, business and cultural arenas.

Being the author of 12 books and having opportunities to provide sports commentary, both on television and in the print media has provided Ron Clarke with an enduring interaction with sport, its people and their organisations. The sport's link has also prevailed in his business ventures. Ron Clarke has been involved in sports footwear, fitness clubs and sporting goods.

His formal education initially led to accountancy, then to sporting affiliated business and of late, to philanthropy as President of the Council for the Encouragement of Philanthropy in Australia Trust.

"Around The Tan" - "The Tan" around Melbourne's Royal Botanic Gardens is my favourite place in the world and, I suppose if you add up the hours of the weeks of the years I have devoted to running around and around it, this is the spot where I have spent the greatest proportion of my adulthood.

It is such a wondrous location. The trees, the river, the gardens, the people, everything about it combines to produce an aura of relaxed energy that makes it impossible not to be enchanted immediately one steps onto the hallowed ground.

Iit also engenders a sense of history and heritage. Hundreds of thousands of runners must have wound their way along the same paths and around the Gardens in the years since they were formed in the 1880's.

The early morning sun streaming through the large oaks with the steam still rising off the river as you stride out towards the Anderson Street hill is the memory I cherish more than any other of my home city.

Certainly in Melbourne, the catch-cry of…"I'll see you 'around The Tan'" is as famous among the generations of Victorian athletes as "Up there Cazally" is with followers of Australian Rules Football.

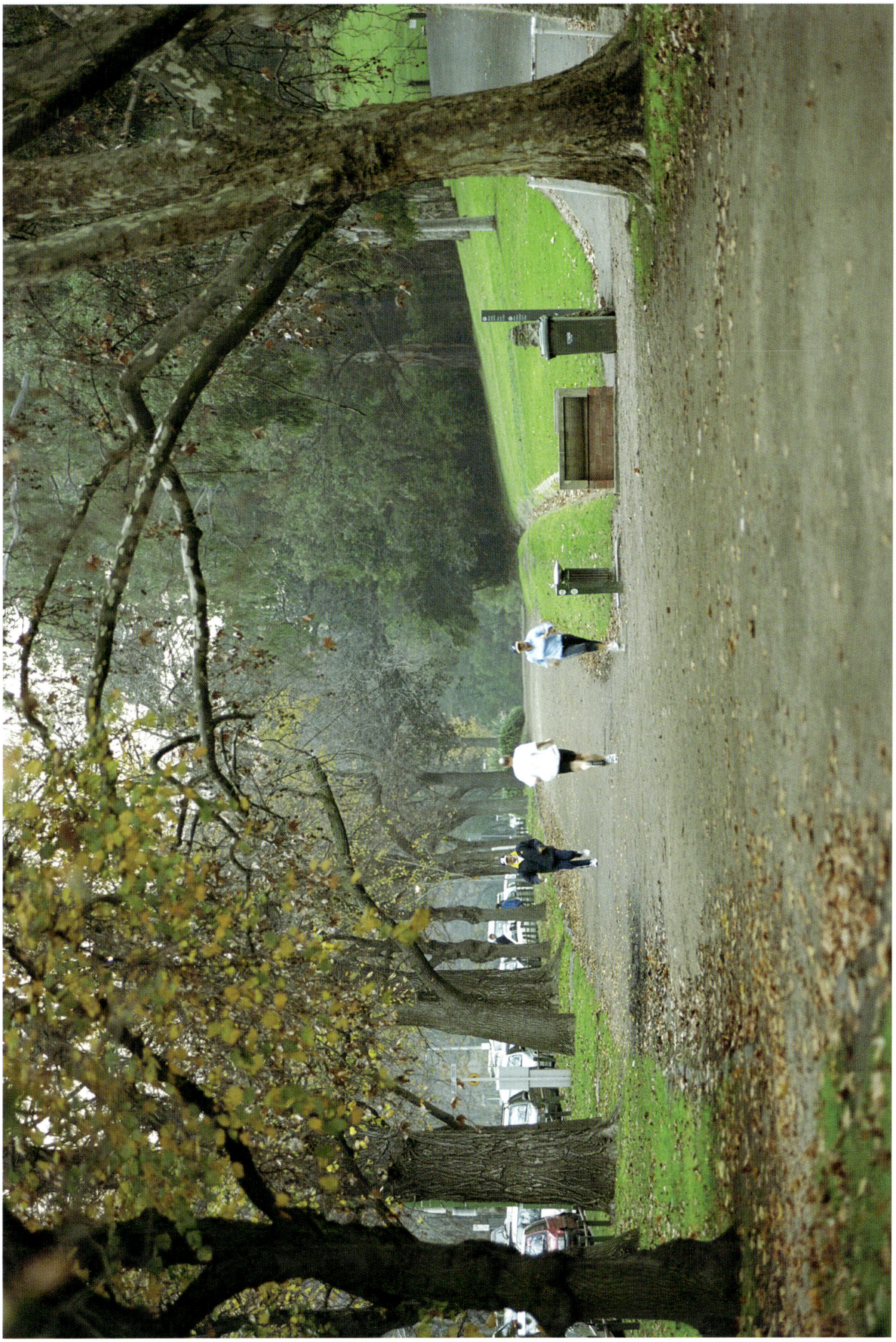

"The Tan"

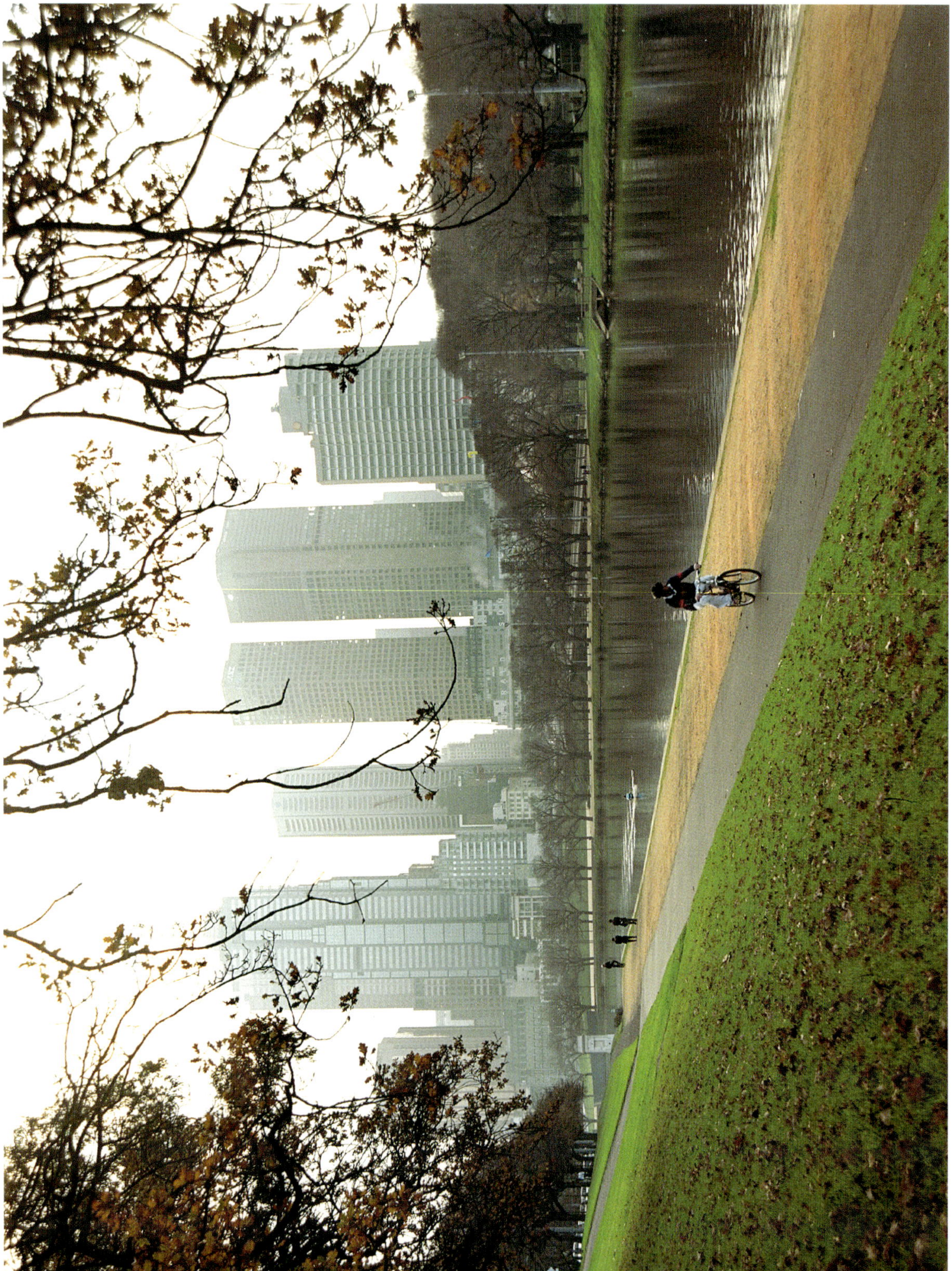

Melbourne and the Yarra River

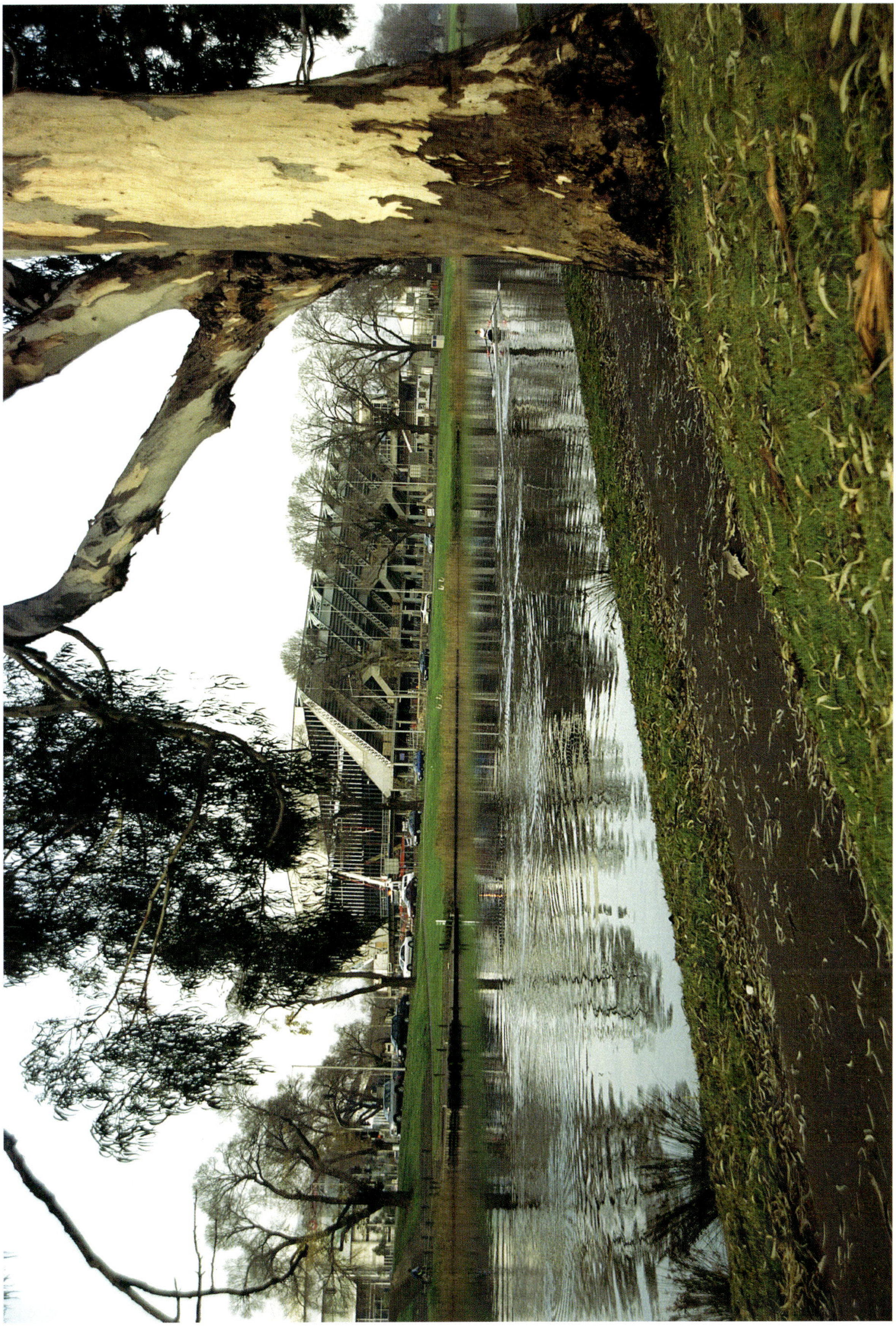

Yarra River

Sir Zelman Cowen

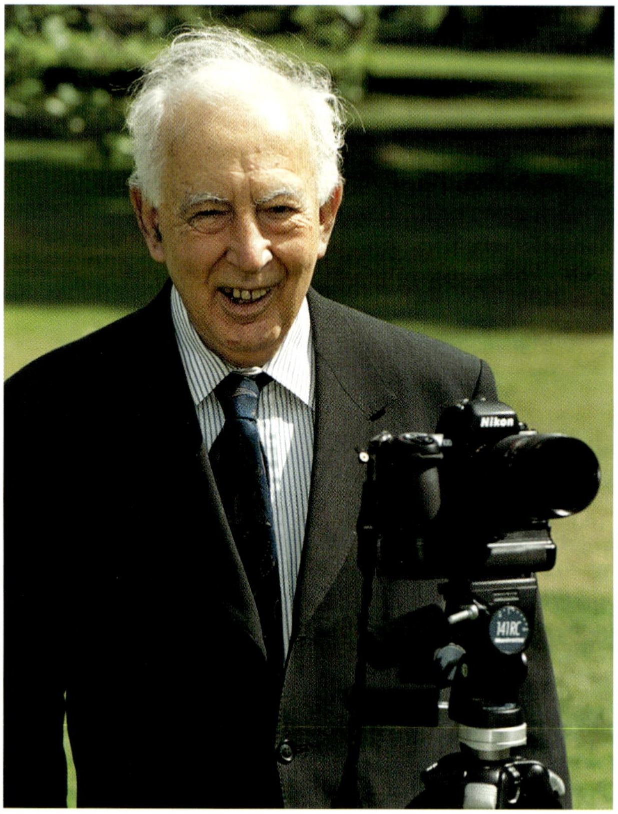

Rt Hon Sir Zelman Cowen AK, GCMG, GCVO, QC, DCL was born in Melbourne on 7 October, 1919. He was educated at Scotch College and the University of Melbourne, where he completed degrees in Arts and Law. In 1940, he was elected as Rhodes Scholar for Victoria, taking up that scholarship in 1945, after war service in the Australian Navy.

At Oxford, he was Vinerian Scholar in Law, and from 1947 to 1950, he was a Fellow of Oriel College. He then returned to Australia as Professor and Dean of the Faculty of Law at Melbourne University. In 1967, he became Vice-Chancellor of the University of New England, New South Wales, and in 1970 became Vice-Chancellor of the University of Queensland. In December 1977, he was sworn in as nineteenth Governor-General of Australia, and served until July 1982. He then accepted the appointment as Provost (Head) of Oriel College, Oxford, his old College. This was Cecil Rhodes' own College. From 1988, he was also a Pro-Vice-Chancellor of the University of Oxford. He retired from these posts in July 1990. In addition, from 1983-1988, he was Chairman of the British Press Council. He was foundation Chairman of the Australian Studies Centre in London from 1982-1990, and was Chairman of the Van Leer Institute in Jerusalem from 1988-95 and is currently its Honorary Chairman. From 1992-95, he was National President of the Order of Australia Association Ltd, and from 1993-1995 he was National President of the Australia-Britain Society. He was Chairman of the Board of John Fairfax Holdings Ltd from 1992-94, and a Director of the Board from 1994-96. From 1995-2000, he was Chairman of the Australian National Academy of Music.

He has written extensively on legal, political and social themes. An edited version of his speeches as Governor-General was published in 1986 under the title *A Touch of Healing*. His Boyer Lectures for 1969 were published as *The Private Man*. Among his books is a biography of *Sir Isaac Isaacs* (1967), 2nd edition (1993), the first Australian born Governor-General.

He was first Knighted in 1976, and is the recipient of other Knighthoods, honorary degrees, fellowships and awards from Australia, the United Kingdom, the United States, Israel and Italy. He was awarded the Knight Grand Cross of the Order of Merit of the Italian Republic, which was conferred by President Cossiga in Rome in 1990.

He and Lady Cowen returned to live in Australia in August 1990. Their principal base is in Melbourne, and they also have a residence in Brisbane.

Treasury Gardens - "These photographs provide an enduring reminder of my great good fortune in living in a *city of gardens*."

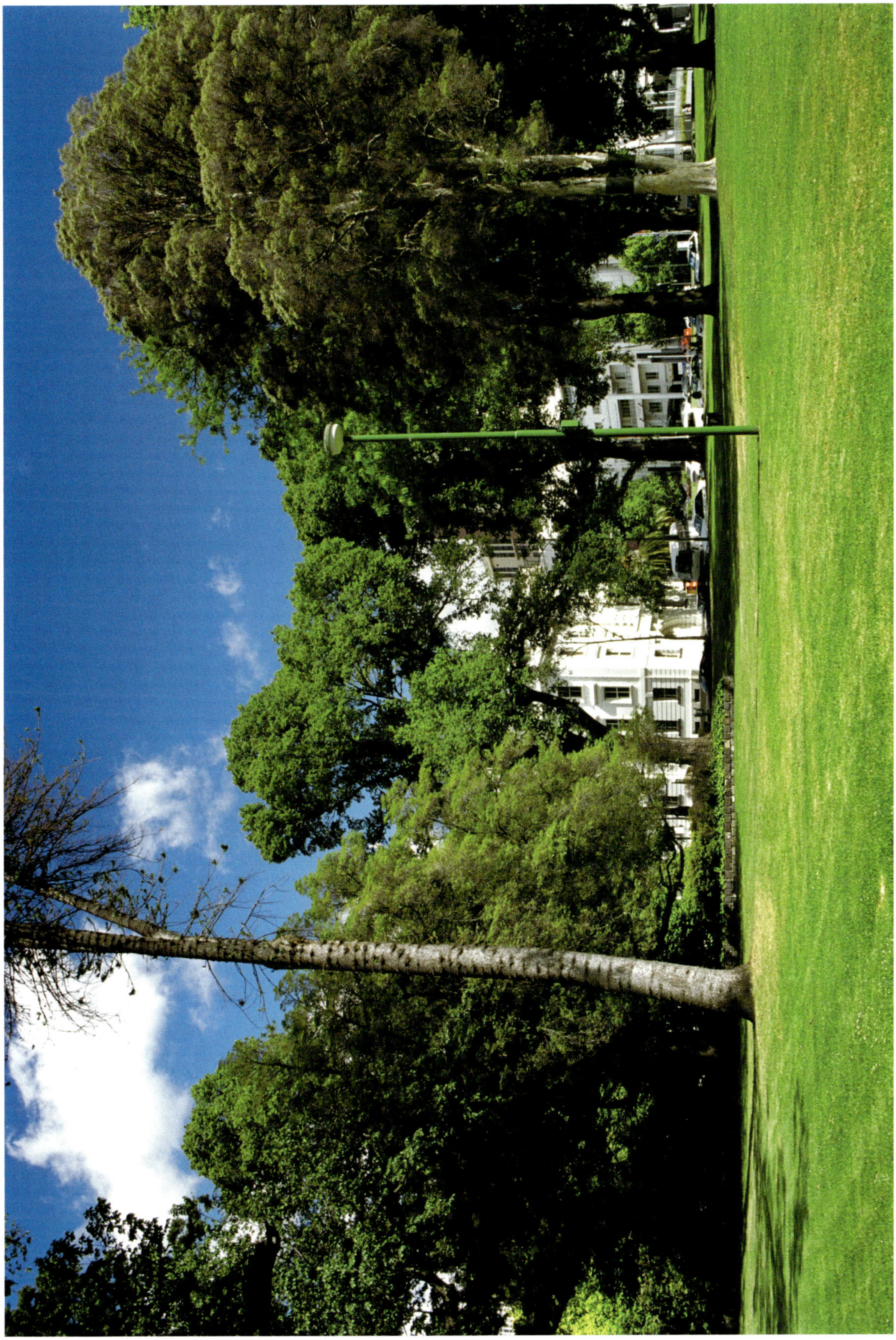

Treasury Gardens

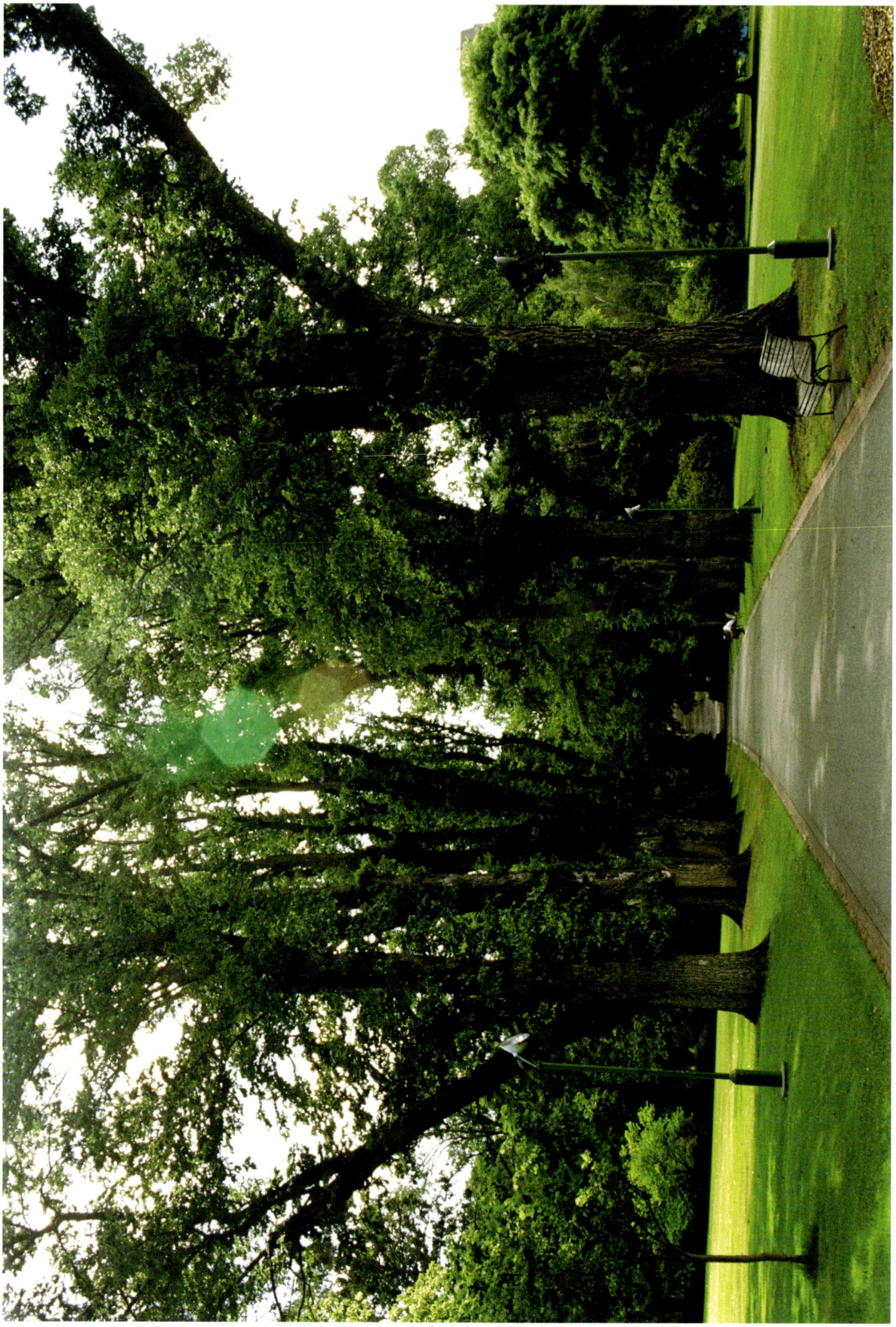

Treasury Gardens

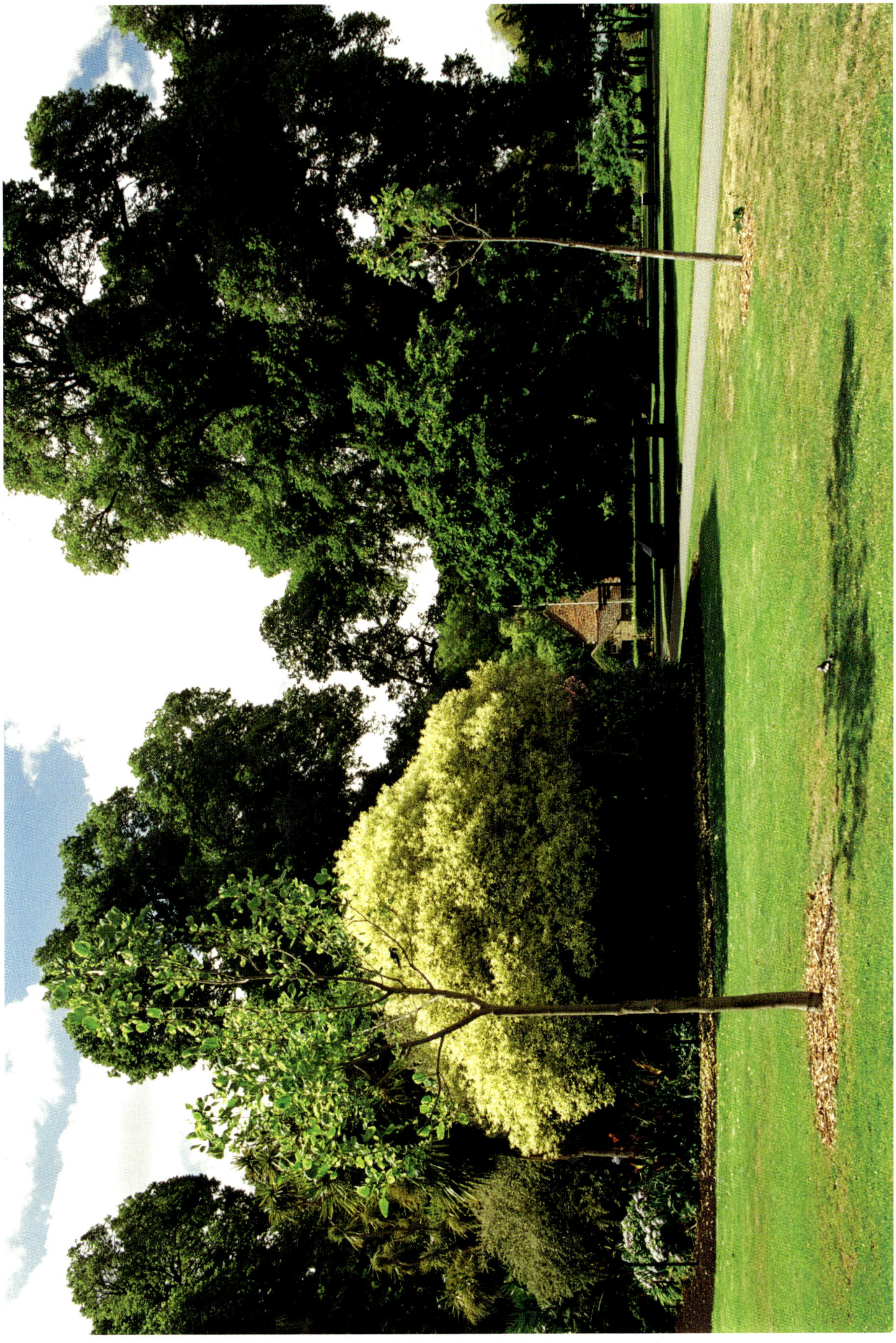

Cook's Cottage

Fabian Dattner

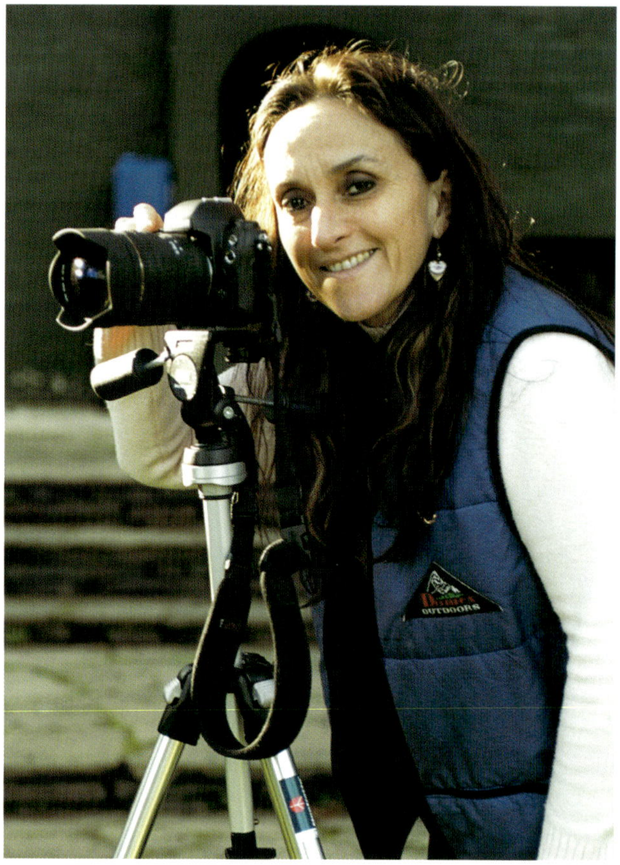

Fabian Dattner, Partner - Dattner Grant.

Fabian is a regular commentator in the media on leadership issues. Through her company, Dattner Grant, Fabian facilitates and supports a range of high profile Australian organisations in leadership development and strategic transformation. She also has a number of commercial and community achievements to her credit.

She has penned three books on leadership and has been included in many others, including works on successful women in leadership in Australia. She is widely recognised as a highly effective change strategist, facilitator, teacher and social entrepreneur.

"Cherry Trees" Eltham - This garden overlooks the Yarra Valley, the lungs of Melbourne. I chose this garden because it is an expression of almost everything precious in my life. I have found fairies in this garden, chased horses, fallen in love, cried over the death of my father, got married, found myself in the depths of despair feeling myself a failure, and then had the opportunity to climb to the very highest pinnacles of joy as I found my way back from the abyss.

I was five when I first saw the garden (and the fairy it contained), 27 when it was sold by my parents, and 40 when my husband and I had the immense good fortune to be able to buy it back.

In a thousand ways it tells the stories of social and political change in Australia. Many of the Whitlam cabinet cried bitter tears of disappointment in its graceful contours at the time of their famous dismissal. Don Dunstan cooked in the kitchen that overlooks the gardens, John Farnham hosted a fundraiser (and I got to wash dishes with he and his wife), painters, poets and aspiring greats have filled every nook and cranny with dreams of change.

Today, it is both my home and also the centre of our business, focusing on amplifying emerging voices in Australia. We work with business leaders from all over the country, seeking to find a more sustainable approach to profitable business in the 21st Century.

For these reasons, I chose this view. Grand reasons, I believe!

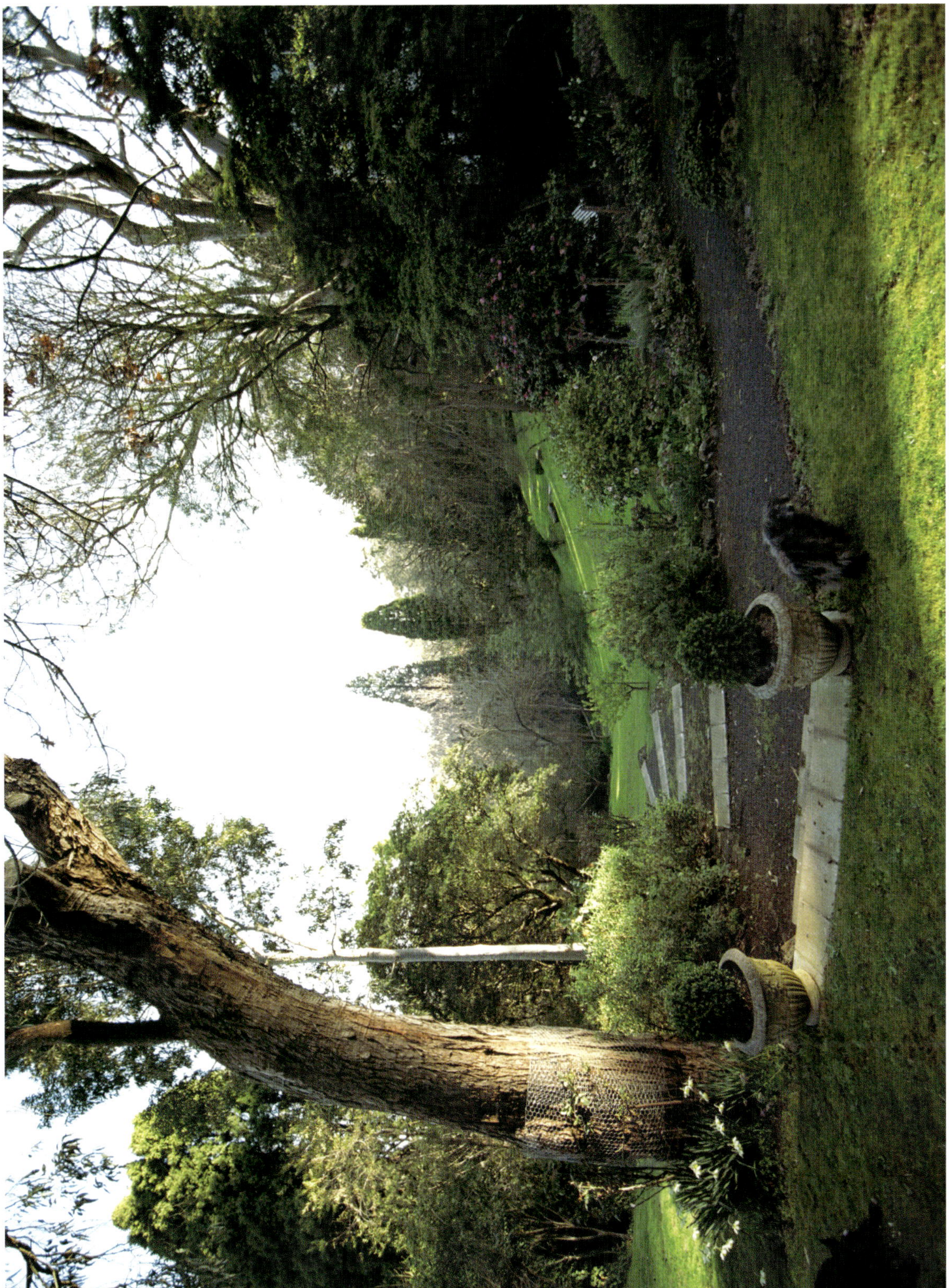

"Cherry Trees"

Diane "Dee Dee" Dunleavy

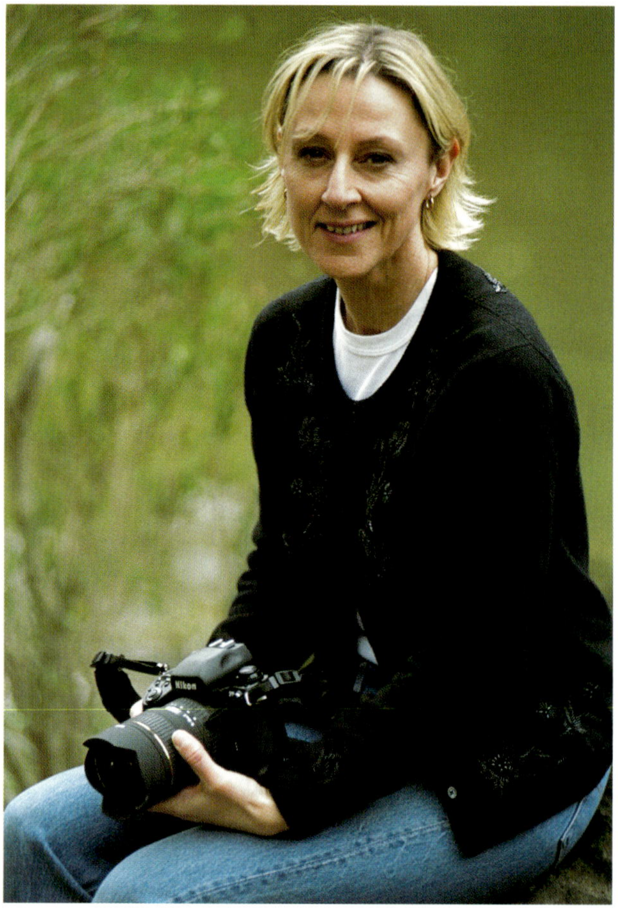

Diane "Dee Dee" Dunleavy, co-host of the popular *"Grubby and Dee Dee Breakfast Show"* on Melbourne's GOLD 104.

She started work as a cadet journalist on Mornington's Town Crier in 1980, moving to The Frankston Standard and then launching her 17-year career in radio in 1986.

She lives in Bulleen in one of Victoria's earliest homes, *Clarendon Eyre* (built in 1862) which she is restoring with her husband Kieran.

Dee Dee has two children: Bonnie, 8 and Bailey, 5.

She's a fanatical St Kilda Football Club supporter and spends most of her spare time rummaging through antiques and second-hand shops, and the rest of her spare time restoring what she finds. And any other little bits of time she has trawling eBay. And if there's any time left she spends it sewing or watching reality TV… or falling asleep at 7 p.m.

The "Changing Moods" of the Yarra River - Bulleen - "The Yarra River gently winds around behind where I live in Bulleen, near the Bolin Bolin Billabong. My children Bonnie, 8 and Bailey, 5 think it's *our* river, which I suppose is right as it belongs to all of us.

Our home, built in 1862, once owned 300 acres in this area and I always feel a sense of history walking through the massive gum trees to our "secret spot" which is visited by kookaburras, rosellas, ducks and the occasional pelican.

In winter we race down after heavy rain for the thrill of seeing the power of the river in flood and in summer, when the waters recede, we wade out and float "boats" made of bits of bark.

It never ceases to amaze me that the madness of the city is only a few kilometers downstream from this tranquil place."

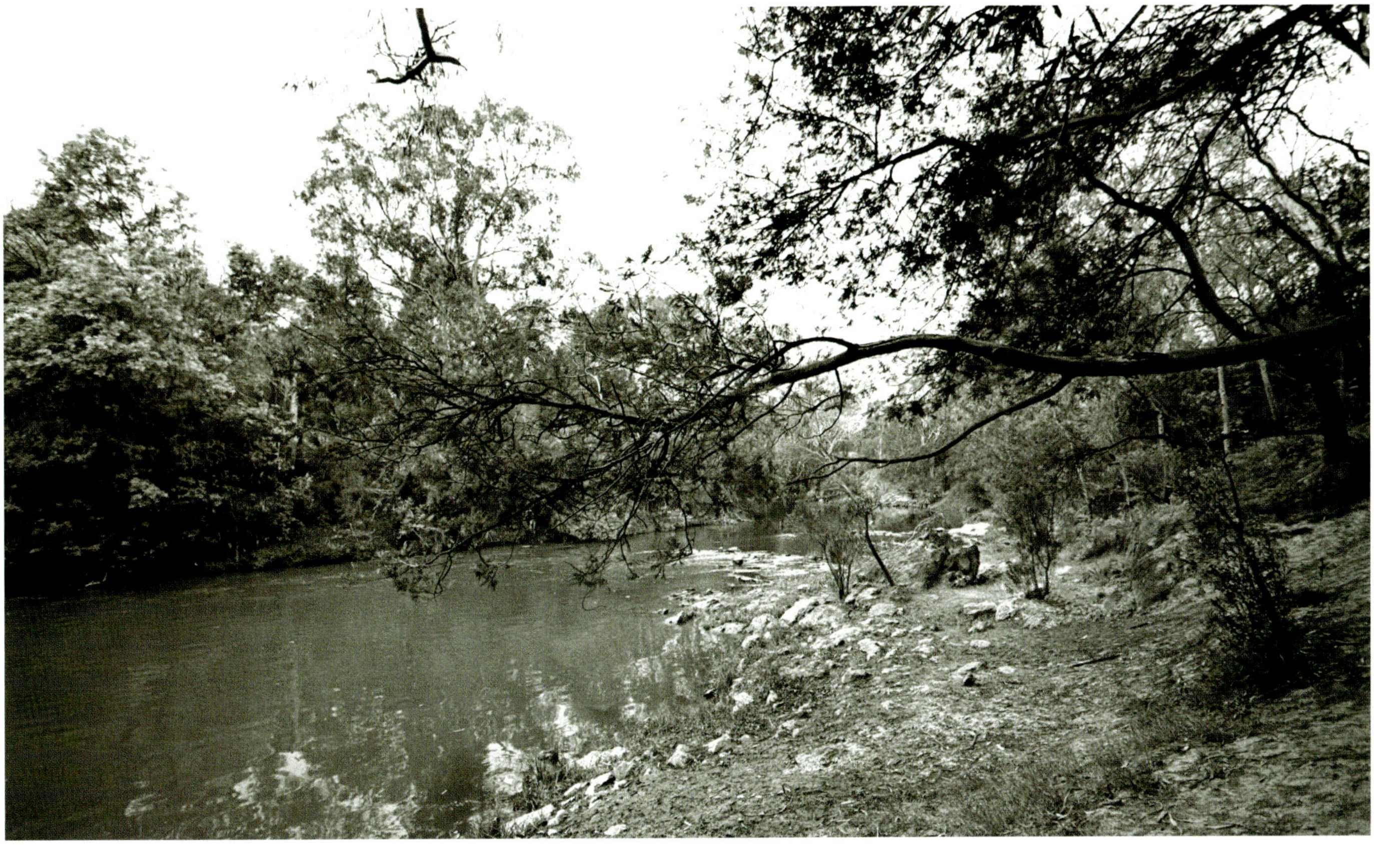

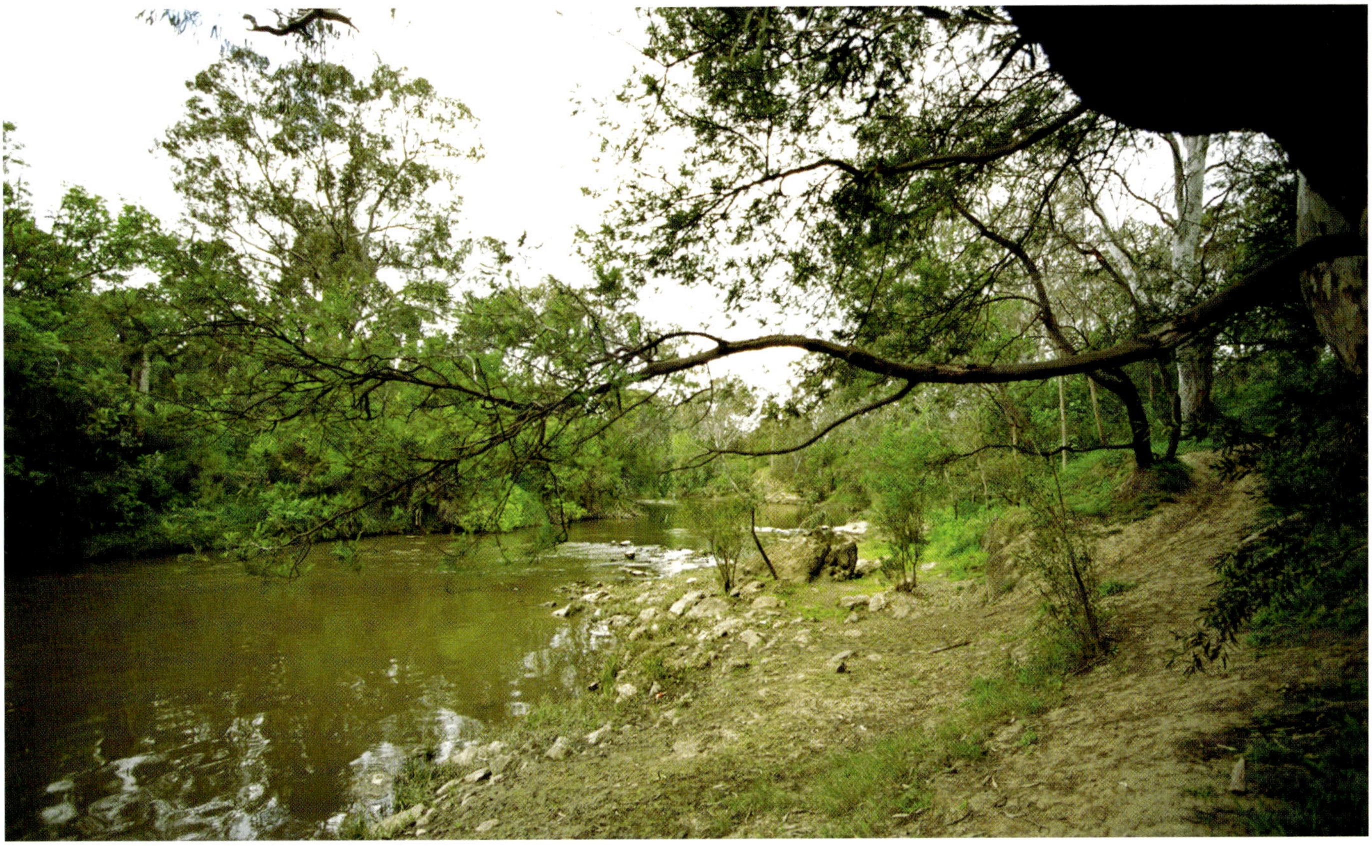

The "Changing Moods" of the Yarra River - Bulleen

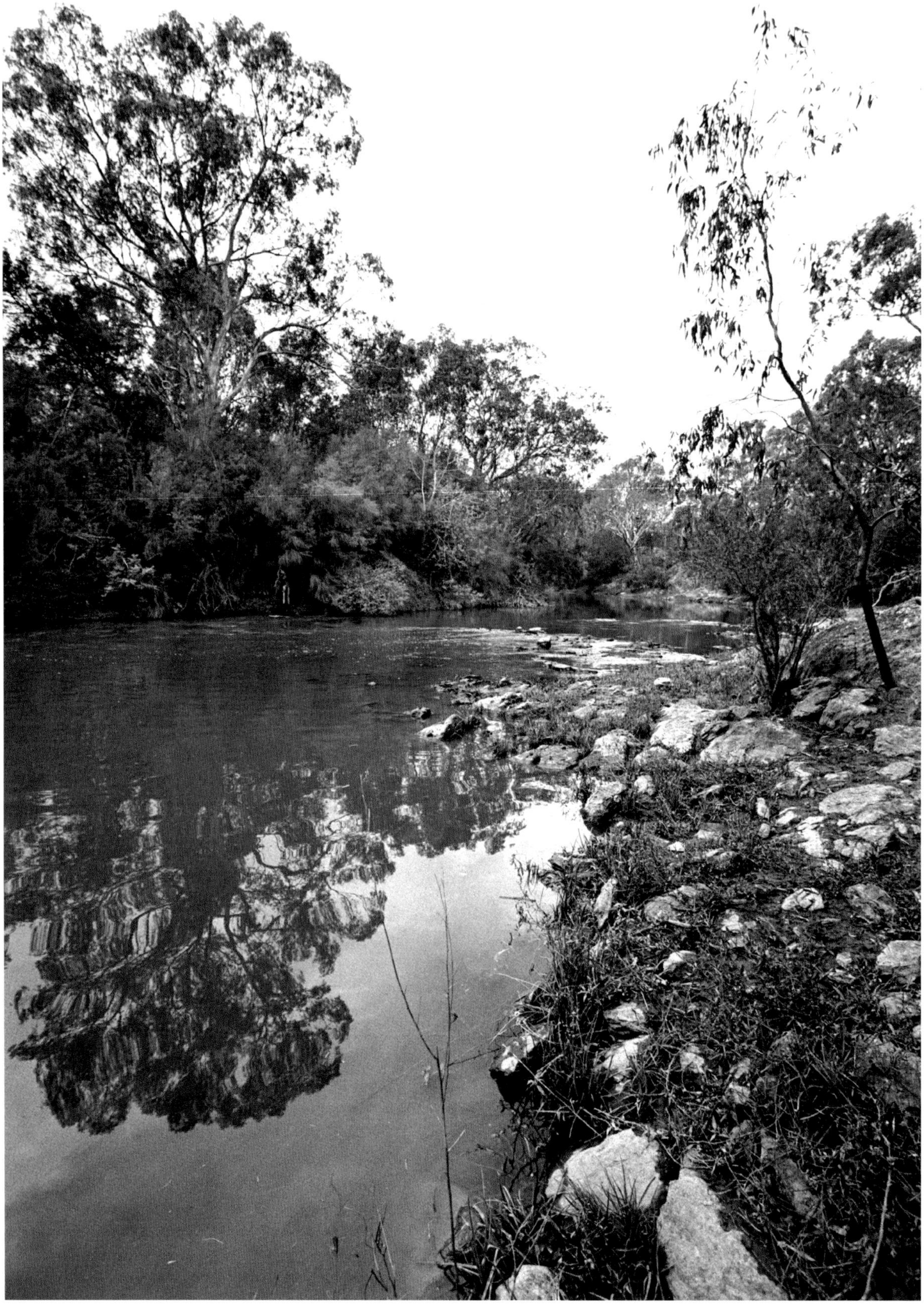

The “Changing Moods” of the Yarra River - Bulleen

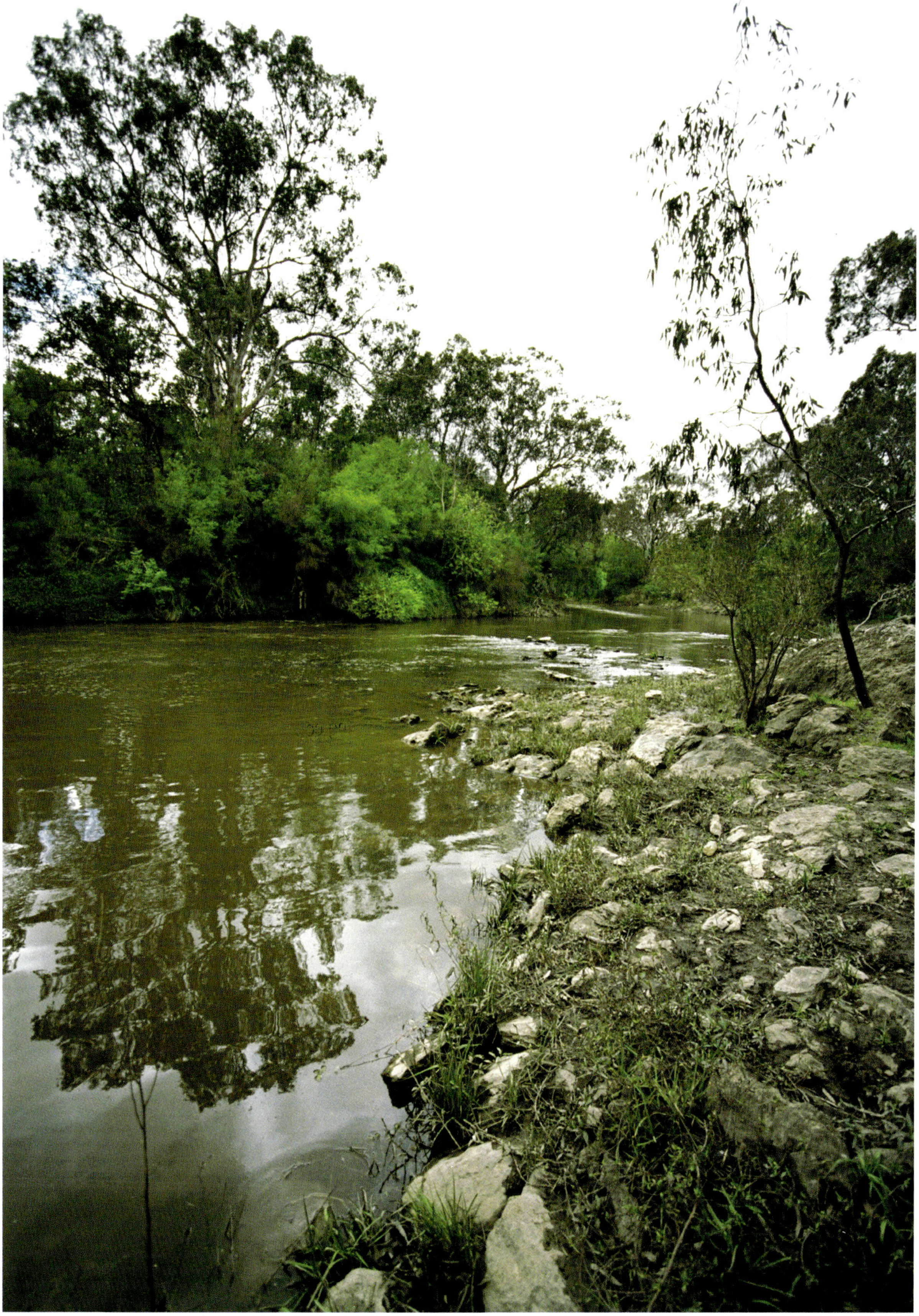

John D Elliott

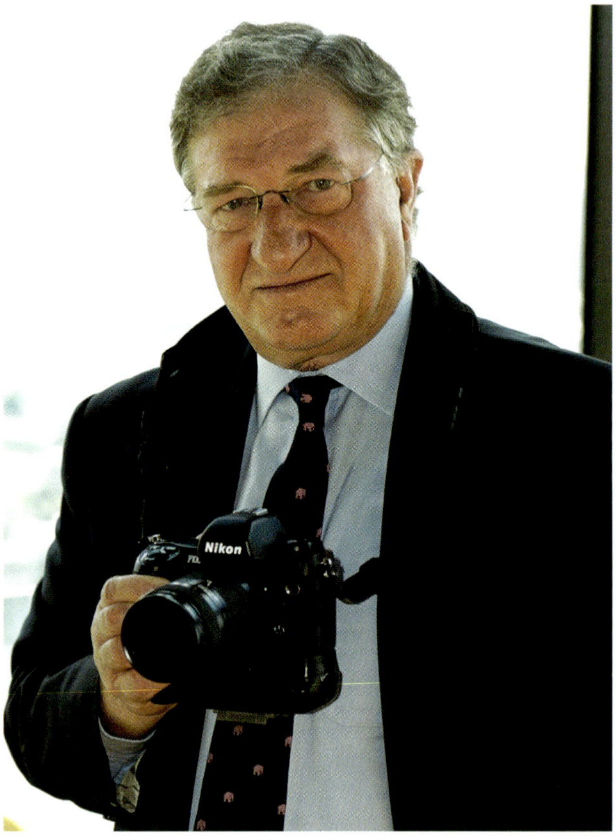

John D Elliott, was born in Melbourne in 1941. Educated at Carey Grammar School and then Melbourne University, where he obtained a Bachelor of Commerce (Hons) and a Master of Business Administration. Following a 2 year term at BHP he joined McKinsey and Co. Inc. and worked on projects in Australia and the United States for 6 years.

In 1972, John Elliott formed a consortium and raised $30 million for the acquisition of Henry Jones (IXL) Ltd., a major food processor.

Following the merger with Elders Smith Goldsbrough Mort Limited and Henry Jones, John was appointed Managing Director of the newly formed Elders IXL Limited. In 1983 the company acquired Carlton and United Breweries Limited for just under $1 billion. The acquisitions of Courage Breweries in the U.K., Carling O'Keefe Breweries in Canada and U.K. based Grand Metropolitan Brewing, made the Group the fourth largest brewer in the world.

John presided over the reconstruction of Elders IXL in 1990 as a single purpose brewing company and then stepped down as chairman and Chief Executive Officer to pursue his own private business interests. He operates business activities in Eastern Europe, particularly Romania, and exports Australian agricultural products around the world.

John played 250 games of Australian Rules Football for his old school until his mid 30's, and was President of the Carlton Football Club for twenty years. He has a well documented interest in politics, having been a member of the Liberal Party for over 30 years. He became Federal President of the Party in 1987, having previously occupied the position of Federal Treasurer, State Treasurer and Vice President in Victoria.

He was Chairman of the 500 Club which he formed 20 years ago and retired last year. He was also the inaugural Chairman of the Committee for Melbourne and is a Director of the Foundation of the University of Melbourne Business School. He has been a Director of a number of public companies

Sunrise over Carlton - "A wonderful view to look at every morning when one wakes up."

Optus Oval - "I've had so much joy looking at what happens on the best football ground in Melbourne. Whenever I looked up I got another view of why this City is so great."

From Le Restaurant - "To the North and East of Melbourne... it encaptures a different view including the CUB Brewery. I haveseen it often and the view is always different."

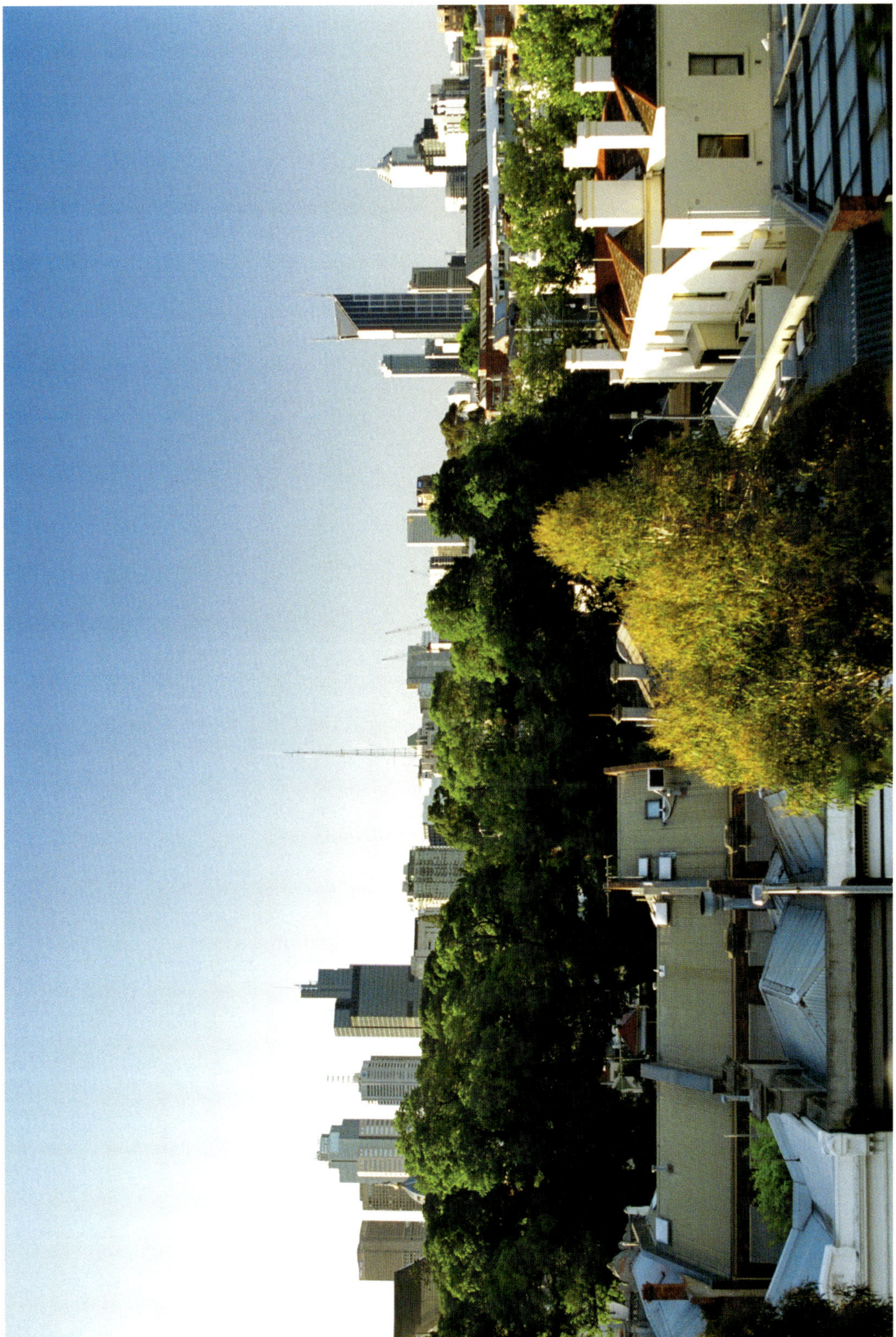

Sunrise over Carlton

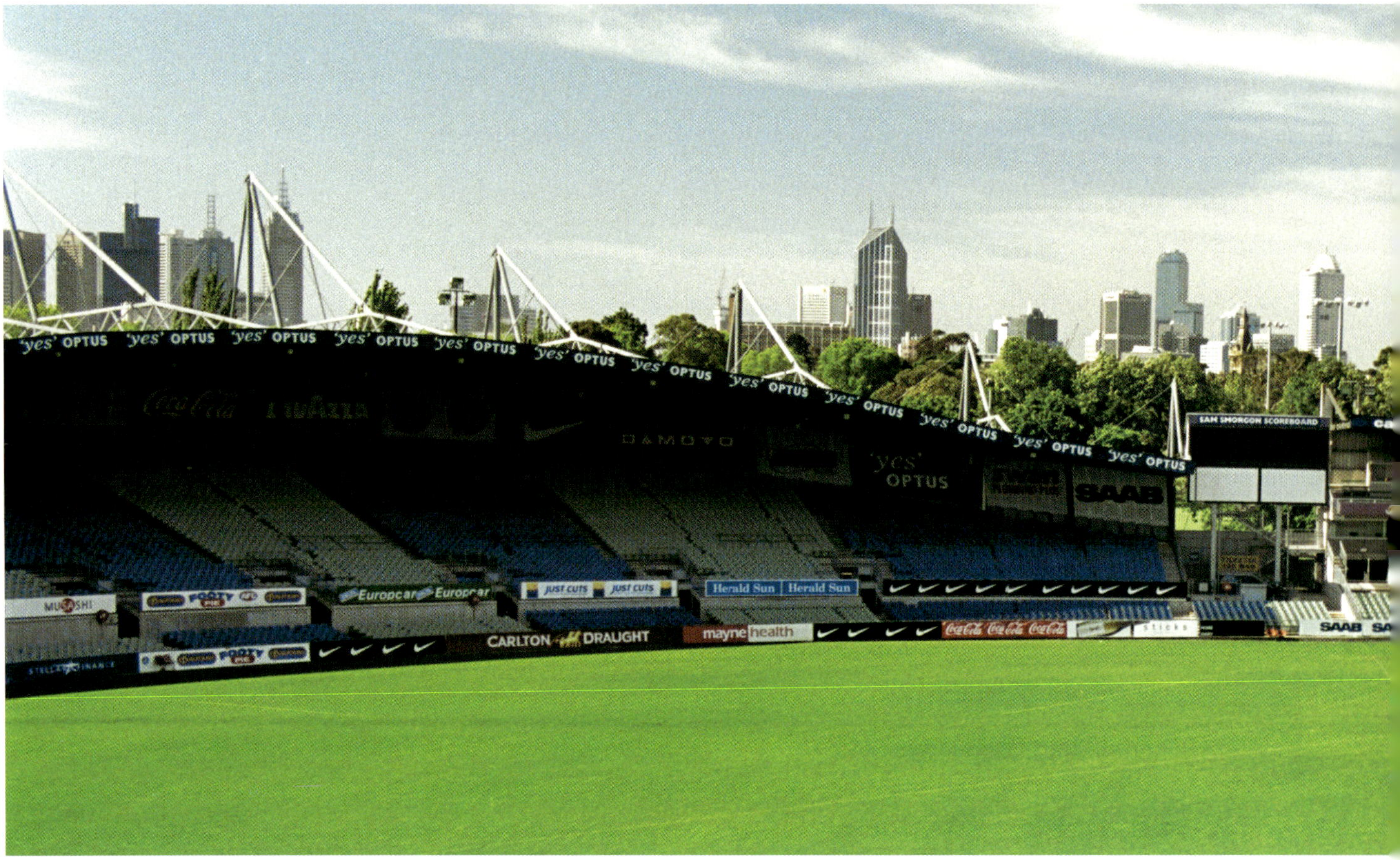

Melbourne from Optus Oval

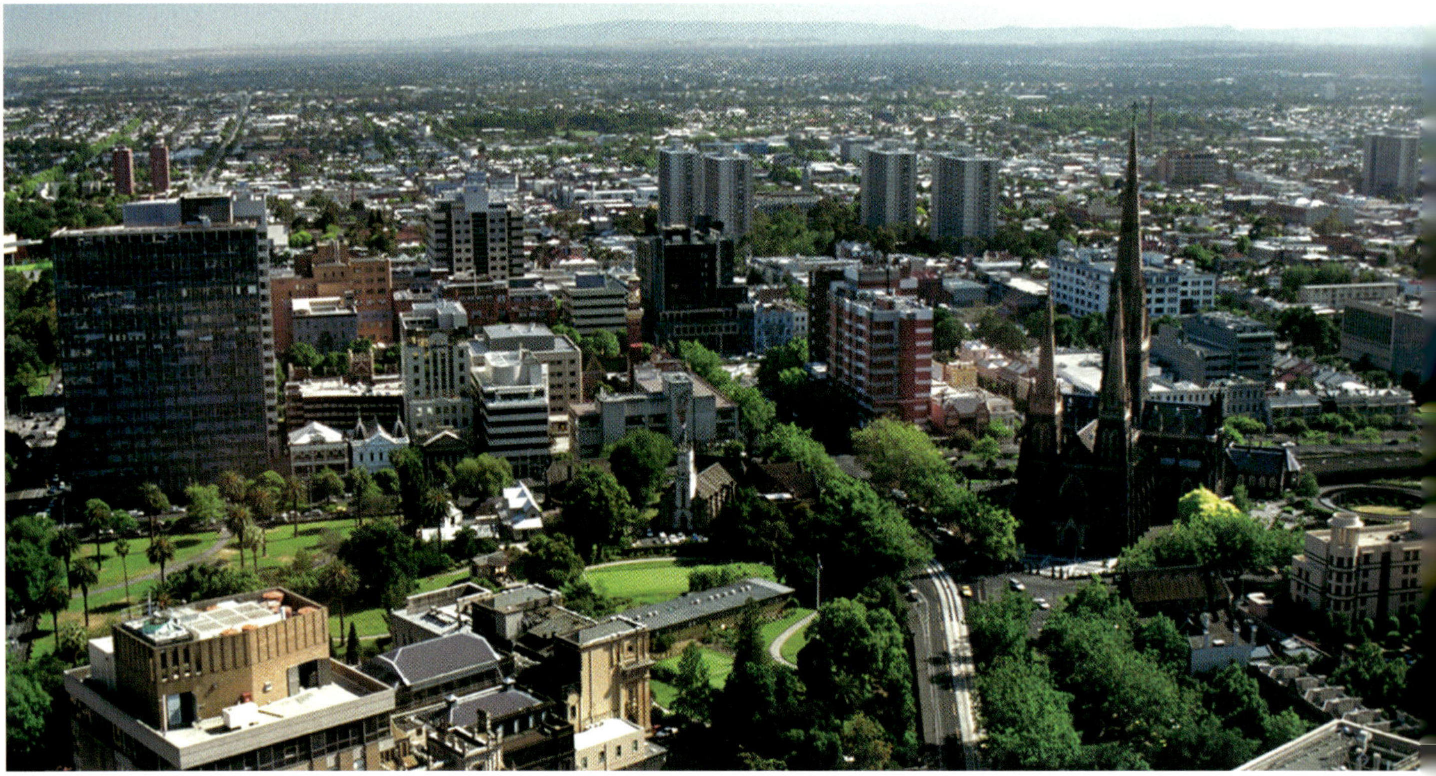
Melbourne to the North and East from *Le Restaurant*

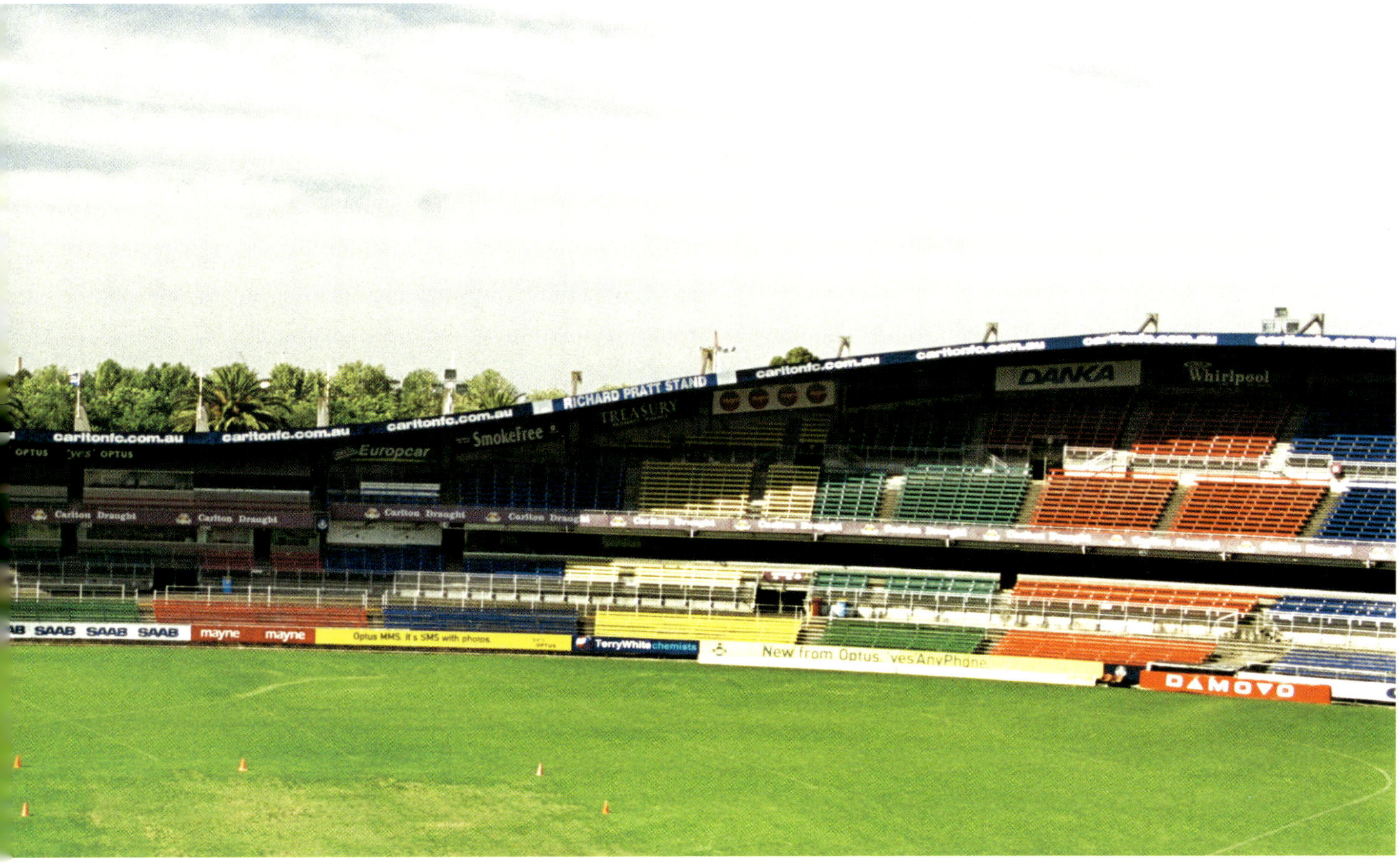
carltonfc.com.au
RICHARD PRATT STAND
DANKA
Whirlpool
TREASURY
SmokeFree
Europcar
OPTUS 'yes' OPTUS
Carlton Draught
SAAB SAAB SAAB
mayne mayne
Optus MMS. It's SMS with photos.
TerryWhite chemists
New from Optus. yes AnyPhone
DAMOVO

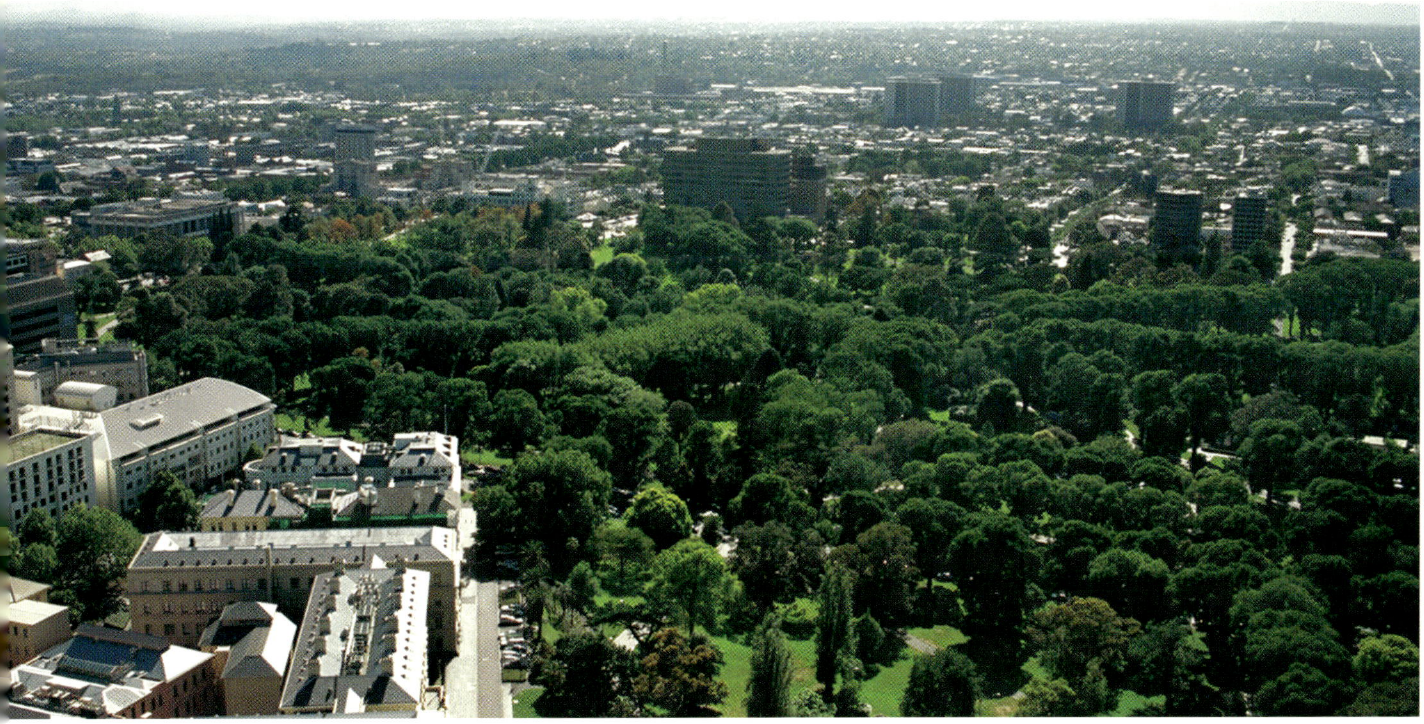

Malcolm Fraser

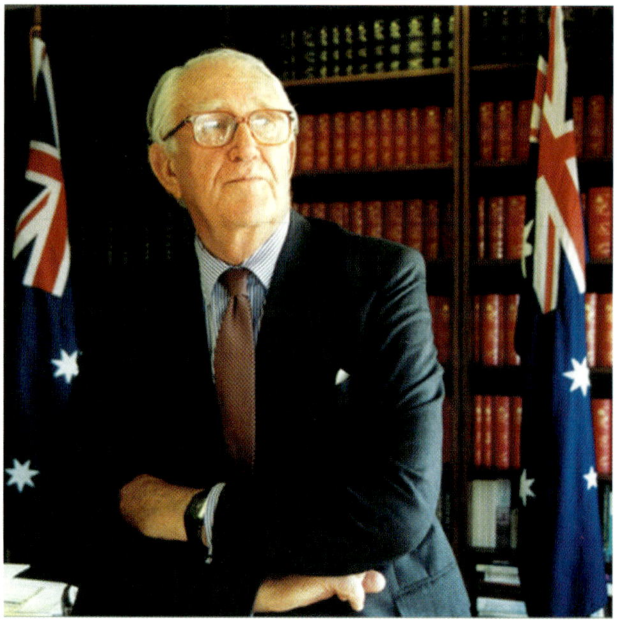

Rt Hon Malcolm Fraser AC CH, was born in Melbourne on 21st May, 1930. He was educated at Melbourne Grammar and Oxford University where he took his Degree in Philosophy, Politics and Economics graduating in 1952.

Under Mr Fraser's leadership, the Liberal and National Country Party Coalition achieved a record majority in the 1975 Federal election. Mr Fraser's Government was subsequently re-elected in the two succeeding elections, in 1977 and 1980. On 25th February 1983, Mr Fraser became Australia's second longest serving Prime Minister. Mr Fraser resigned from the Parliament in April 1983 after nearly 28 years as the Member for Wannon.

Mr Fraser was Chairman of CARE Australia from 1987 to December 2001. He was President of CARE International from 1990-1995, and was Vice President from 1995-1999.

The Human Rights and Equal Opportunity Commission awarded Mr Fraser the 2000 Australian Human Rights Medal.

In 2002, Mr Fraser published his book "Common Ground – Issues that should bind and not divide us".

Mr Fraser is married with four children, and ten grandchildren.

Mr Fraser likes to devote any spare time to his interests of photography, fishing and vintage cars.

Mornington Peninsula - Located SE of Melbourne, has many wonderful views. The rolling hills and colour present many photographic opportunities.

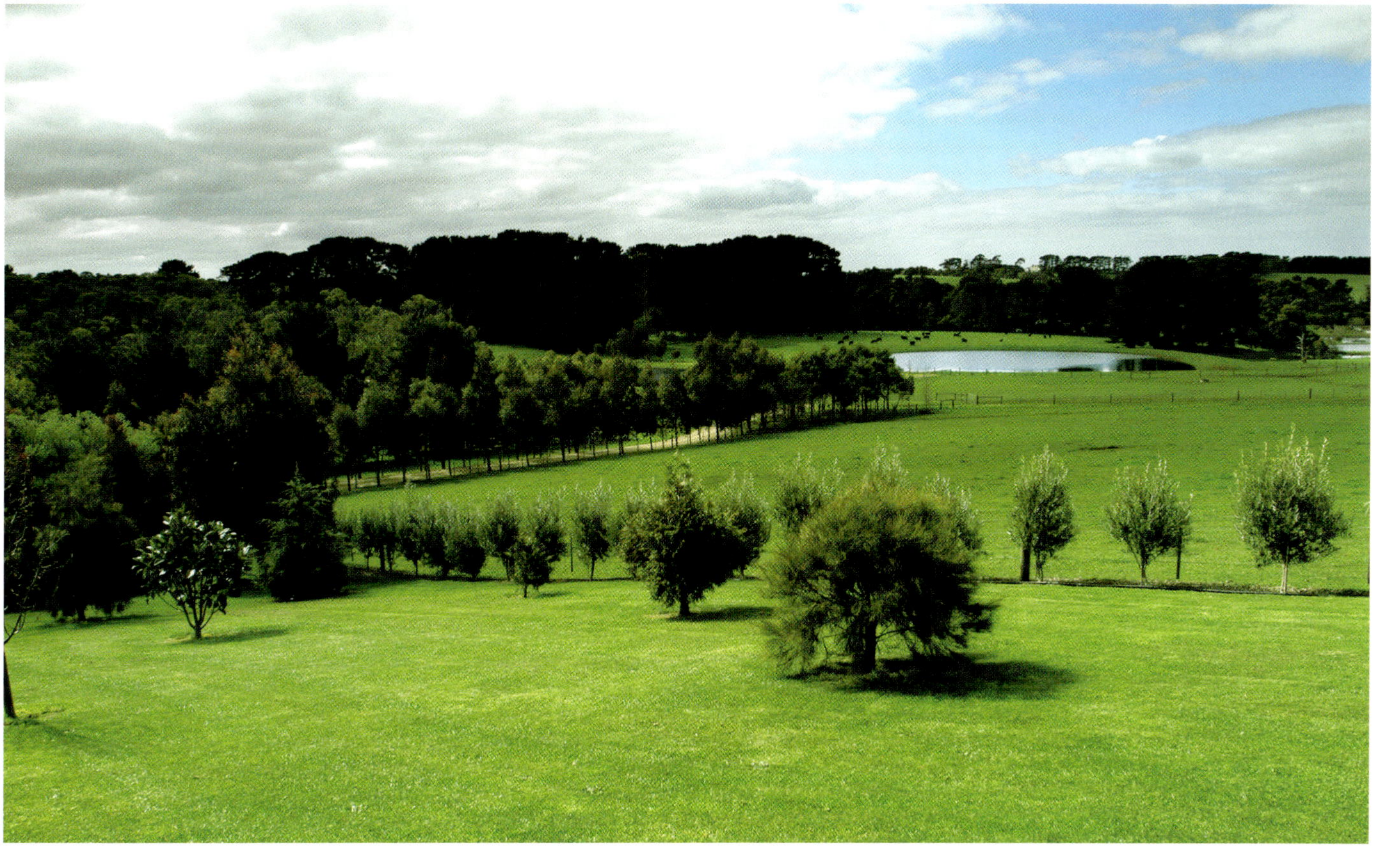

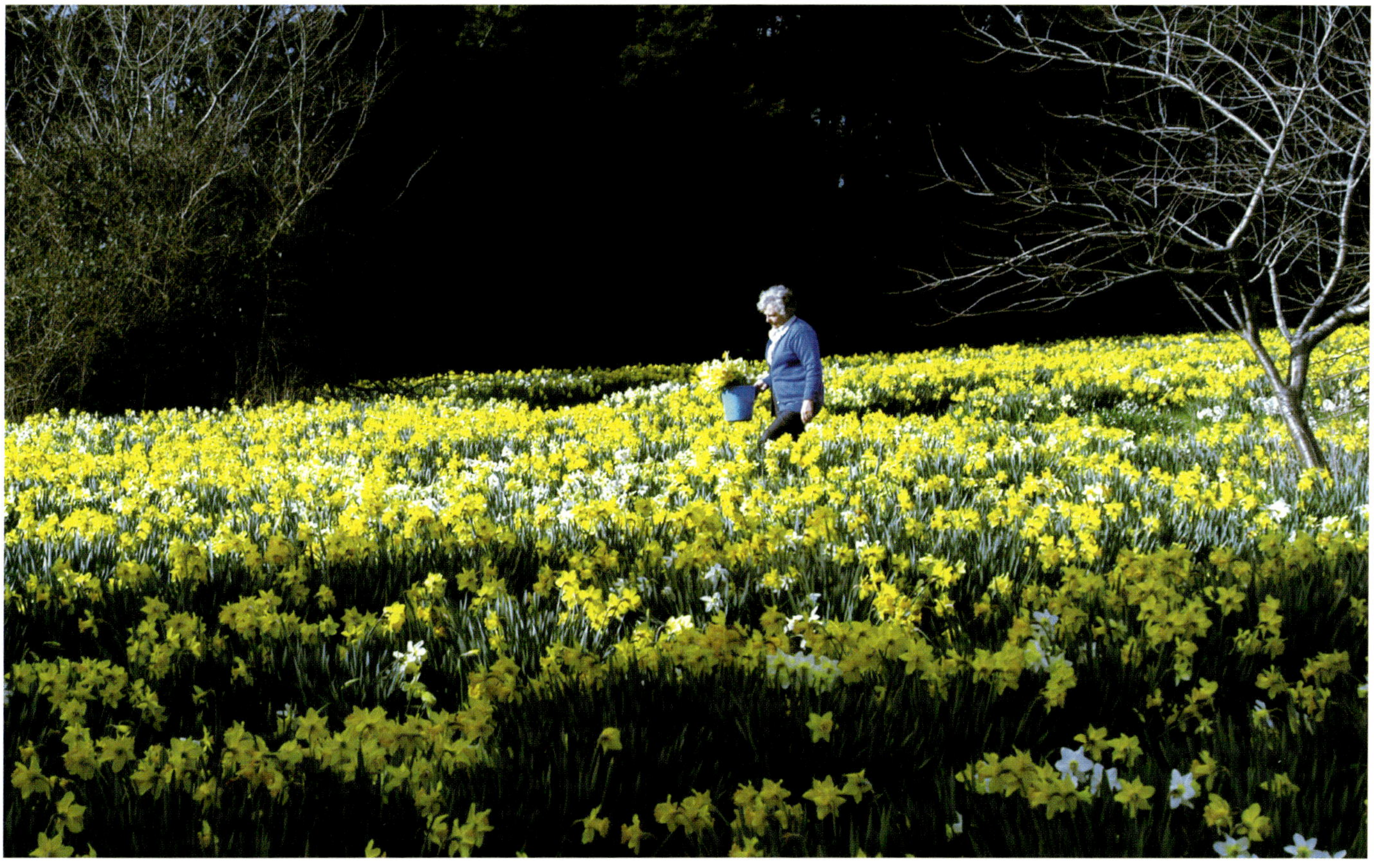

Mornington Peninsula

Charles Goode

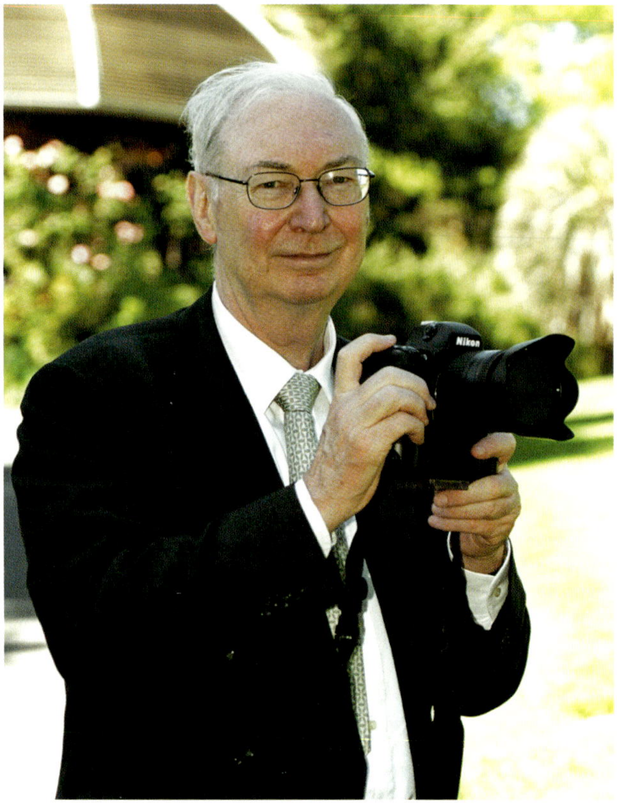

Charles Goode AC, is the Chairman of the Australia and New Zealand Banking Group Ltd., (ANZ) a position he has held since 1995.

He is also Chairman of Woodside Petroleum Ltd., Australian United Investment Company Ltd and Diversified United Investment Ltd, and a Director of Singapore Airlines Limited.

Mr Goode has a wide range of community interests which include serving as Chairman of the Ian Potter Foundation and President of Howard Florey Institute of Experimental Physiology and Medicine. The former, founded by the late Australian financier, Sir Ian Potter, is Australia's largest private philanthropic foundation.

Mr Goode holds degrees from Melbourne University (Bachelor of Commerce with Honours) and Columbia University, New York (Master of Business Administration), an Honorary Doctorate from the University of Melbourne (Doctor of Law, honoris causa), and an Honorary Doctorate from Monash University (Doctor of Law, honoris causa).

Royal Botanic Gardens – A beautifully landscaped garden with different views around every turn in the paths. It provides a peaceful reflective environment where one is in touch with nature.

ANZ Gothic Building – This reflects a wonderful restoration of the ANZ Banking Group Ltd's fine gothic building of the 1880's, situated on the corner of Collins & Queen Streets.

Skyline of Melbourne – This shows Melbourne as a modern city with relatively clear views of city buildings and Port Phillip Bay. It depicts an environment within which an active commercial world is at work.

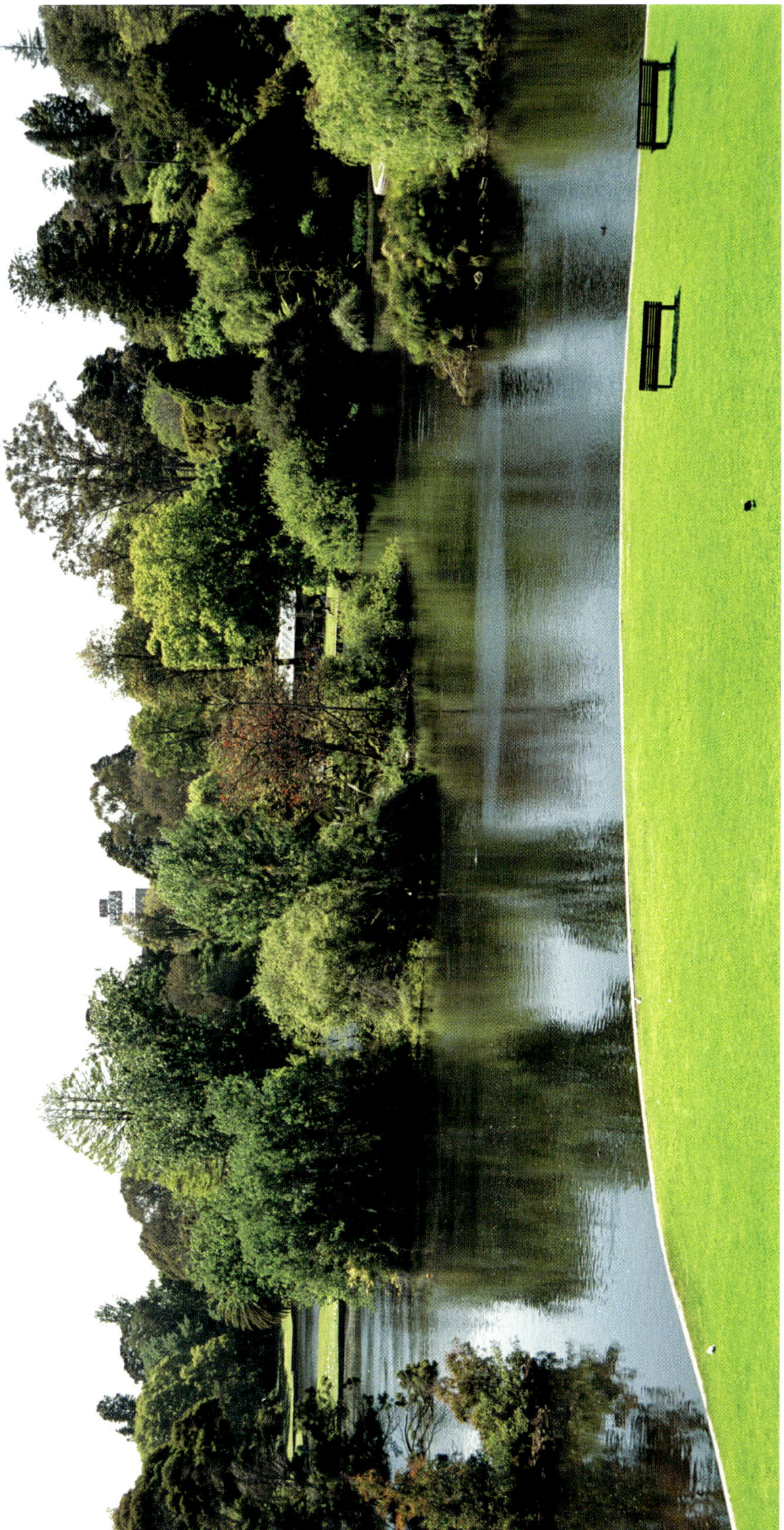

Royal Botanic Gardens

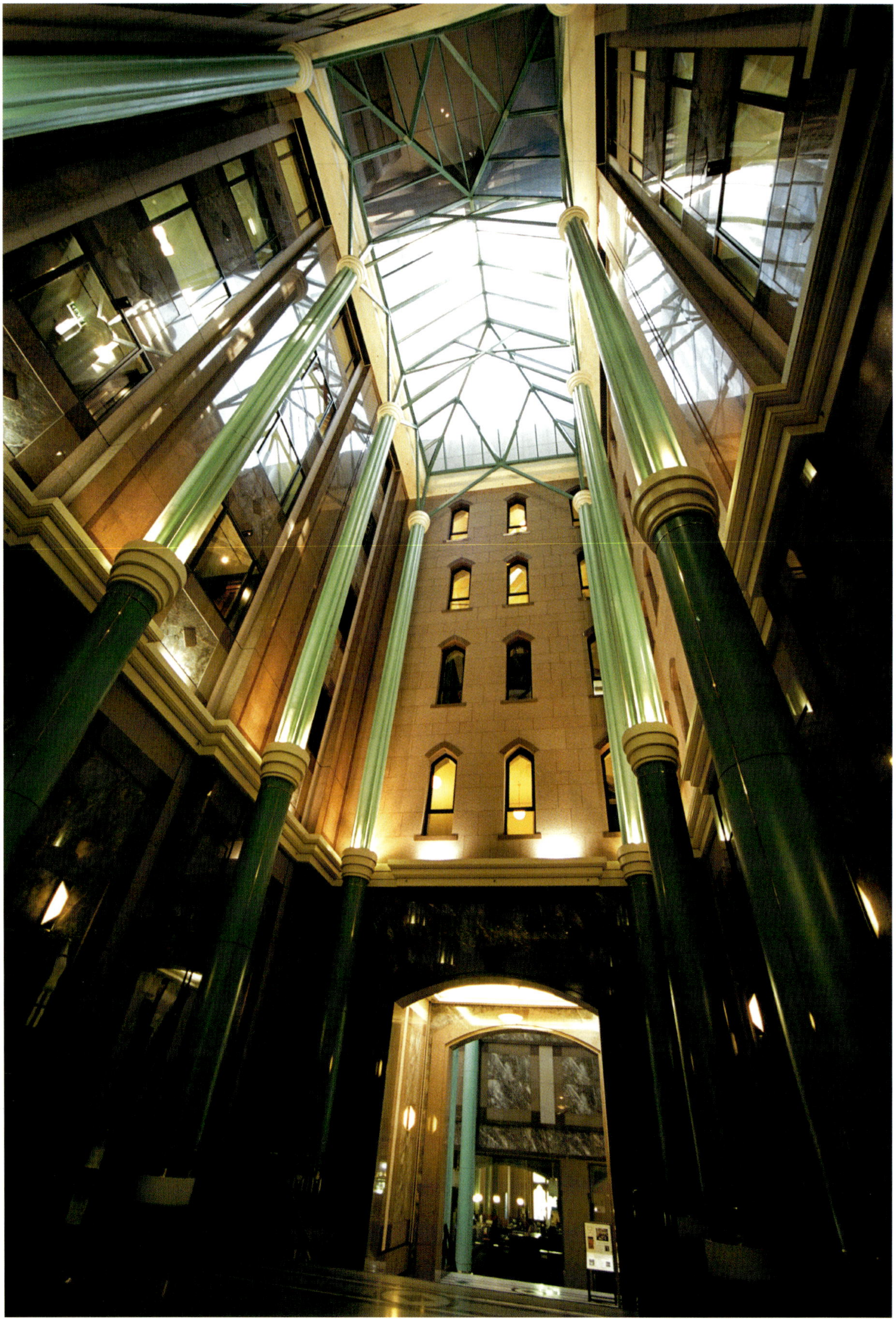

ANZ Gothic Building

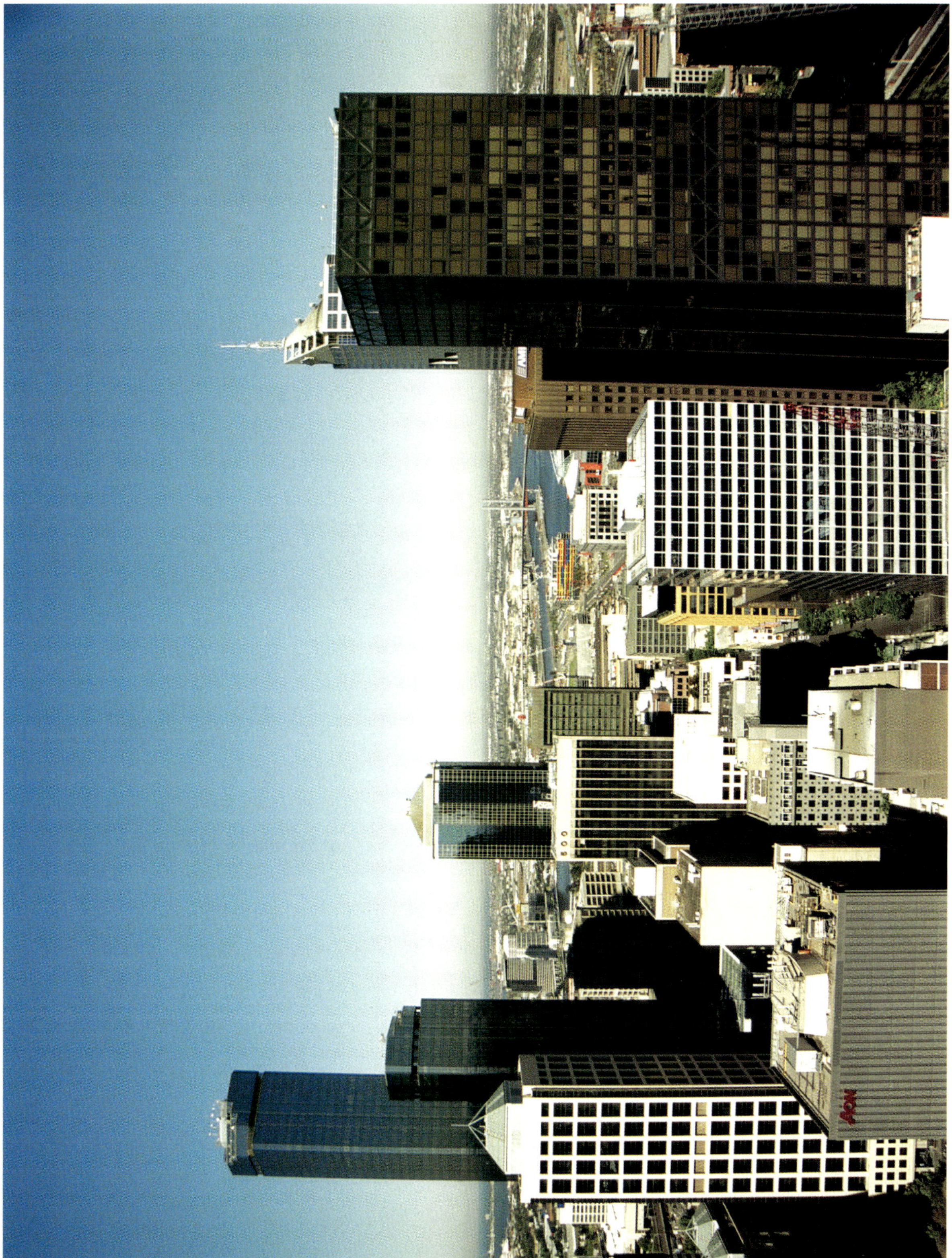

Skyline of Melbourne

Michael Gudinski

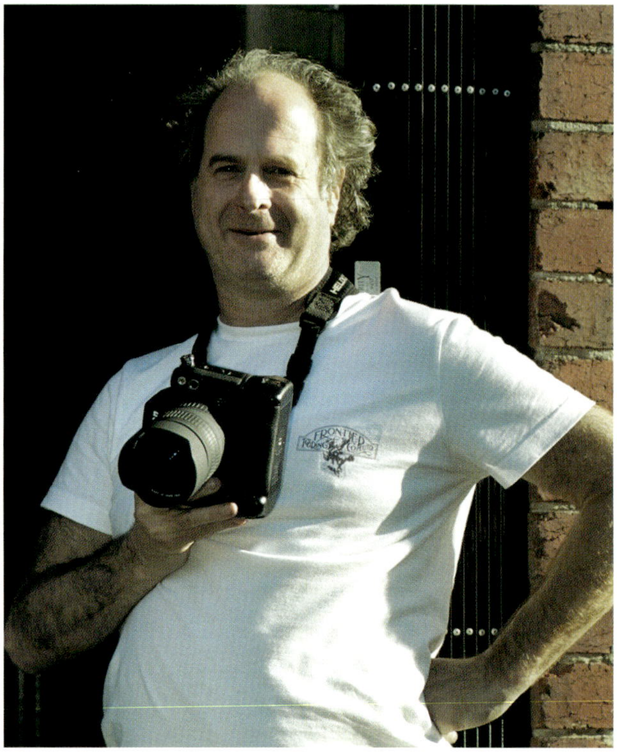

Michael Gudinski, Chairman, Mushroom Group of Companies

He's been called the rock guru, the music mogul, the mushroom man, and is widely recognised as one of the most important figures in the history of the Australian music industry. Irrefutably, he is a man of many faces and his many business interests reflect the multiple facets of both his personality and his talents.

Born to Russian immigrants in 1952, the future success of Michael Gudinski could probably have been predicted back in 1959. At the ripe old age of seven years, Michael showed his entrepreneurial side on Caulfield Cup day when he charged race goers for parking spaces in a vacant block next to his home. From there he never looked back, promoting gigs at Melbourne halls for alternative acts like *Chain* and *The Aztecs* and developing his first taste for what would be a life long love affair with the music industry.

In 1972, Michael and business partner Ray Evans staged, managed and booked all the entertainment at the legendary new Sunbury Festival. In the same year, Michael simultaneously founded Mushroom Records – which was to eventually develop into the largest independent record label in Australian music – and Mushroom Music, which is today the principal independent music publishing company in Australia.

Since its formation in 1979, The Frontier Touring Company has become the leading tour promoter in Australia, been twice voted the "No 1 International Touring Company In the World"

1998 also saw Michael awarded the prestigious "Ted Albert Award" for Outstanding Services to Australian Music at the APRA (The Australian Performing Rights Association) Awards. In 1999, the AMI (Australian Marketing Institute) awarded Michael "The Sir Charles McGrath Australian Marketer of the Year Award" – the highest accolade for personal achievement an individual can receive from the AMI.

In 2003, at the International Live Music Conference in March, Michael received the "ILMC 'Bottle' Award", the equivalent to a life time achievement award. He continues to work across all facets of his companies, and is frequently trekking from pub gig to entertainment centre, in Australia and abroad, looking for the next big thing to promote – be it through management, his record label, touring companies or his publishing arm.

The Winning Post - Flemington Racecourse - Having grown up 100 yards from the Caulfield racetrack I have always wanted to own or part own the winner of the Melbourne Cup at Flemington. One of my horses, Frontier Boy did run 5th and 21st in this race, but I'm still waiting for the big one!

Dundas Lane - With over 20 years of memories of great music, great people, many changes and a lot of fun - this building to me represents the spirit of Mushroom, its fantastic artists and terrific staff.

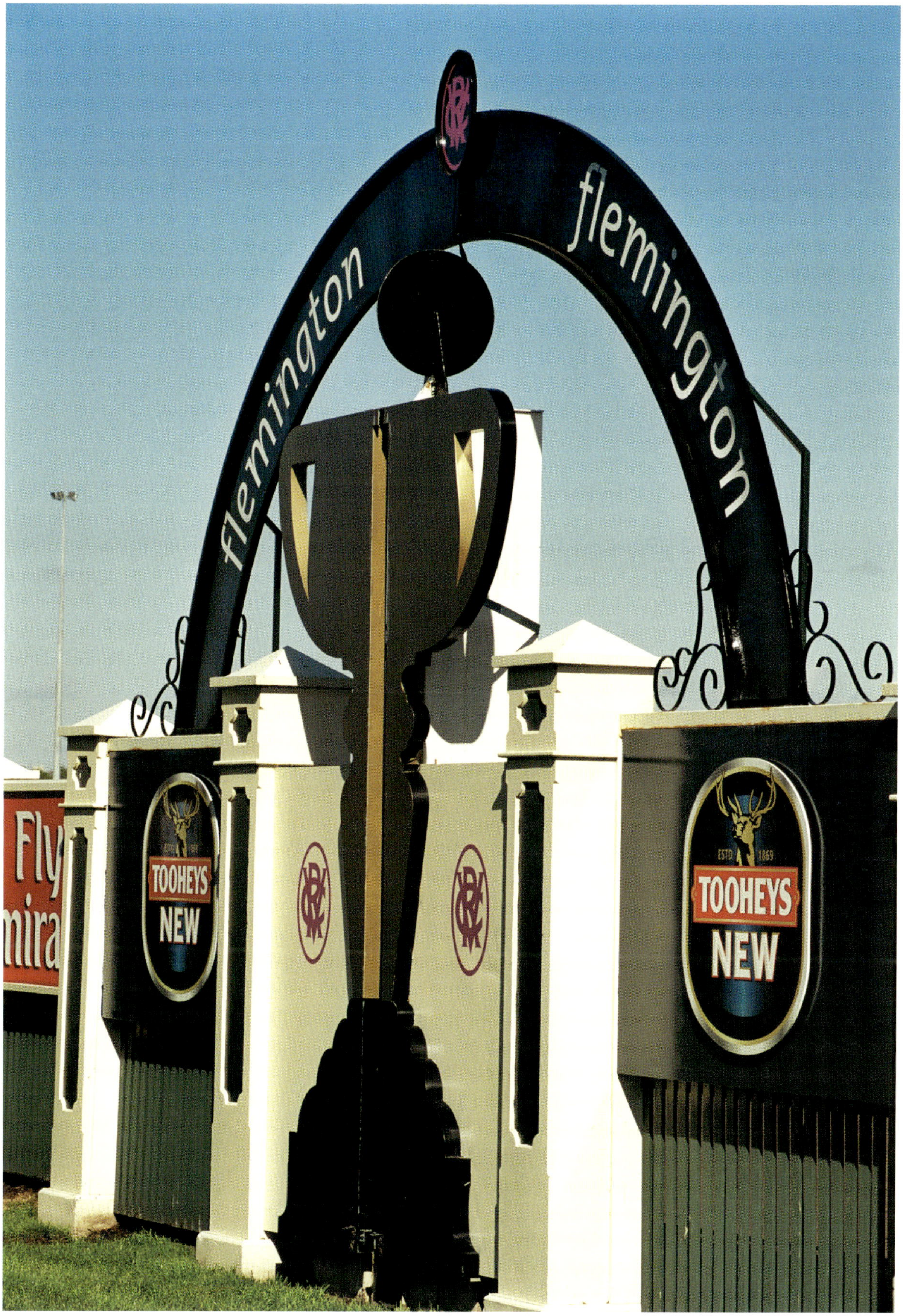

The Winning Post - Flemington Racecourse

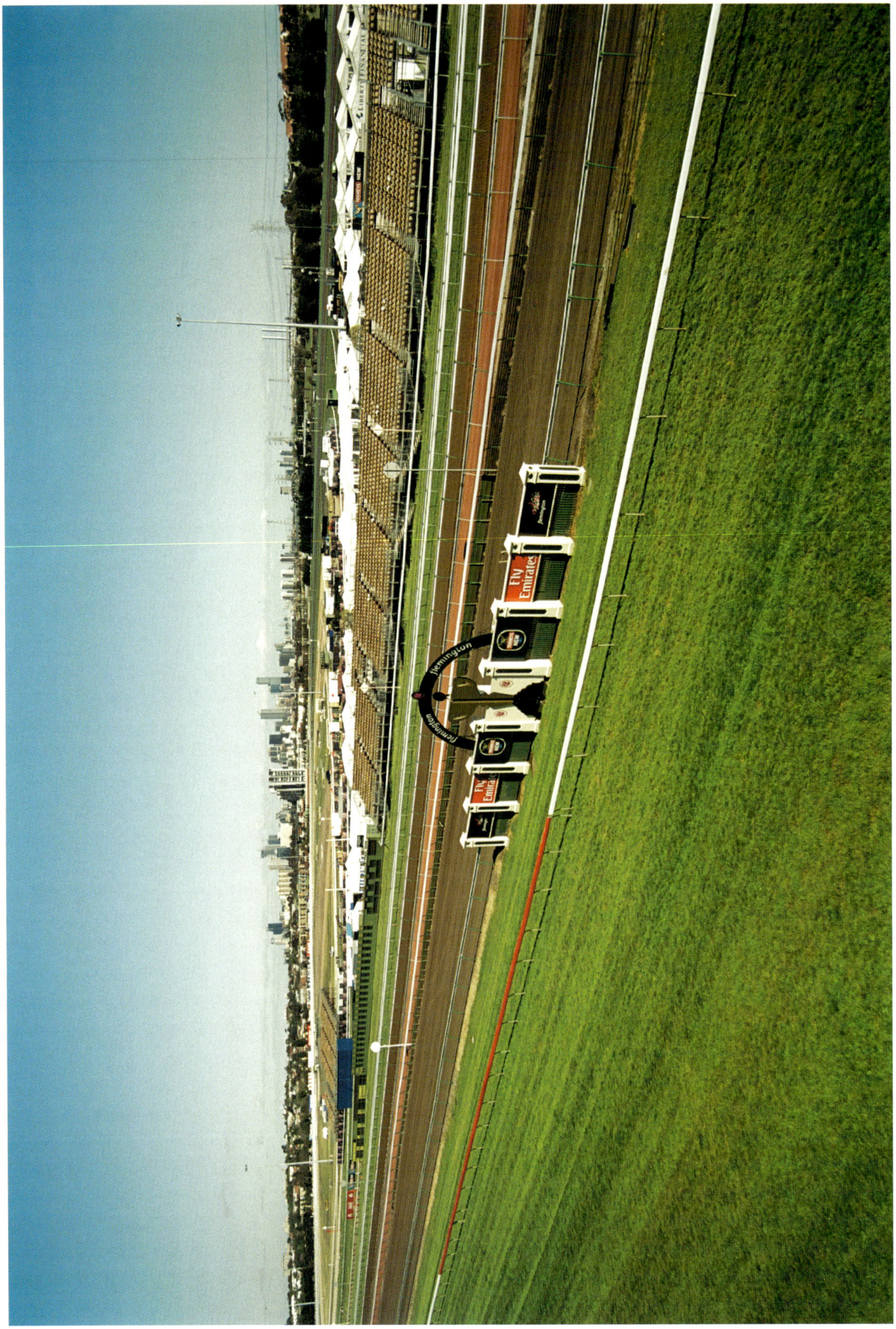

Melbourne and Flemington Racecourse

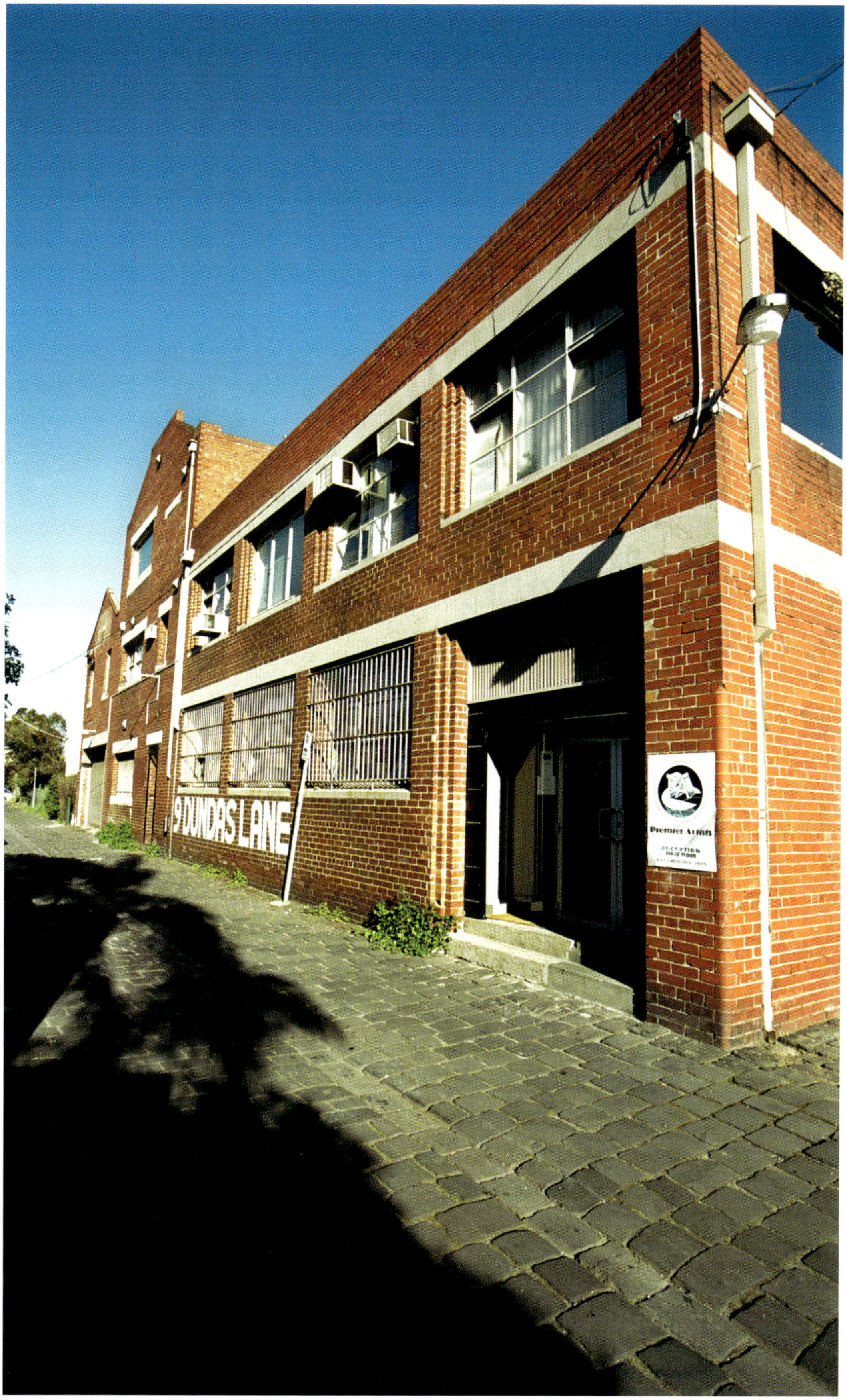

Dundas Lane - Albert Park

Jo Hall

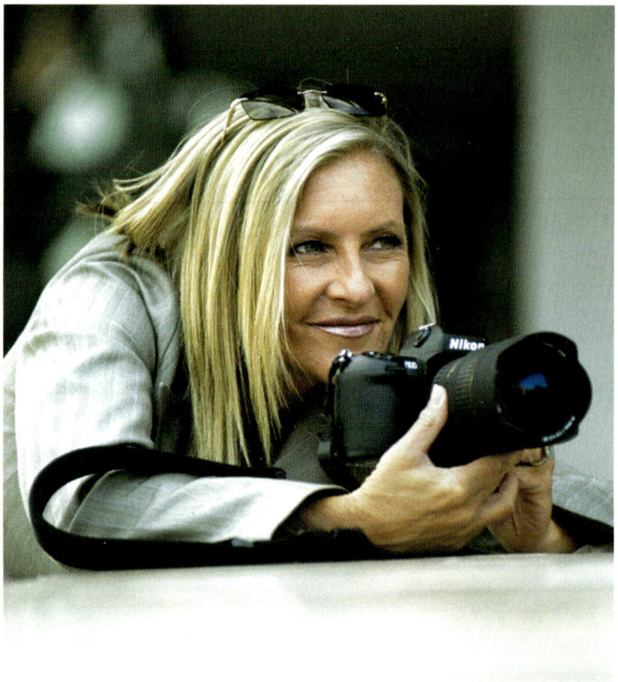

Jo Hall, National Nine News (Melbourne).

Jo joined National Nine News in 1979, after beginning her cadetship with a Melbourne suburban newspaper. She always wanted to be a journalist and imagined herself hunched over a typewriter, not in front of a television camera.

During her 23 years with National Nine News, Jo has become a familiar face to the people of Melbourne, both as newsreader and reporter.

In 1990 she was presented with a prestigious Thorn Award - the National Award for Journalism for her report on the siege at Hawthorn Kindergarten in May 1989. Jo was the first woman to win the award since its inception 16 years earlier.

"That was a shocking story, absolutely awful," reflects Jo. "The parents would arrive not knowing if their child was one of those being held hostage. You can't imagine their anguish, and as a parent I never lost sight of that."

Another story almost cost Jo her life. Covering the Ash Wednesday bushfires at Anglesea, Jo and her supporting camera crew were confronted by a wall of fire. "I jumped behind the wheel of the car and the crew hopped in the back. Had the engine not started I believe we wouldn't be here now," Jo recalls.

Today Jo is the chief presenter of National Nine News' weekend service which consistently wins its time-slot. It is among the top ten most watched programs in Melbourne each week with an average audience of 550,000 viewers. Jo anchors news bulletins weekdays and takes over the chair in Peter Hitchener's absence.

Jo admits that stories about children affect her most, and she can still be moved to tears by a story. It is this closeness with children that sees Jo working with the Variety Club on McHappy Day and the club's Underprivileged Children's Christmas Party. She is also Patron of Bonnie Babes, an organisation researching miscarriages, premature births and which provides counselling to grieving parents.

Jo has hosted three top rating Melbourne specials: "Zoos – The Bigger Picture", "From The Ground Up" and "All You Can Eat" (Part 2).

Jo Hall is married to Jason Danda and has four children, Rhyss, and Tysyn, and twins, Emmerson and Fynn.

Federation Square - Has been the subject of a lot of controversy. Not everyone has embraced its' unusual angles and design. From the early days of construction I loved its' appearance and felt it was a flattering, modern contrast to the "old" Melbourne, much the same as the glass pyramid at the Louvre in Paris.

Brunswick Street - Has always been interesting but in the last few years has come alive. There are so many different places to eat and you can lose yourself in some of the shops. I love clothes and it's one of the best places to find something unusual. It also has the very best florist!

Flemington Racecourse - The Spring Racing Carnival is truly lovely time to be in Melbourne… The weather is usually fine and Flemington Racecourse is such a great place to be… My mother (who died 12 years ago) loved Oaks Day and it's become a bit a of tradition for us to go each year… She so loved the roses… My photograph holds memories of a wonderful day, my three friends I shared it with are in the shot.

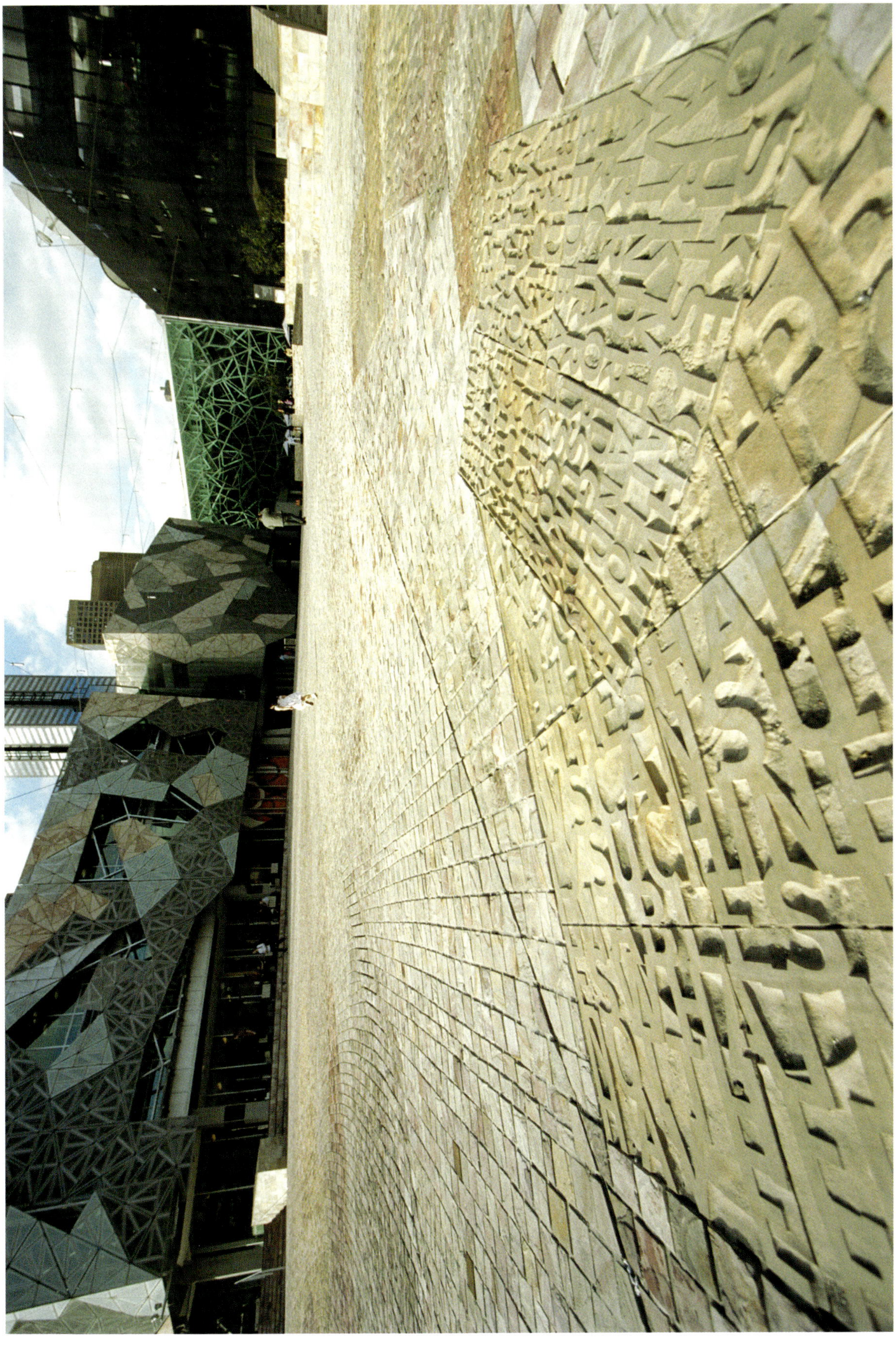

Federation Square

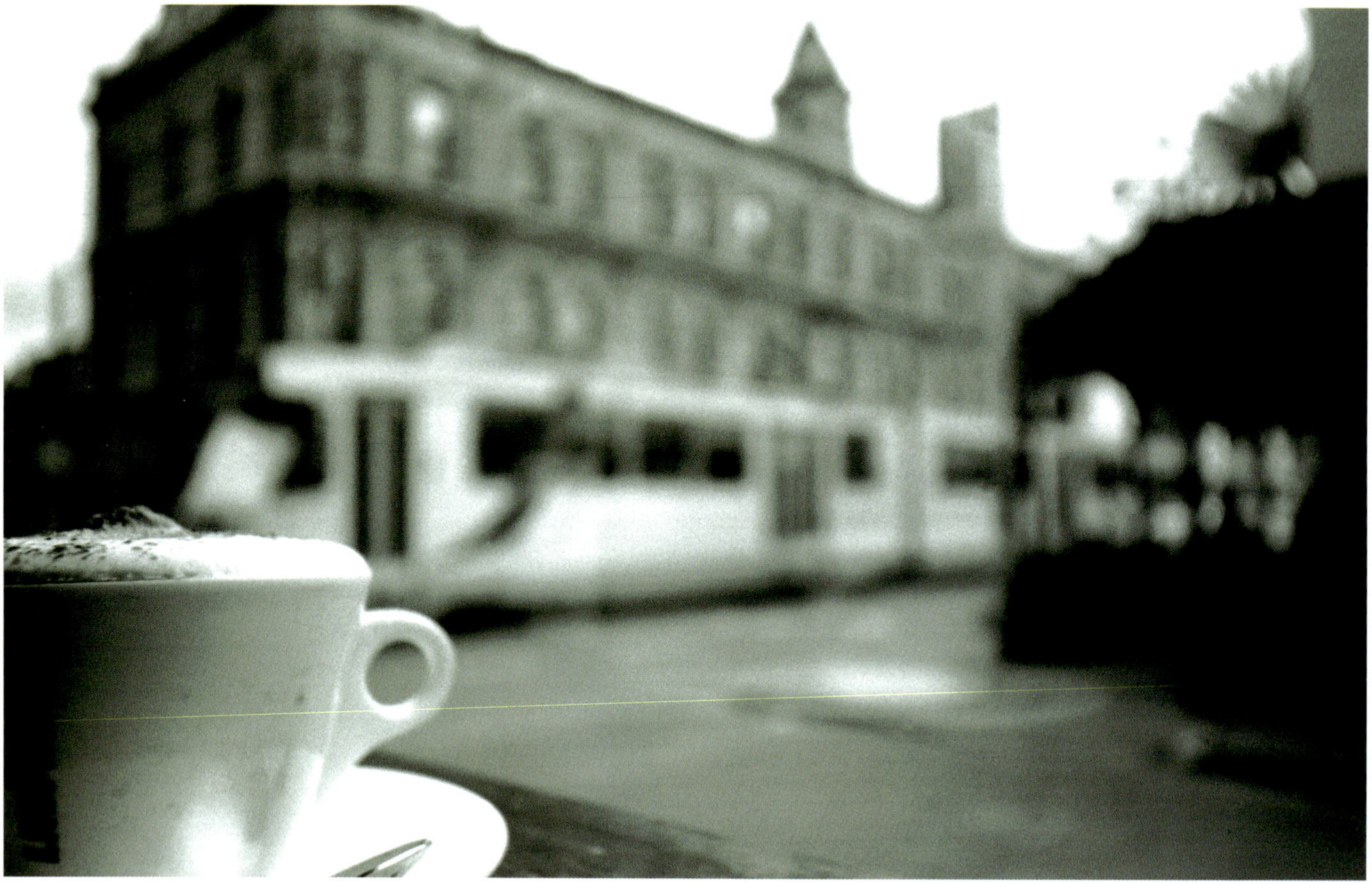

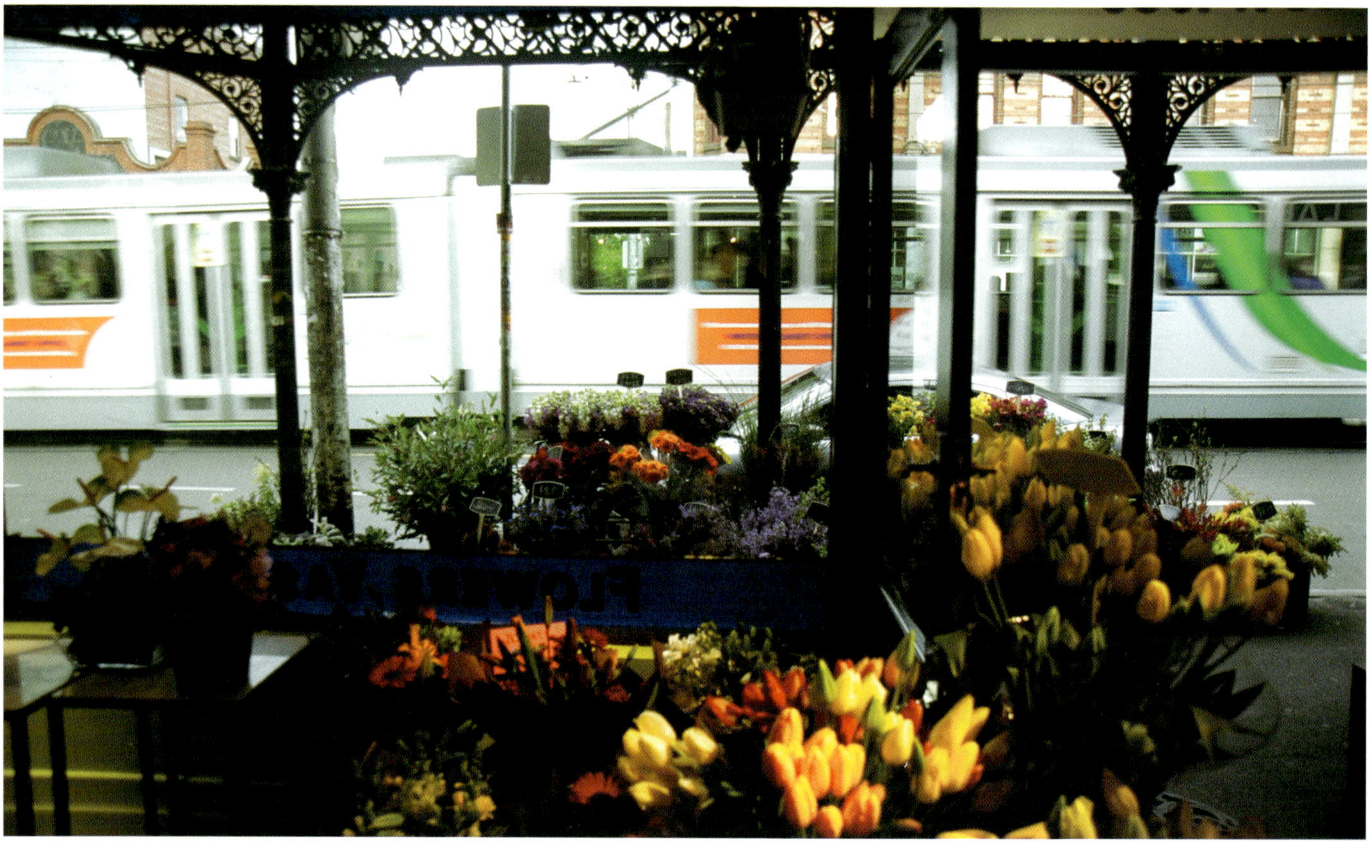

Perspectives of Brunswick Street

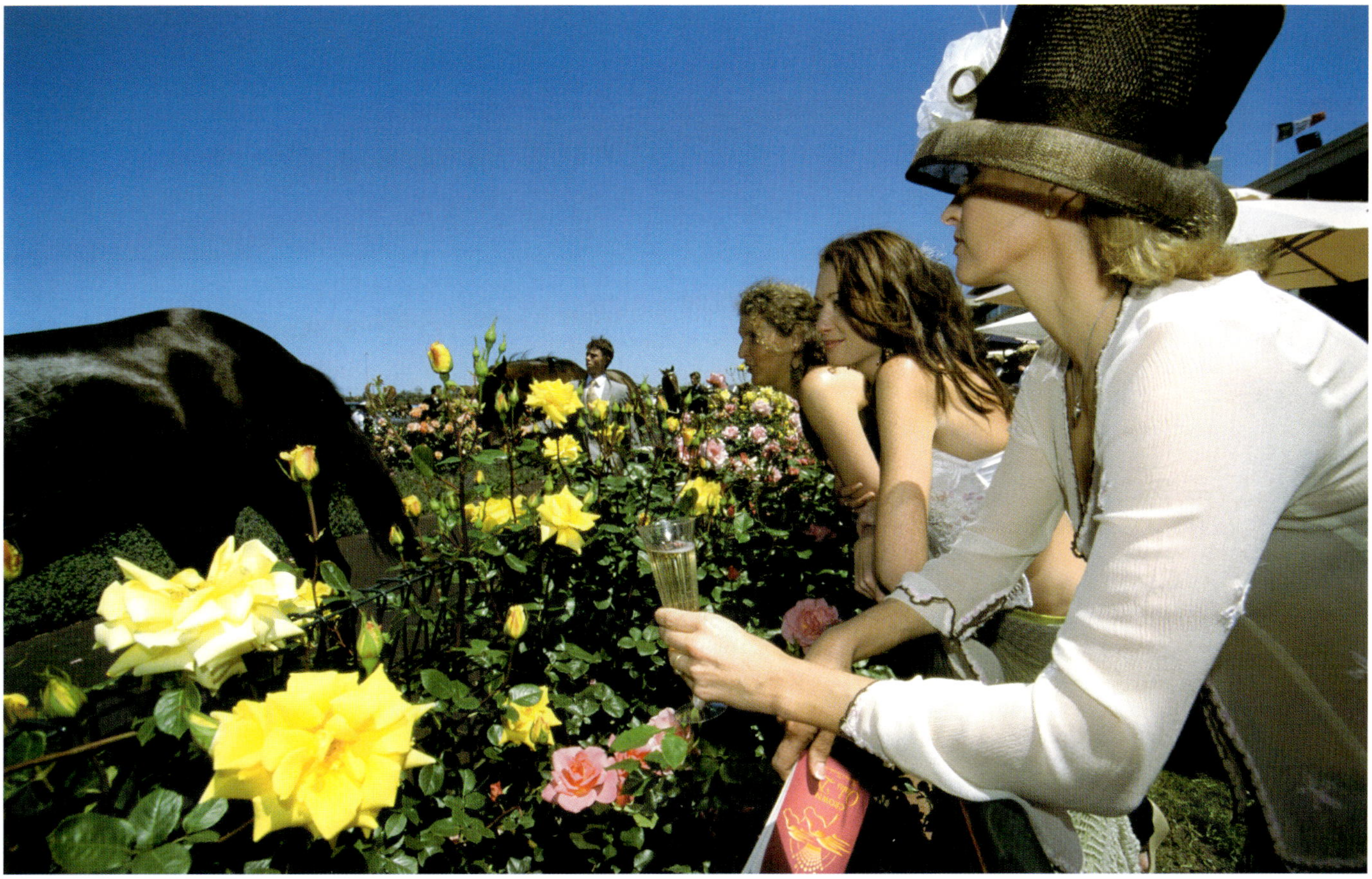

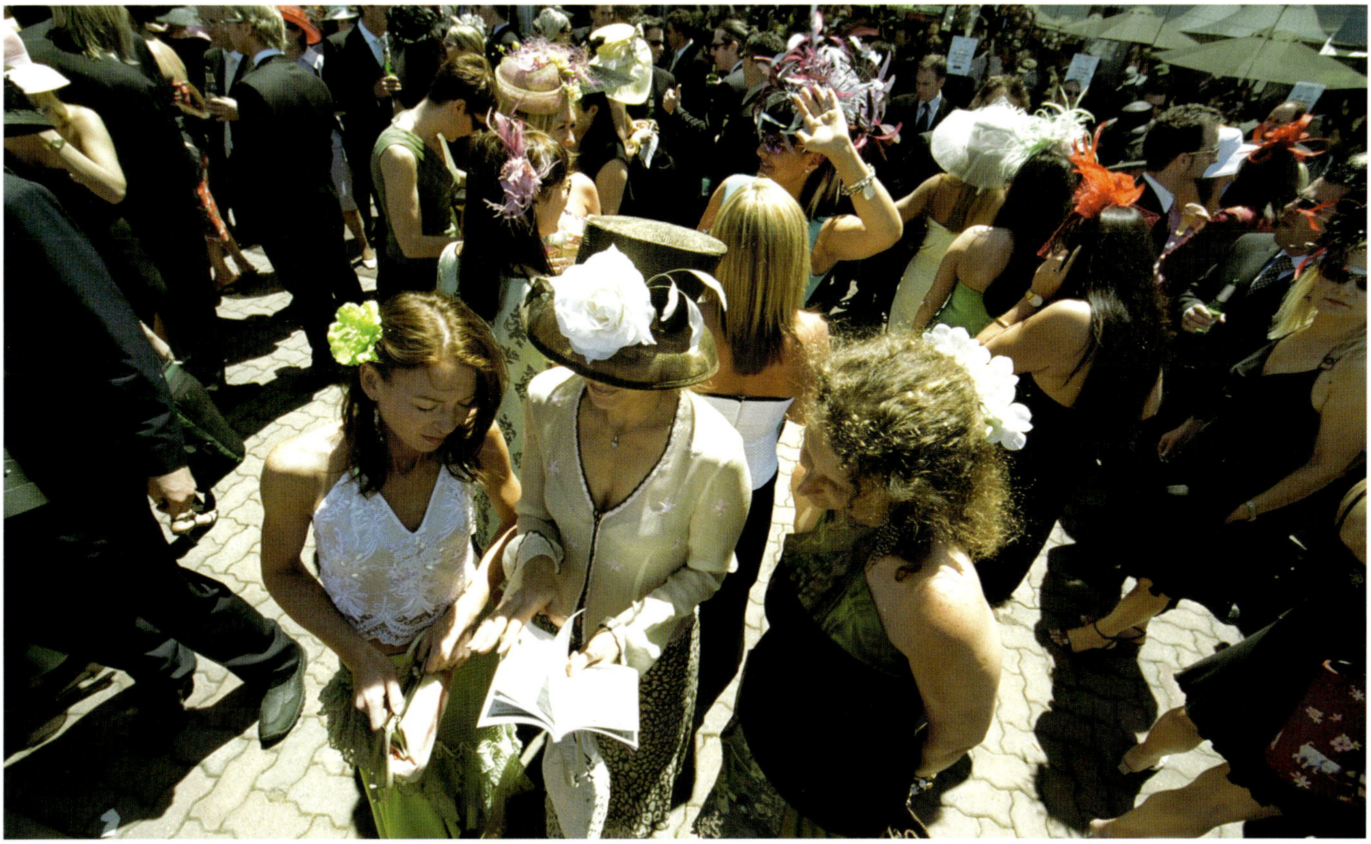

Oaks Day - Flemington Racecourse

John Ilhan

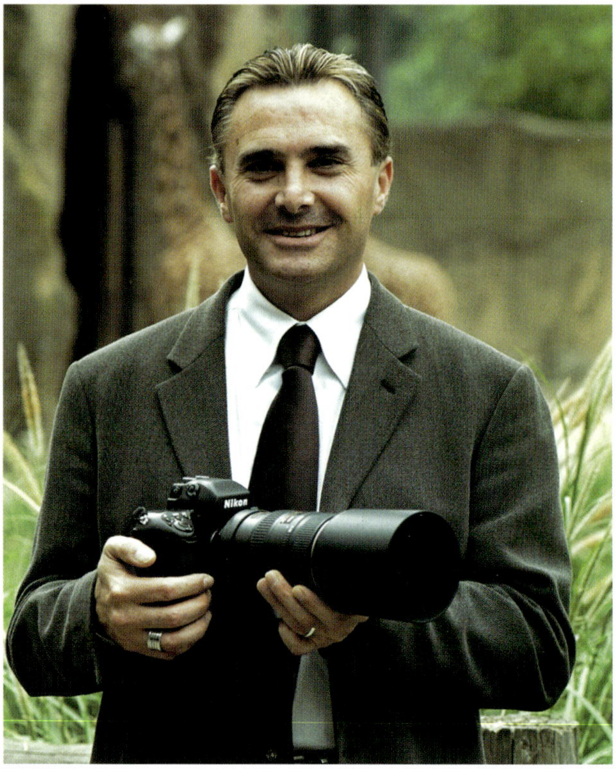

John Ilhan, CEO "Crazy John's"

Having developed his skills in several sales roles, including the mobile phone industry, in the early 1990's, John Ilhan identified a gap in the mobile phone marketplace – customers were crying out for good service and advice at the best price.

So with an entrepreneurial flair and a winning formula, John established the first Crazy John's store in 1991 in the Melbourne suburb of Brunswick.

Twelve years later, Crazy John's has over 80 stores in Australia catering for retail and business cutomers, offering the largest range of telecommunications requirements from mobile phones to key systems and PABX systems for small business up to corporate clients and everyone in between.

Crazy John's is Australia's number one Telstra MobileNet Dealer and FixedNet Dealer.

With the growth in the business, Crazy John's is no longer a one-man band. Crazy John's staff now number over 500 and like everything else this figure is growing.

So why the name? Many people thought that John Ilhan going out on his own was a "crazy" idea. With deals so good, "he must be crazy."

He is. He's Crazy John. And now he provides the best solutions for everyone's telecommunications needs throughout Australia.

Melbourne Zoo – When I was younger my mates and I would drive down to the ocean and sit for hours watching the water. I loved the water because it was so peaceful. I also found the same sense of peace watching the animals at the Melbourne Zoo. They were so strange and fascinating that I would spend hours just watching them.

To me the world is an amazing and curious place that I never get tired of learning about.

So why did I choose to photograph the giraffes out of all the animals at the zoo? To me they seem curious. What are they for? What do they do? Watching these strange animals taught me to love life for its mystery.

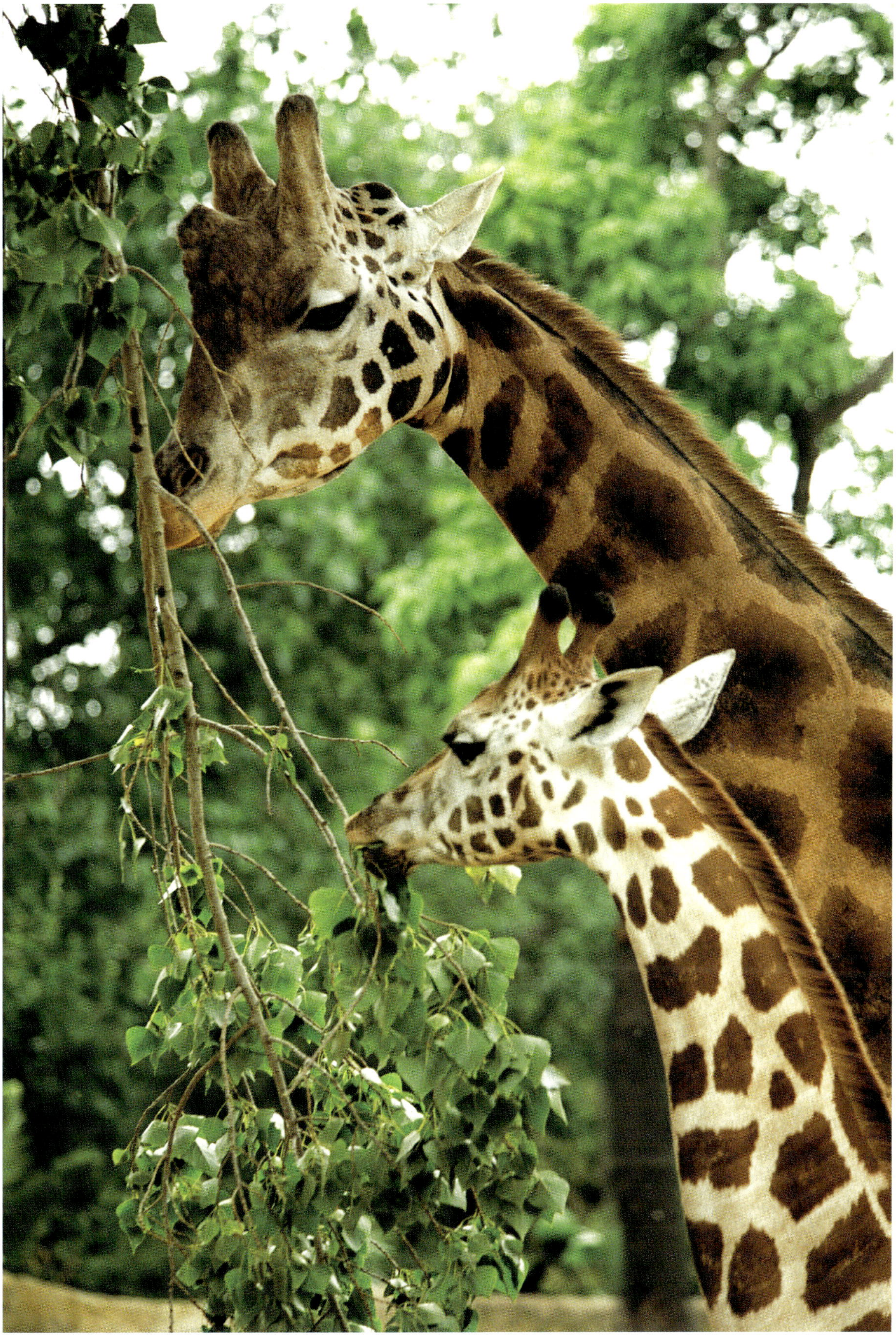

Giraffe Enclosure Melbourne Zoo

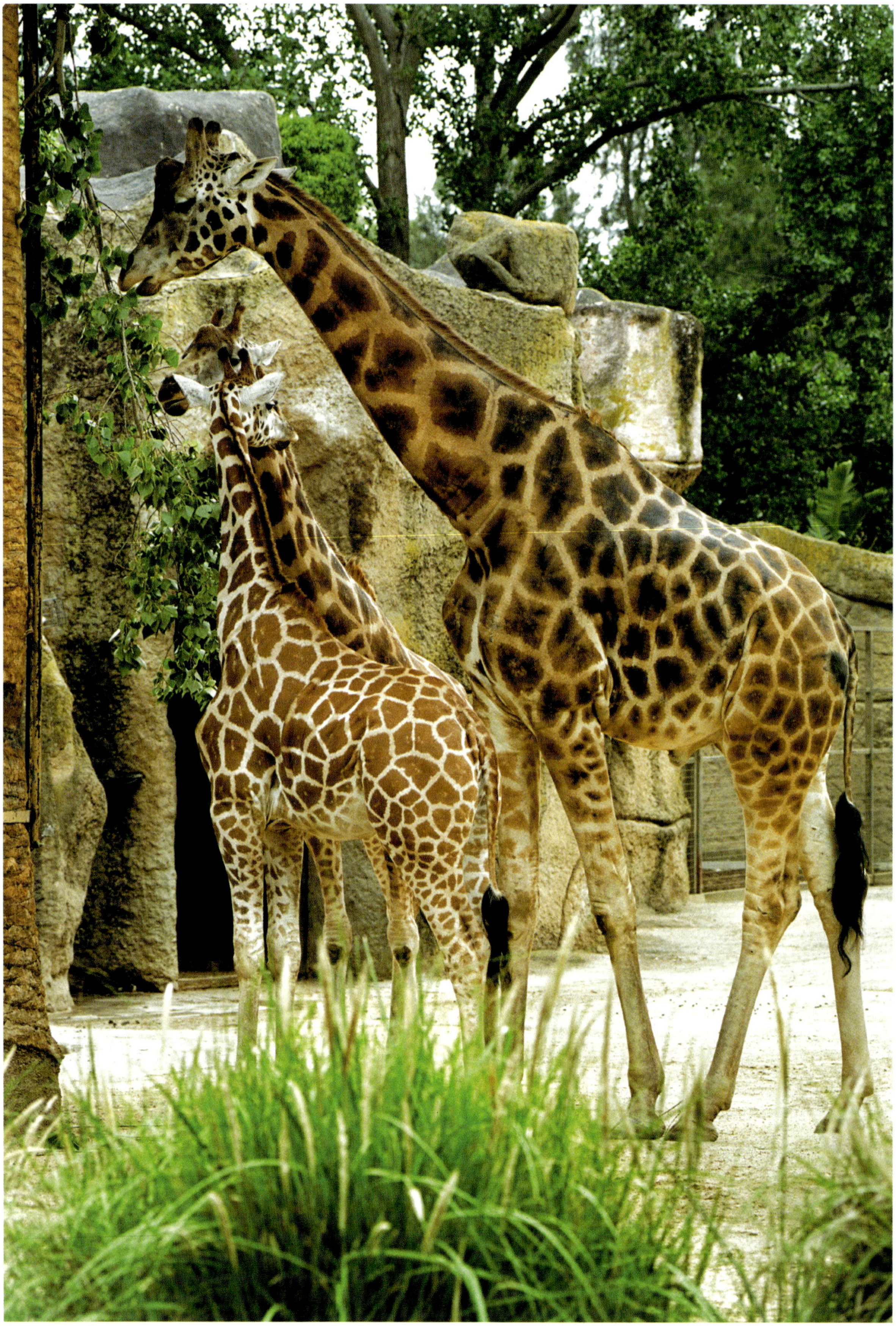

Giraffe Enclosure Melbourne Zoo

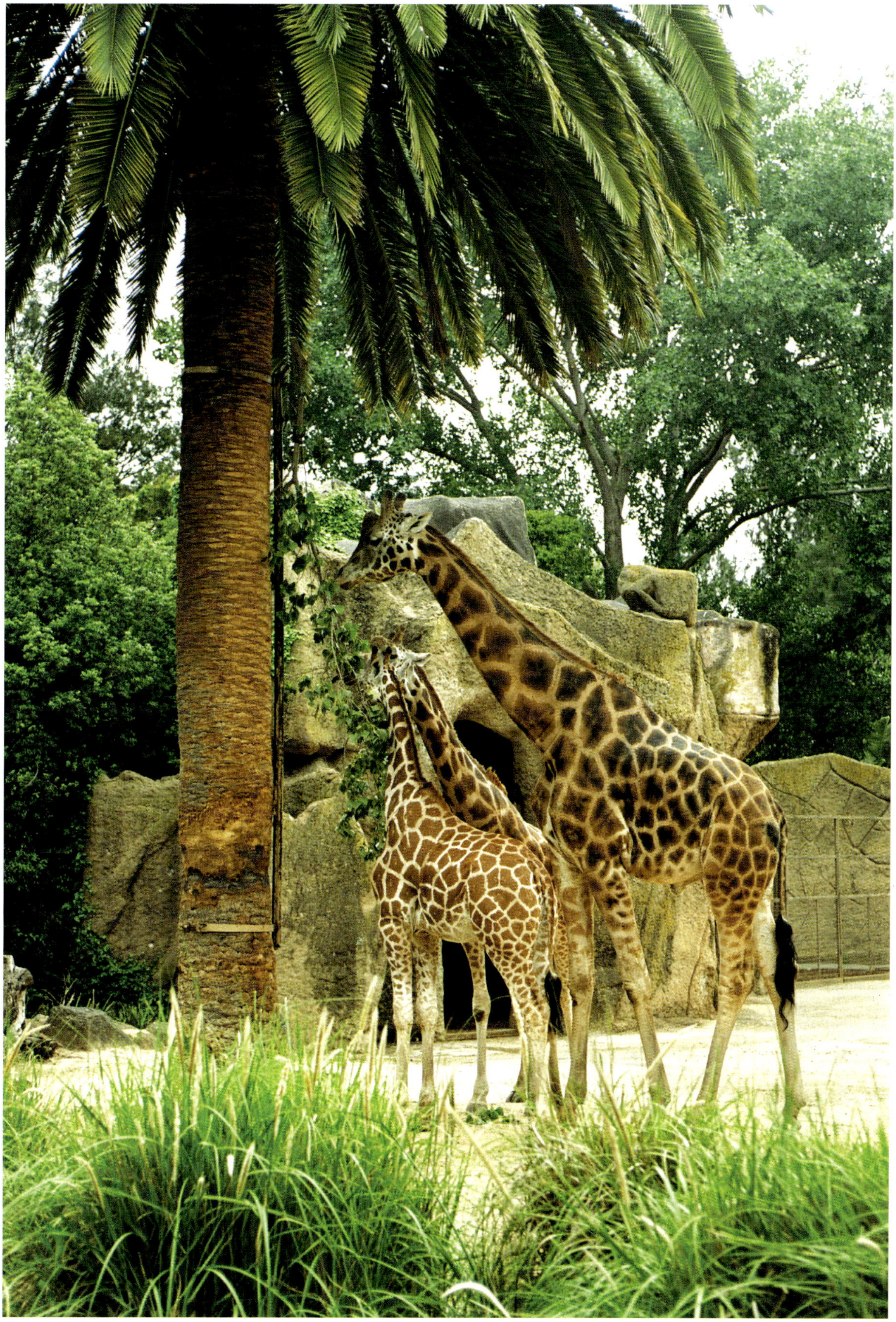

Jennifer Keyte

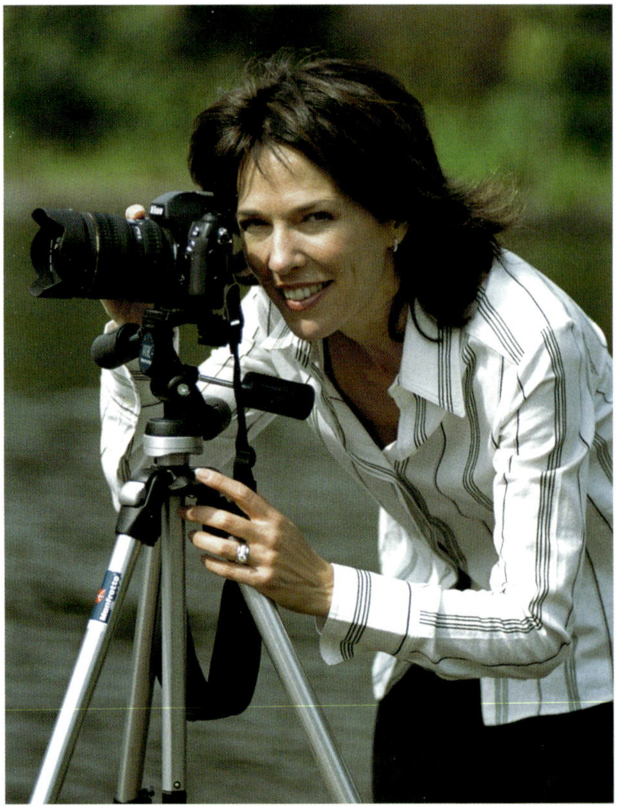

Jennifer Keyte, is an accomplished journalist, newsreader, presenter, MC and guest speaker and brings a sophistication and glamour to all her roles.

After beginning an Arts Degree at La Trobe University, Jennifer realised her passions lay in the area of journalism. She had no hesitation in accepting a cadetship with radio station EON-FM in 1980. In a matter of months she had proved her ability and was a graded journalist moving to radio 3XY where she worked as a journalist and wrote and read news bulletins.

In 1982, Jennifer made the move from radio to television, joining Network Ten. Here Jennifer gained invaluable experience working in all major areas of journalism including state politics, crime, courts and general news.

In 1987, Jennifer joined the Seven Network and and began reading the main evening news bulletin with Glenn Taylor, and eventually went solo. Jennifer also did the news on 'Tonight Live' with Steve Vizard.

In 1996, Jennifer made an exciting career change joining the Nine Network to host "Good Medicine" and a one off series "Moment of Truth" along with hosting various other specials.

Seven and half years later in August 2003, Jennifer returned to the news desk at the Seven Network in Melbourne to take up the position of Weekend Newsreader. Jennifer described the move as a "wonderful homecoming" and that she never lost her passion for news. "It's in your blood, I have to say I found it very hard watching big stories break on the TV. I wanted desperately to be part of it again. It just bubbles away inside you".

With the joy of motherhood and working weekends, time is limited but Jennifer admits that her new role with Seven suits her down to the ground and gives her the week to be Mum to her two boys James, 3 and Alexander, 1, along with husband Ben.

When the opportunity allows, Jennifer is a keen theatre goer, a passionate Essendon Football Club supporter and enjoys travel, cycling, walking and reading. Jennifer is committed to contributing to society and gives her time in her chosen charities of the Royal Women's Hospital and Breast Cancer Institute of Australia. She is also a World Vision sponsor.

"The Royal Botanic Gardens is one of my favourite places in Melbourne. I have lived nearby for many years and have spent many hours, pounding "The Tan", picknicking by the lake, and just wandering through the gardens. I love the tranquility of the gardens, the colour of the flowers, the size of the old trees and the aromas from the herb gardens. I now take my 3 year old son along the 'secret' paths before we buy an ice-cream and find a private spot to listen to the sounds of the gardens, the piercing bell-birds, the honking ducks and swans and the distant fruit bats. The perfect spot to stop and smell the roses!"

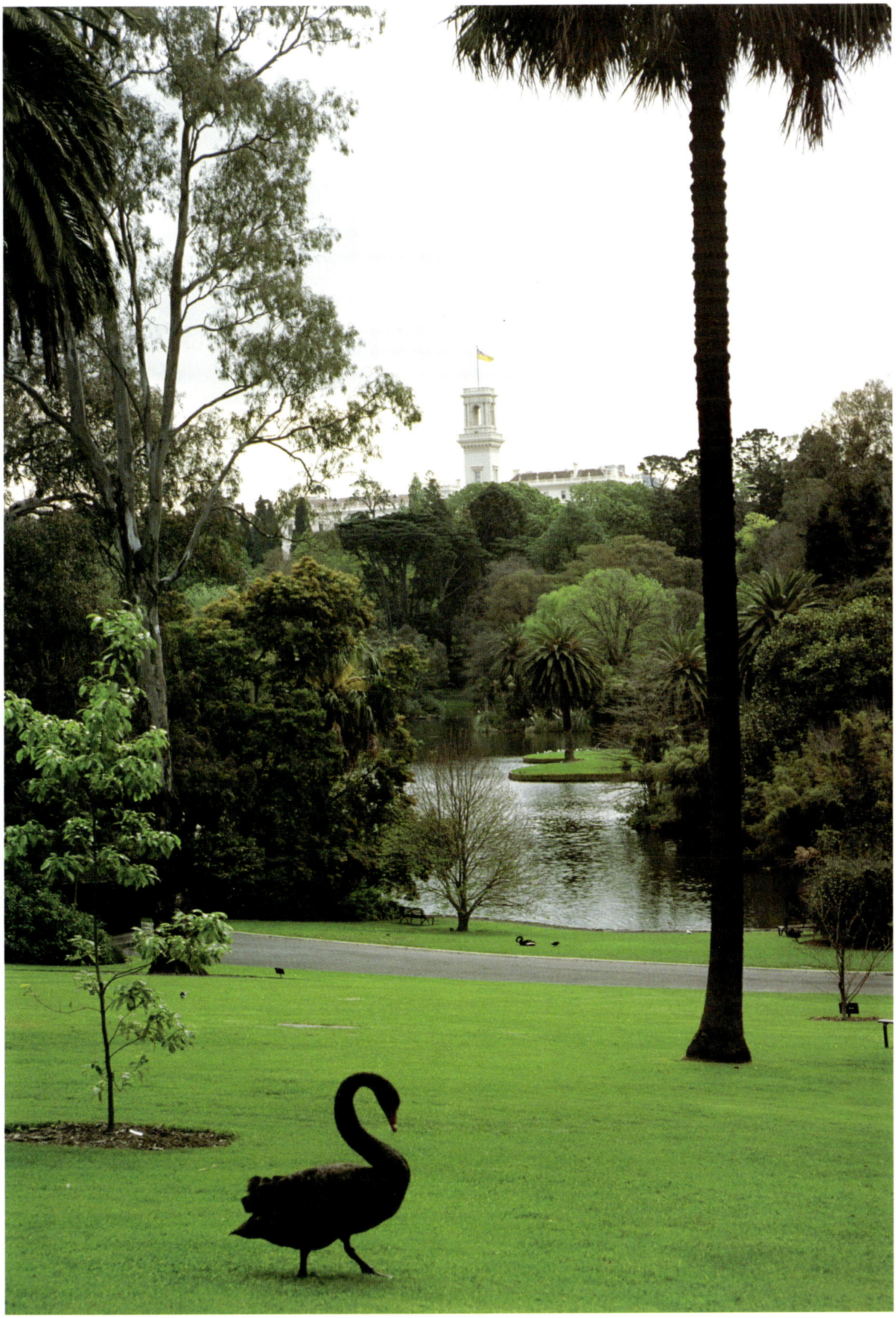

Royal Botanic Gardens

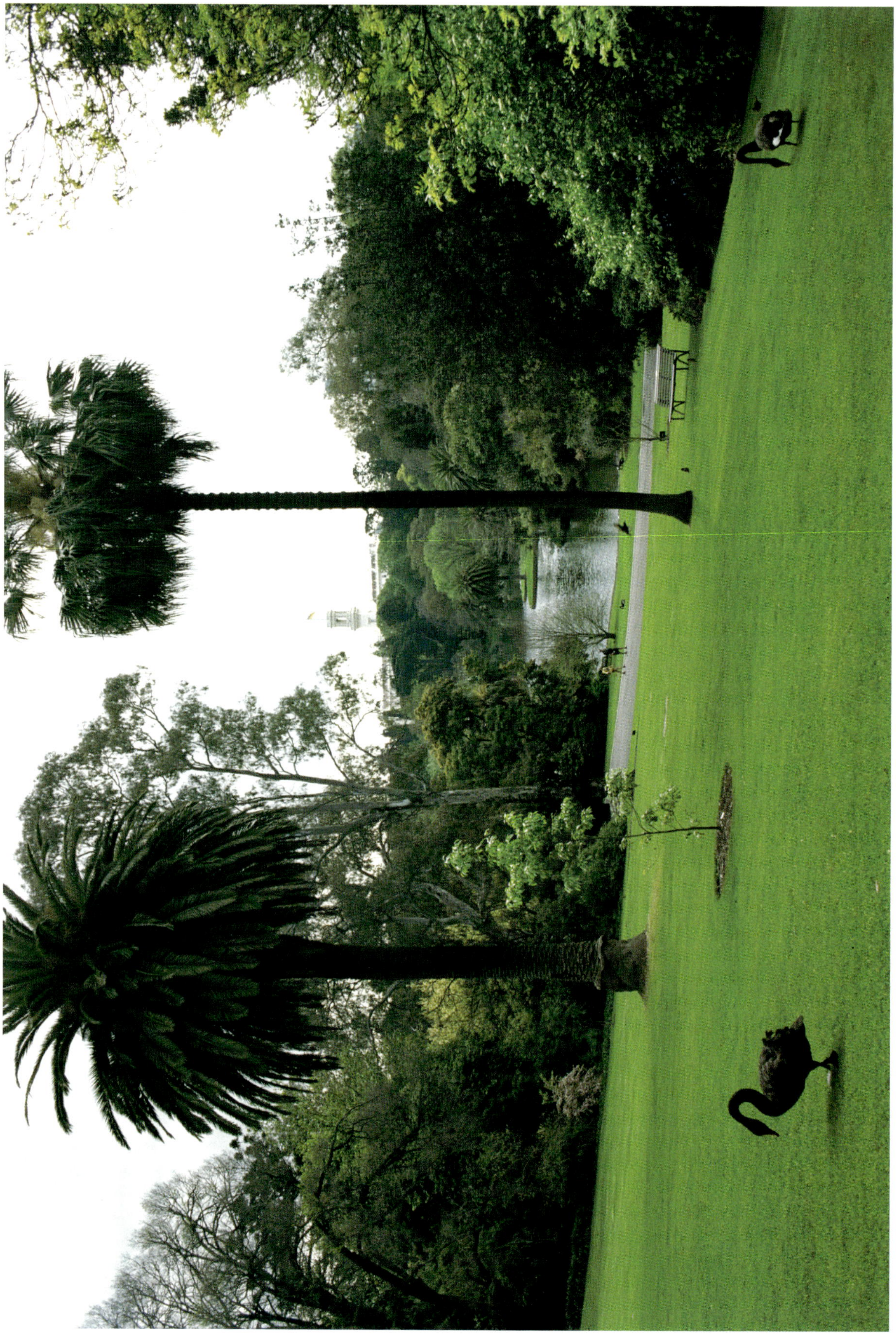

Royal Botanic Gardens

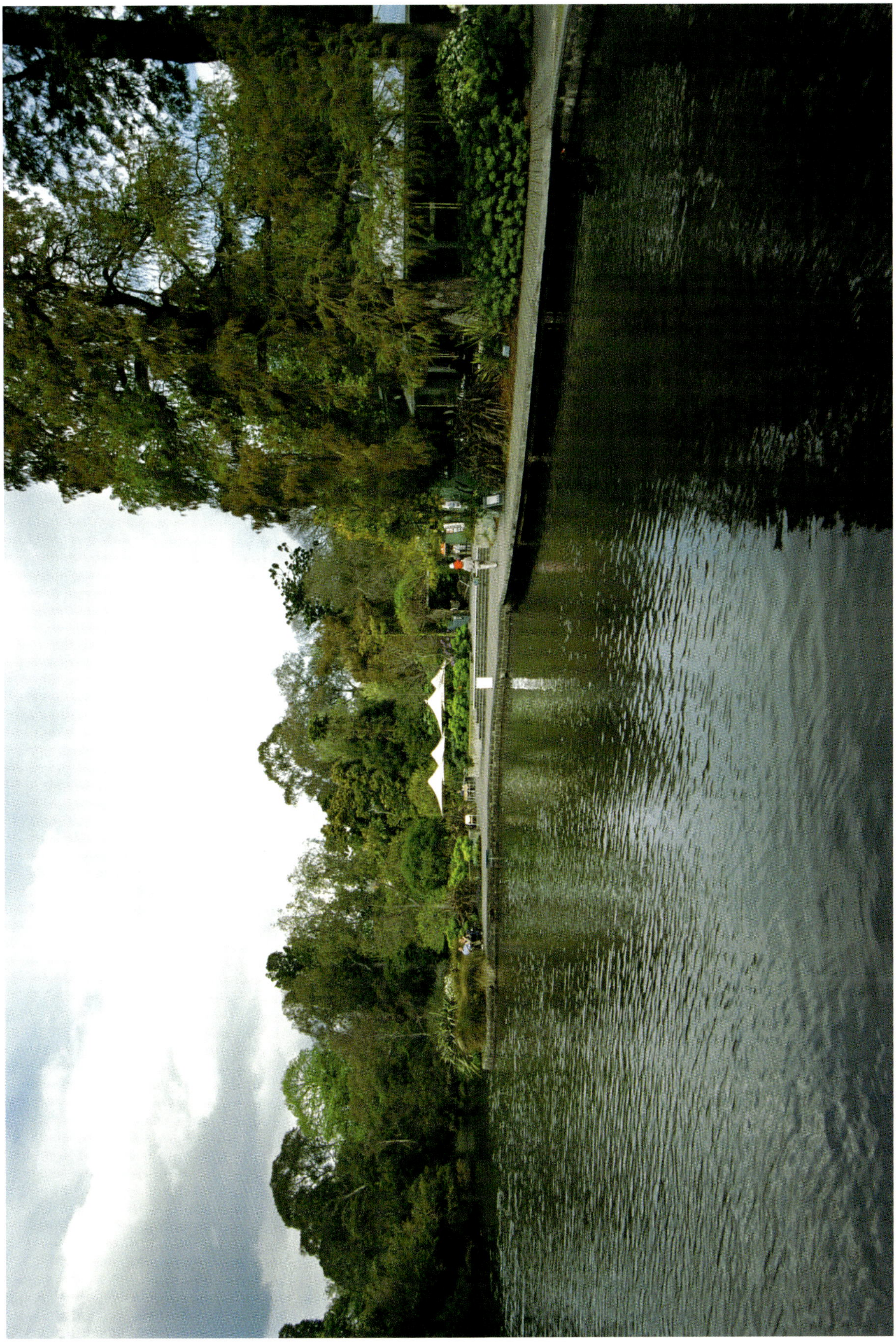

Martin Kingham

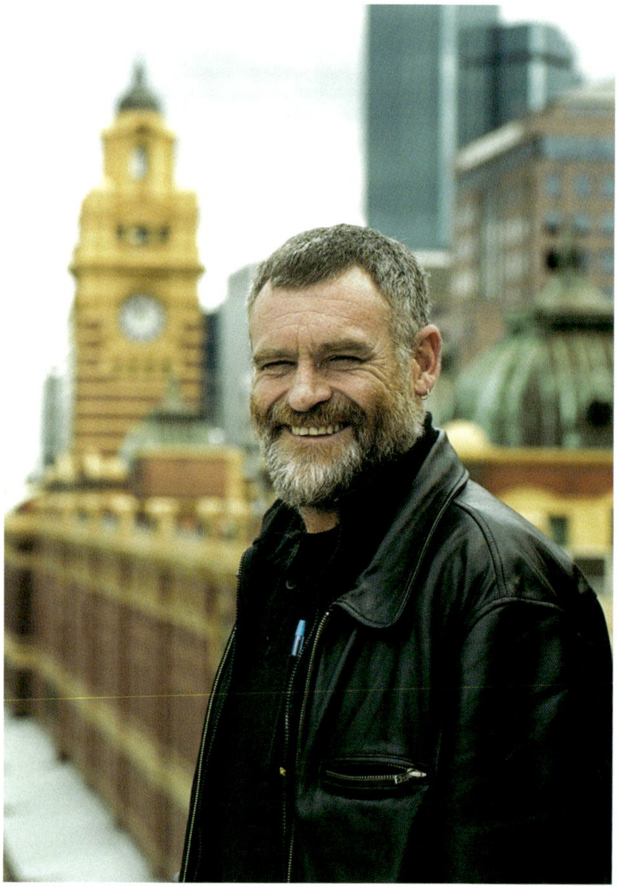

Martin Kingham, State Secretary of the Construction, Forestry, Mining and Energy Union (CFMEU).

Martin grew up in Queensland and moved to the UK when he was 18 years old. There he took up an Apprenticeship in London and became a qualified carpenter. He moved back to Australia in 1980.

From 1983 to 1986 Martin was employed on the major redevelopment of the Flinders Street Station site, which he fondly calls a "very special place."

In 1986, he accepted his first role as a union official and in 1992 he was appointed State Secretary of the CFMEU.

No one can deny that Martin is a man of passionate beliefs, driven by a strong sense of social justice and guided by a clear set of values.

Martin describes his family as critically important – he's been married for twenty four years and has two grown up sons.

Flinders Street Station - "The redevelopment was a special job for me. It is usual practice for a building site to be securely fenced off from public access – to be closed off to the outside world. However, with over 100,000 commuters and pedestrians passing through on a daily basis, Flinders Street Station provided a unique opportunity for interaction with the people of Melbourne.

This interaction allowed those working on the site to get to know people, particularly the homeless, who spent much of their time sitting on the stairs beneath the famous clocks of Flinders Street Station. A little know fact is that in the final days of the Station reconstruction, heating elements were installed in these steps to make life just that little bit more tolerable for those spending so much time sitting there escaping their reality.

Flinders Street Station has many sensational views; long platforms, domed roof, the clock with people waiting or walking beneath to the many arches. It's as unique in its look as it is in the method of its construction."

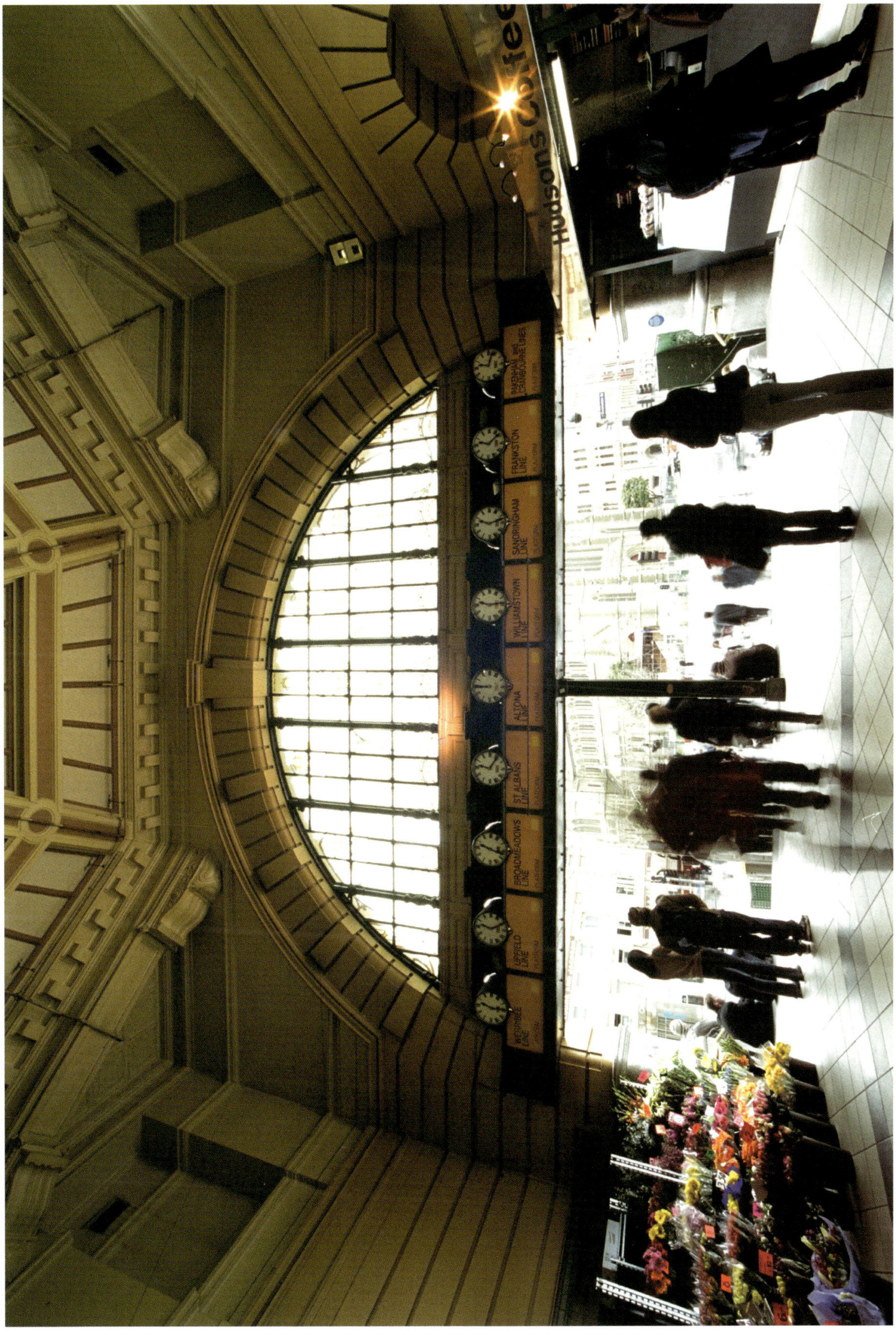

Flinders Street Station Entrance

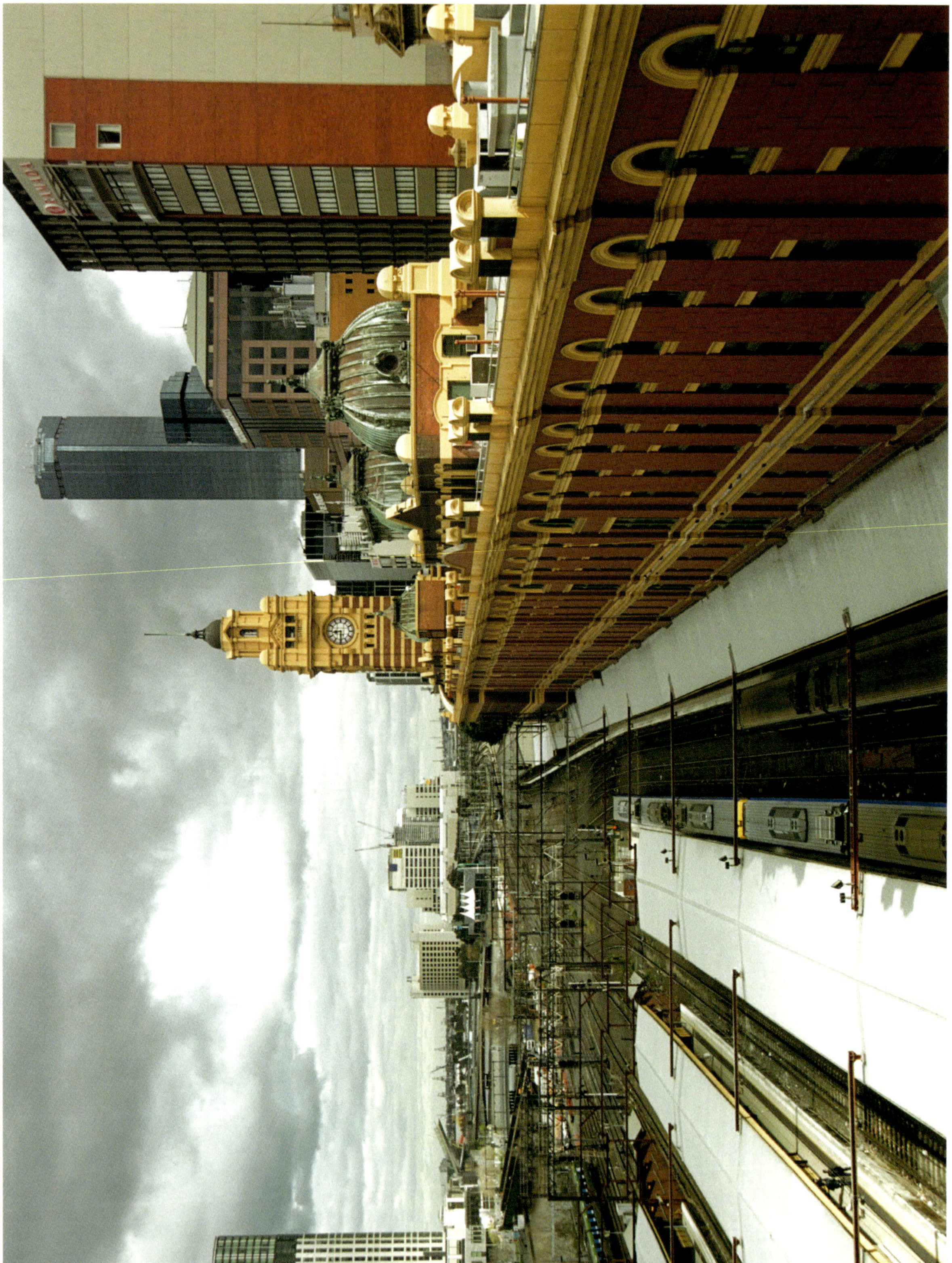

Flinders Street Station "On the Roof"

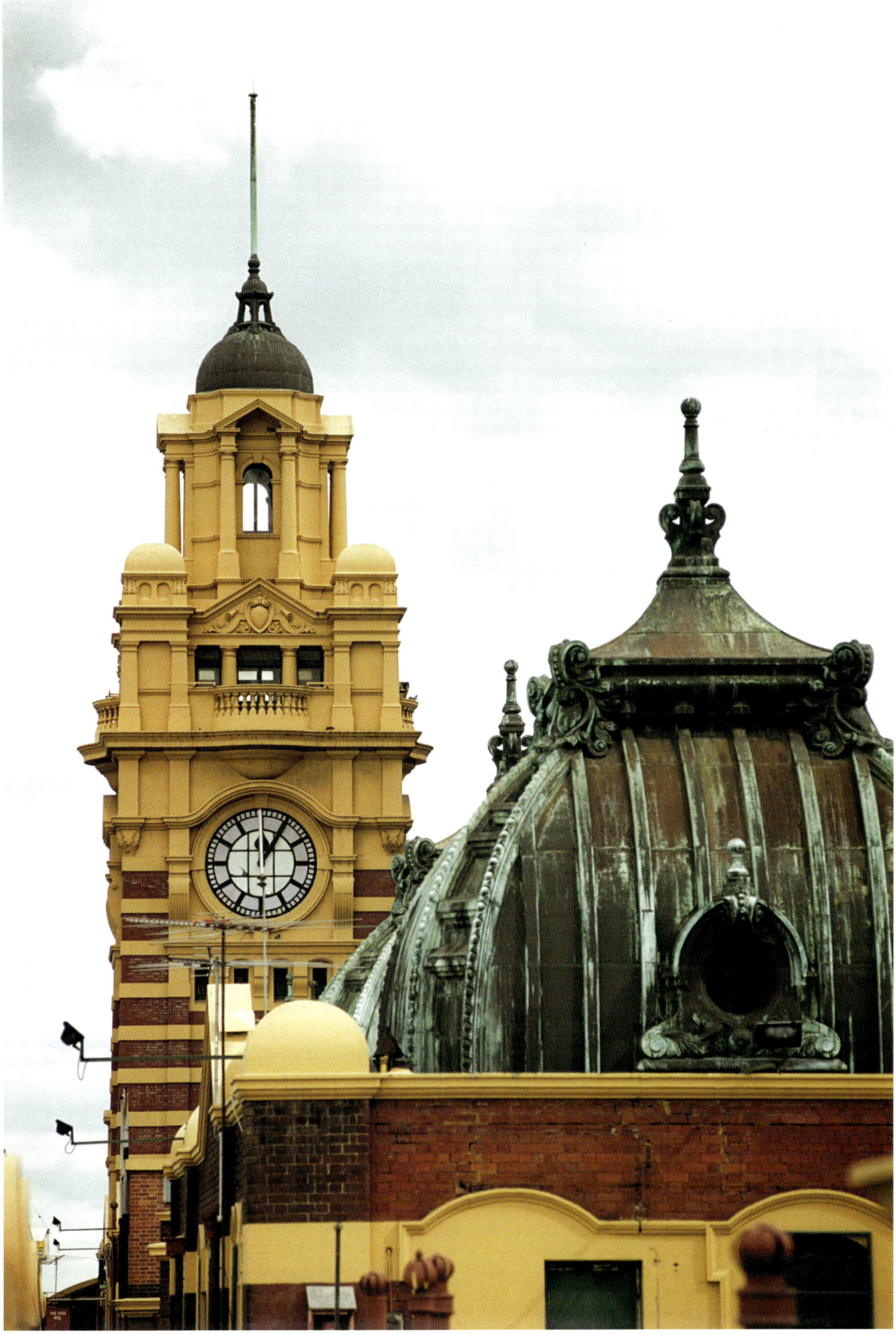

Flinders Street Station

Michael Kroger

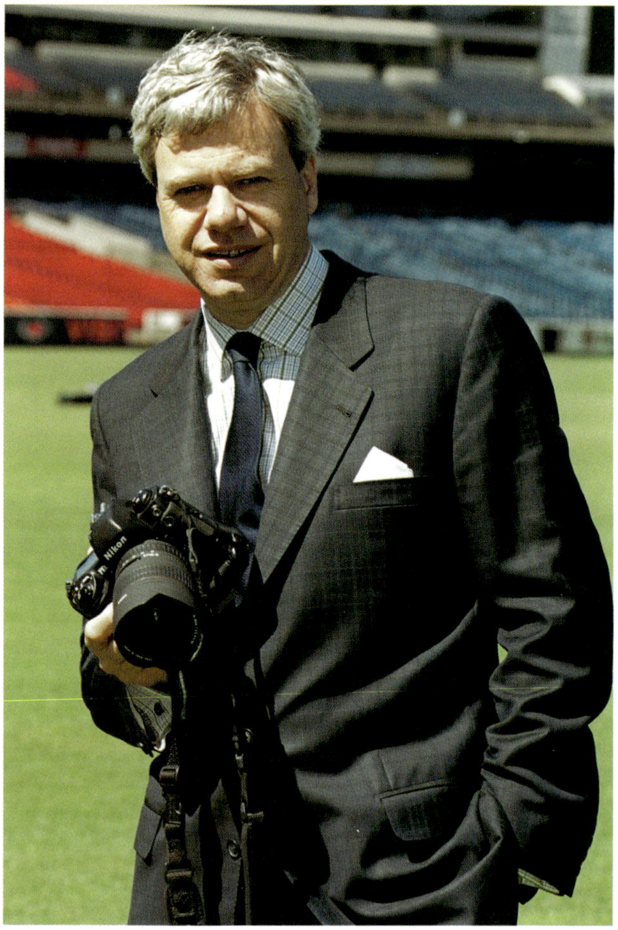

Michael Kroger, Chairman JT Campbell & Co. a Melbourne-based corporate advisory business.

Prior to his current role Mr Kroger was a Principal of Kroger & Kroger Solicitors, specialising in labour, employment and industrial law.

Mr Kroger studied at Monash University and holds degrees in Jurisprudence and Law. He was President of the Victorian Division of the Liberal Party from 1987 – 1992.

Melbourne Cricket Ground - The MCG is one of Australia's greatest monuments. The events that take place on its hallowed surface provoke both tears of triumph and tears of sorrow. For any Australian who loves sport the MCG is a compelling and magnetic institution which demands our presence no matter what the sport.

My father started taking my brother and I to the MCG when we were young boys. It has been part of our lives as it has for so many Australians, ever since. Later in his life Dad became the Returning Officer in Melbourne Cricket Club (MCC) elections, a Volunteer Guide at the wonderful sporting Museum and he had the difficult task of checking Member's signatures during the football finals just to ensure no Member had inadvertently lent his MCC medallion to a third party. The great deeds performed on its luscious turf have inspired generations and hopefully it will forever be thus.

Wesley College - During his working life my father was a teacher at Wesley College where he was a Master for some 40 years. Teaching is a noble profession and he was one of its finest exponents. He was the wicket keeper for Prahran for many years and played at least one game for Victoria, an achievement of which he was exceptionally proud.

He was for many years Master in Charge of Cricket and the school honoured him by naming its front turf in St Kilda Road "The H J Kroger Front Turf".

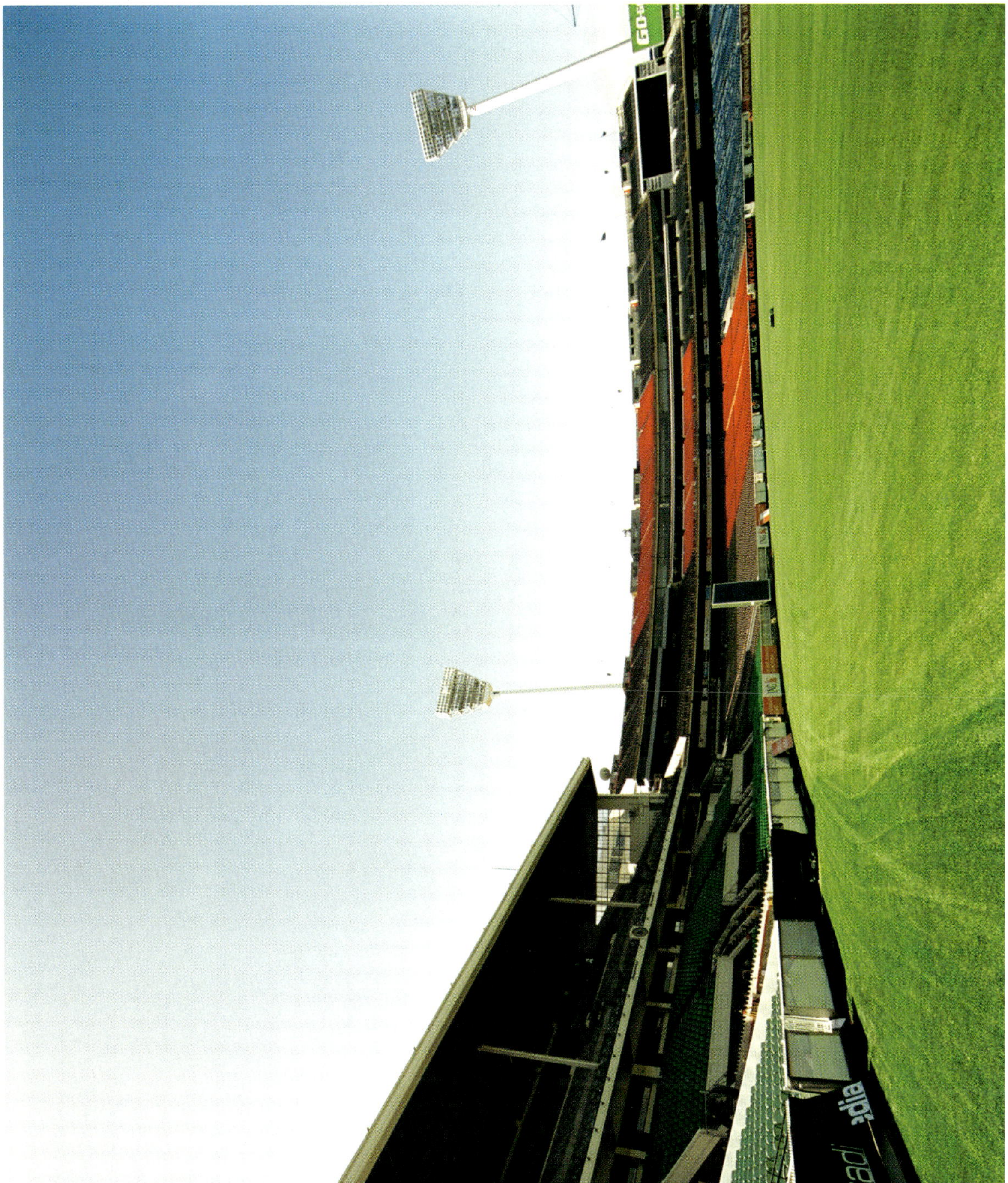

"The Day before Demolition" - Members Stand Melbourne Cricket Ground

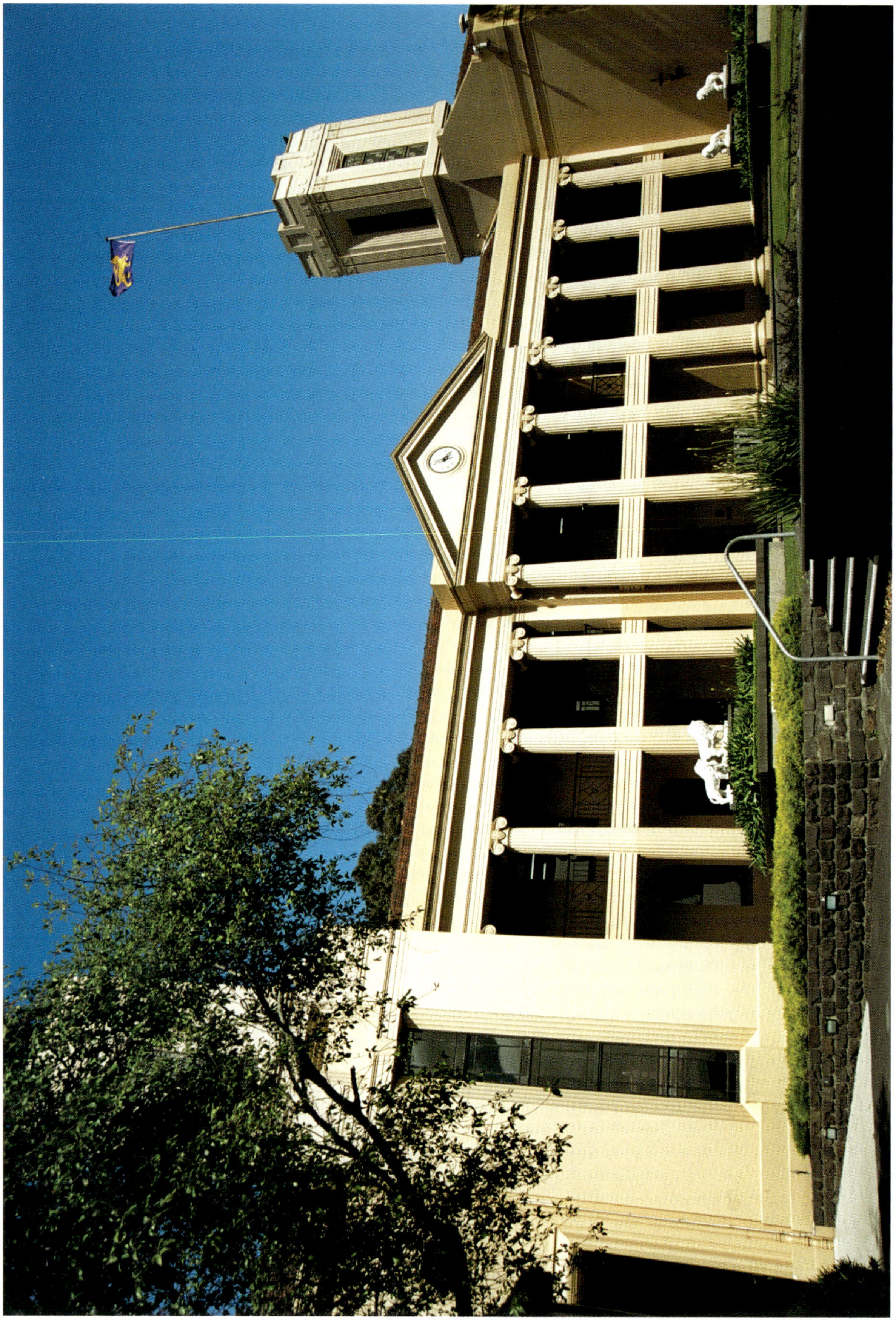

Wesley College

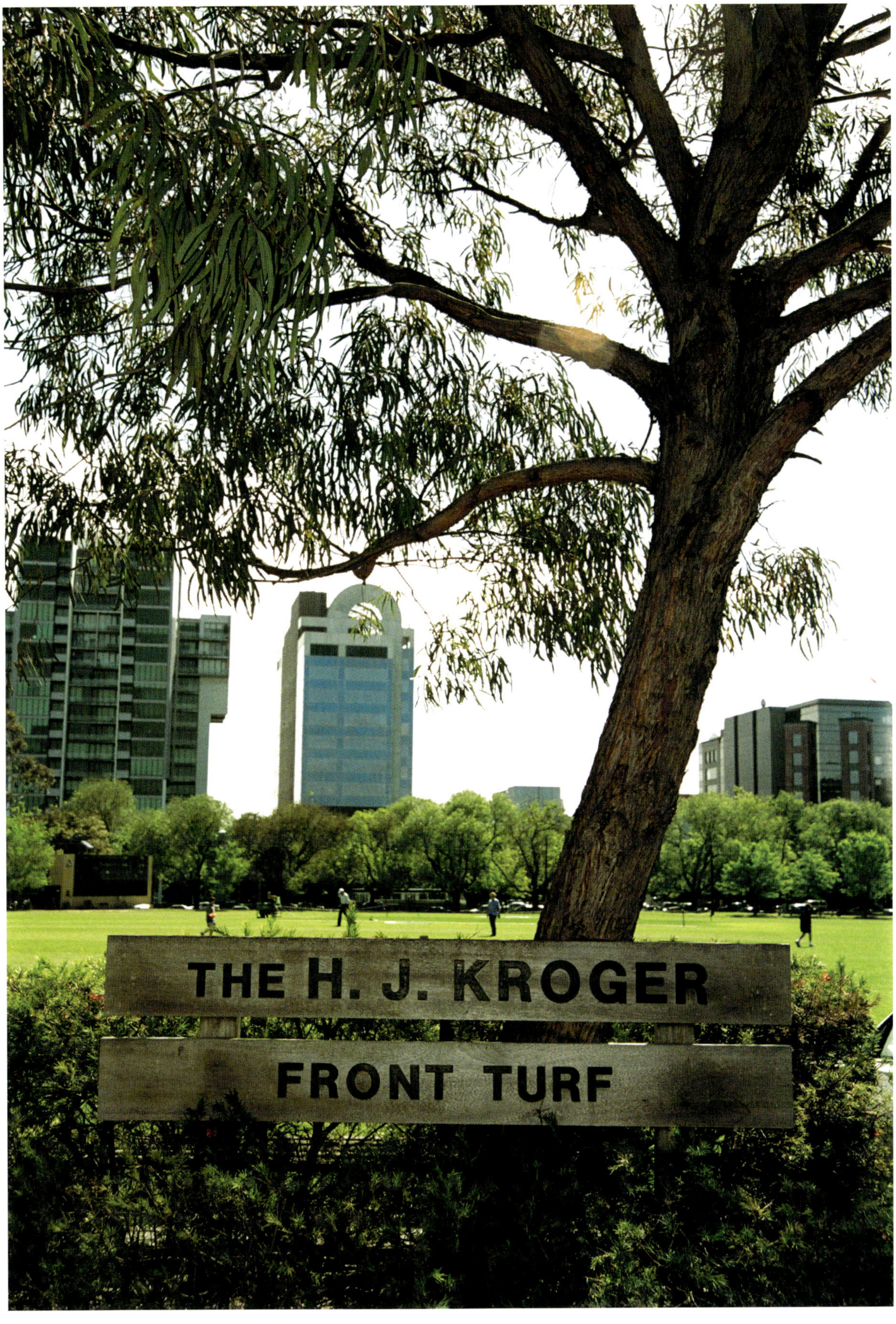

The "H.J. Kroger Front Turf" Wesley College

Ted Kunkel

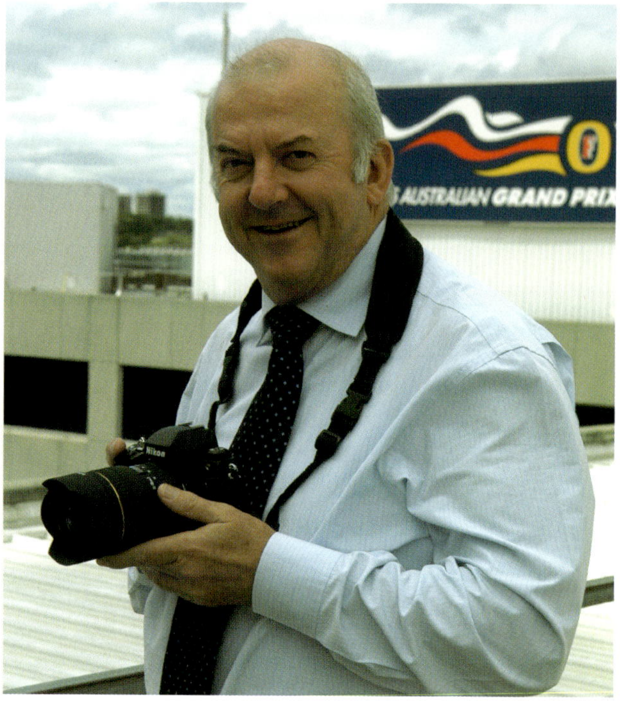

Ted Kunkel, President & CEO Foster's Group Limited.

Ted Kunkel was appointed to this position in 1992. He also serves as a Director on the Board of Foster's. Educated in New Zealand, he has a Bachelor of Science in Chemistry and Zoology from Auckland University.

Ted Kunkel has been in the adult beverage business all his working life. Following a year in the New Zealand wine industry he joined CUB in 1968 as an assistant brewer. He then held a series of progressively senior positions in CUB, Carling O'Keefe Breweries and Molson Breweries.

He is 60 years of age, has three daughters and his main recreation is golf.

Brighton Beach Foreshore - "As a Kiwi, where the sea is an integral and always visible part of life, I find its ever changing landscape very appealing."

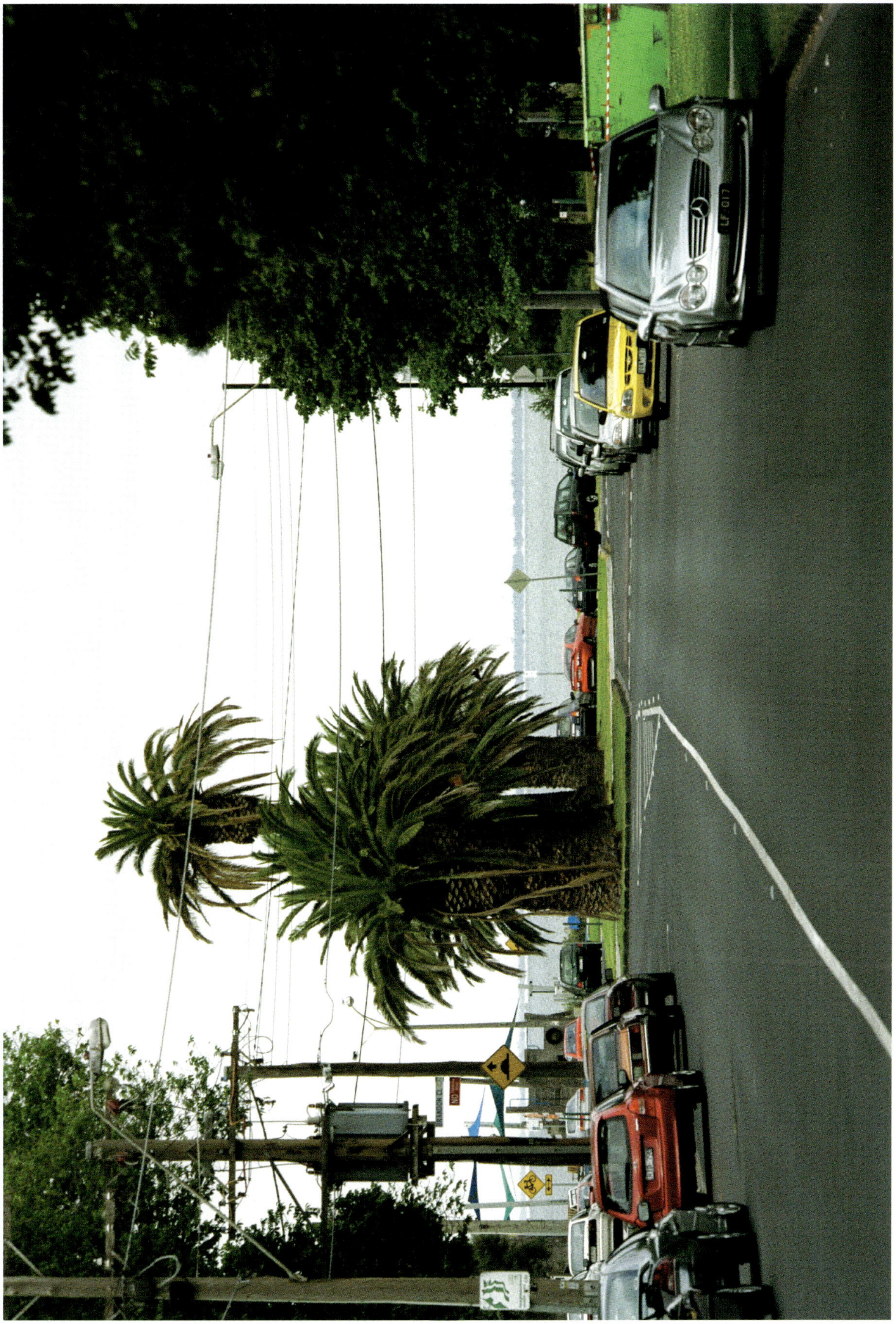

The road to Brighton Beach

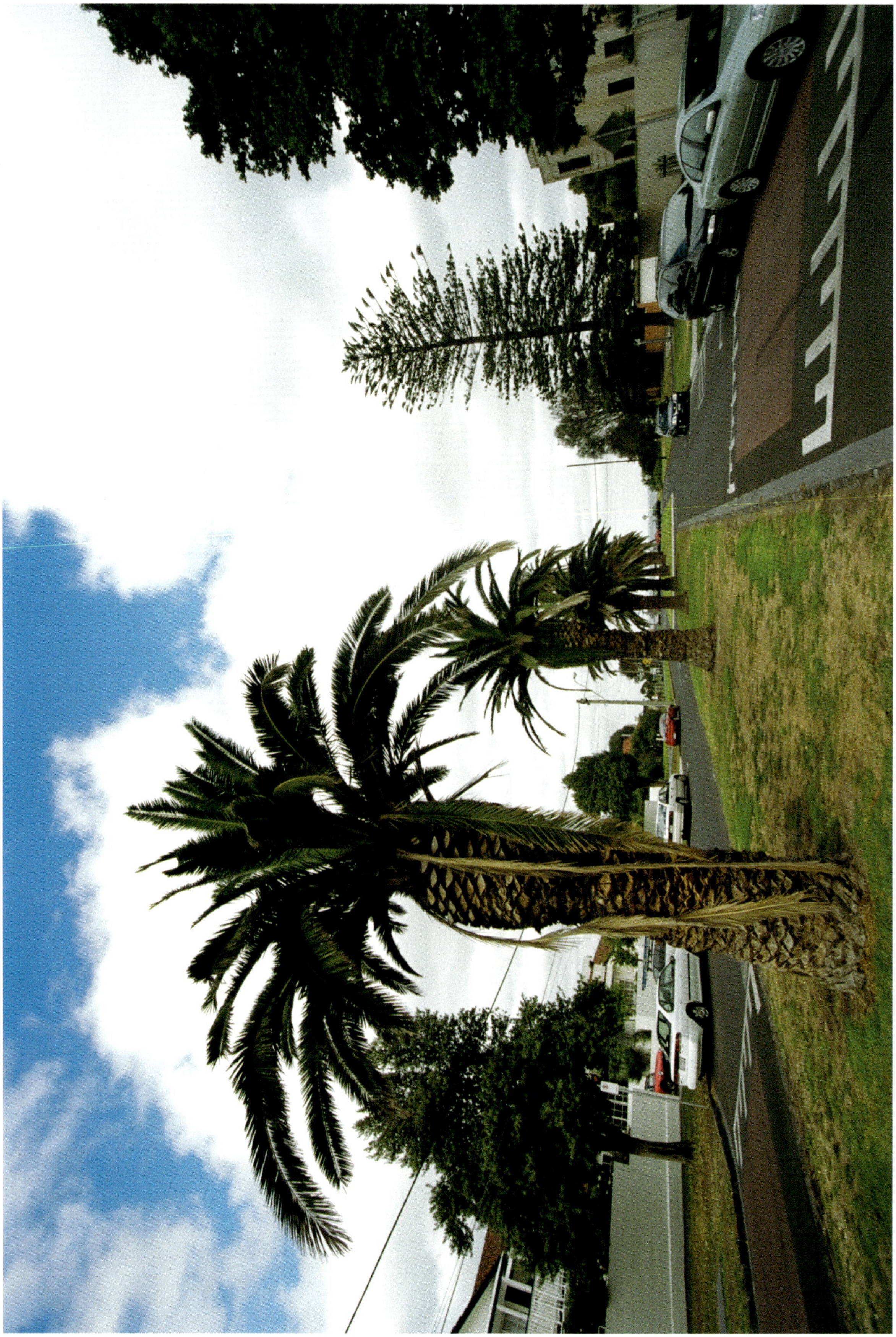

The road to Brighton Beach

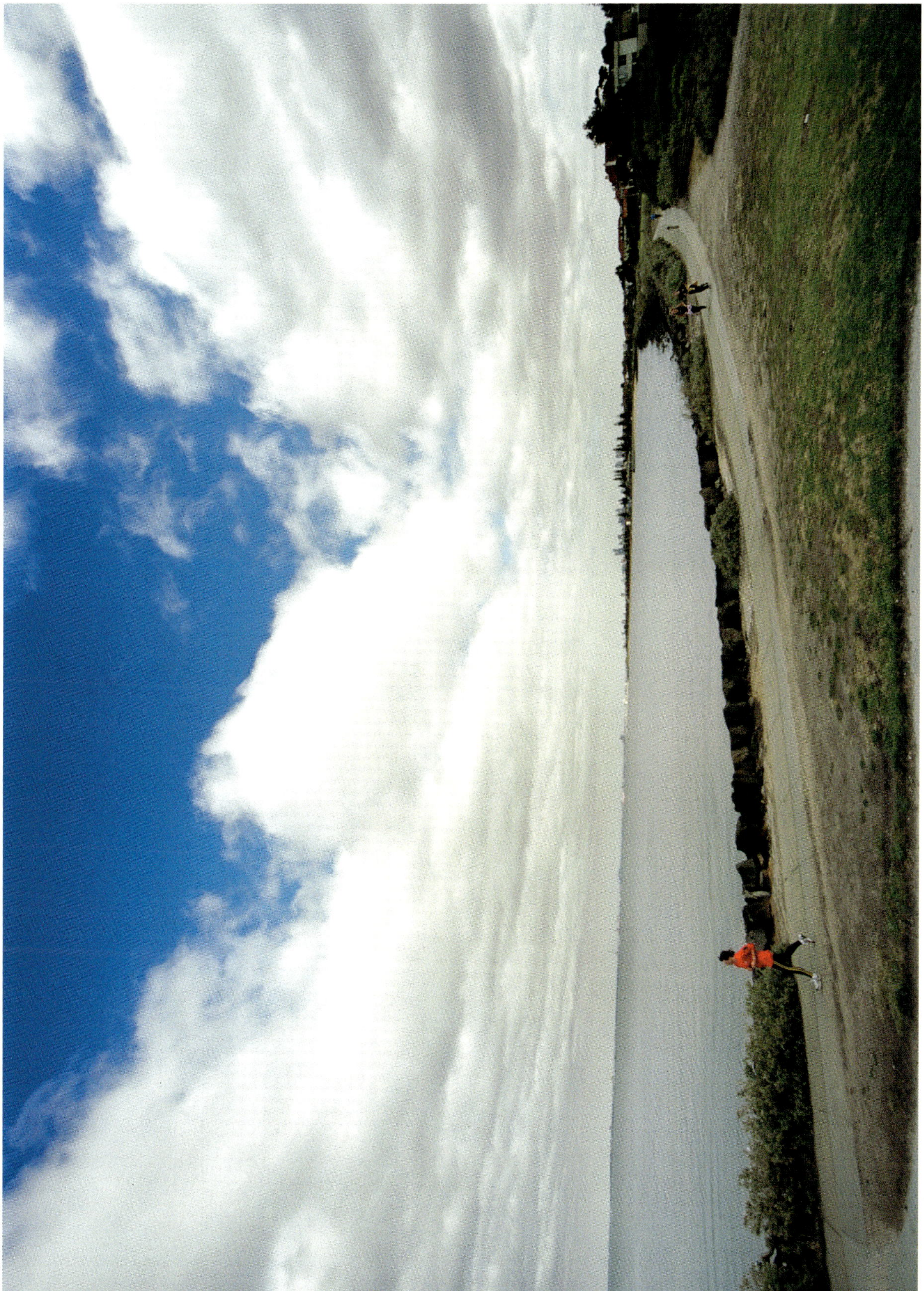

Brighton Beach

Judy Maddigan

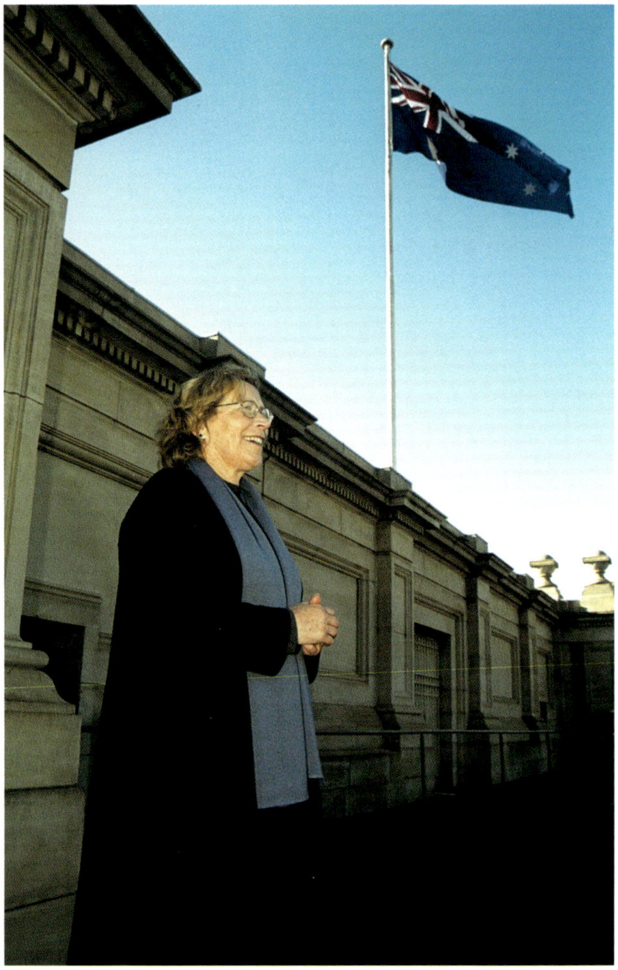

Judy Maddigan MP, Speaker Victorian Parliament.

Judy Maddigan is the first female Speaker of the Victorian Legislative Assembly.

Her prior employment in the Public Sector, as a councillor with the City of Essendon and as a Member of the Victorian Parliament since 1996 has provided her with a solid grounding to undertake her role as the Speaker.

Judy's interest in the community extends beyond her political role. She has chaired many local Essendon based forums, been a committee member on local legal, historic and commerce committees as well as maintaining a strong representation concerning community libraries.

Judy is married and has an adult daughter.

The view from the roof of Parliament - "Parliament was built at the top of Bourke Street, to be an important landmark of democracy in the early days of Victoria. Unfortunately, it has never been completed but should have a dome above it, which is one and a half times the height of the Parliament building. It is believed that Alfred Deakin cancelled the completion of the building as Victoria moved towards the end of the 19th century. However, some of the original drawings still exist.

Whilst by 2004, buildings around have overtaken it, the view from the roof gives a unique perspective of other important buildings such as the Princess Theatre, a reminder of the days when Melbourne was "marvelous."

The Parliament itself, a symbol of our gold rush days is a beautiful building of which all Victorians can be proud."

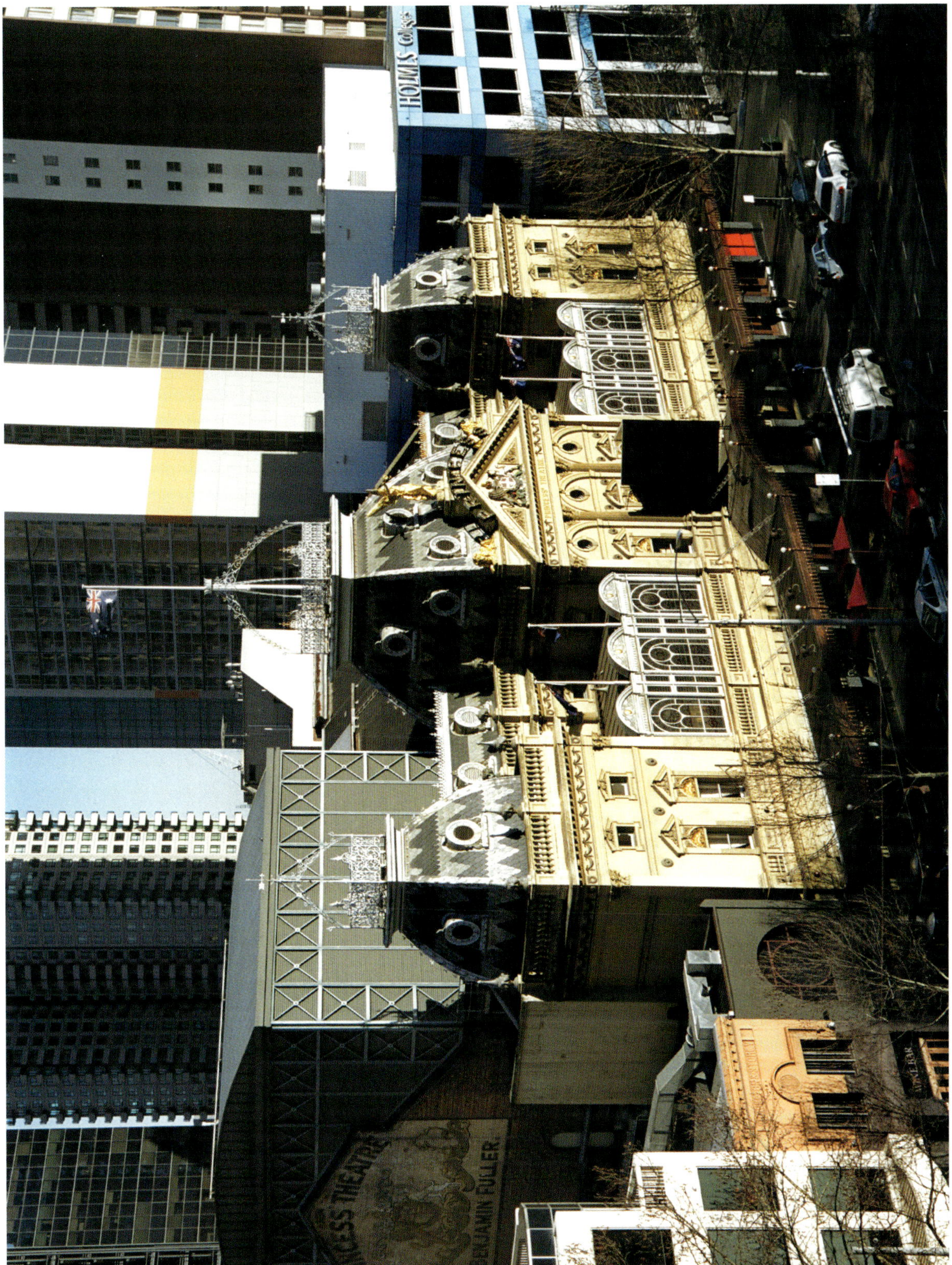

Princess Theatre

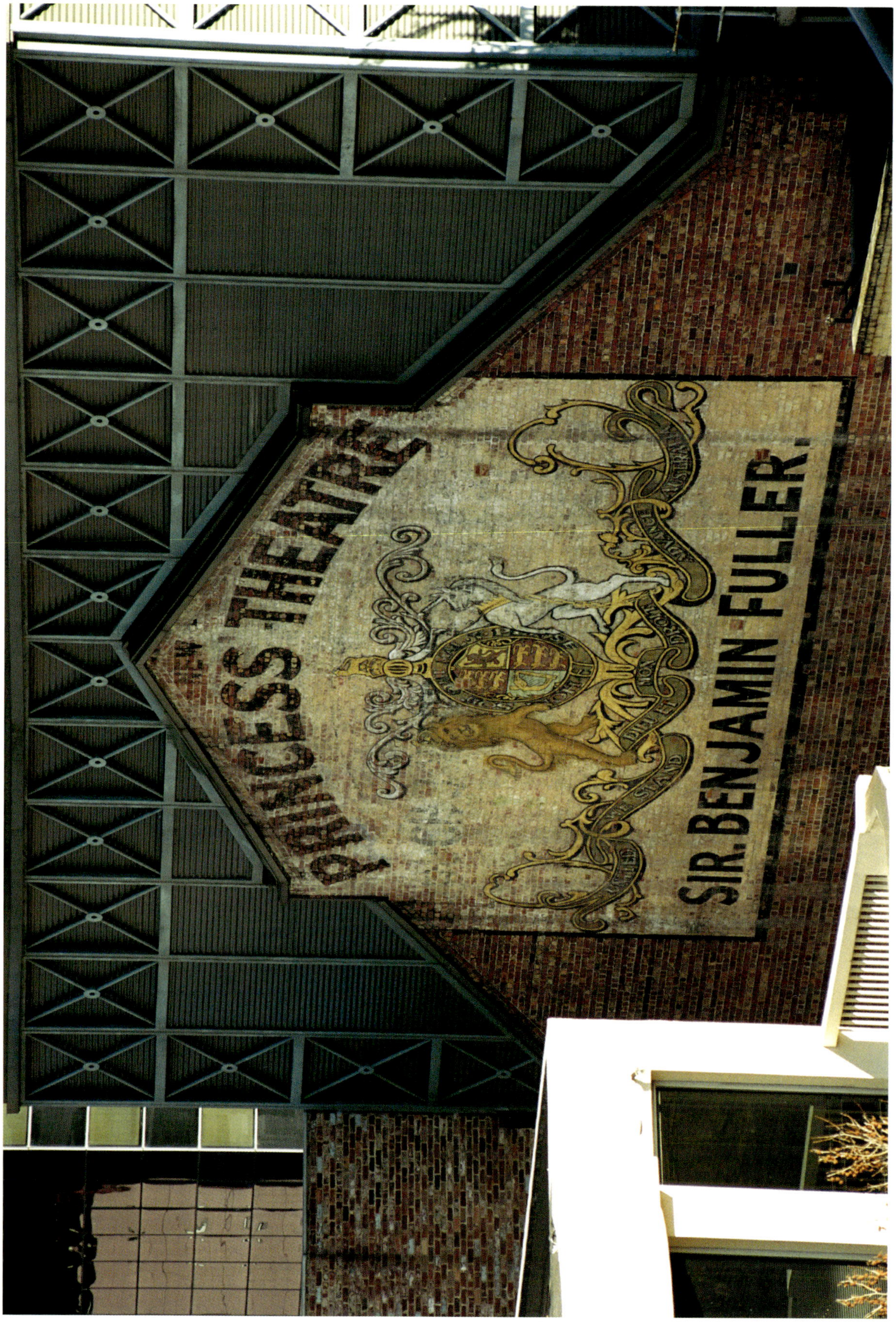

Princess Theatre

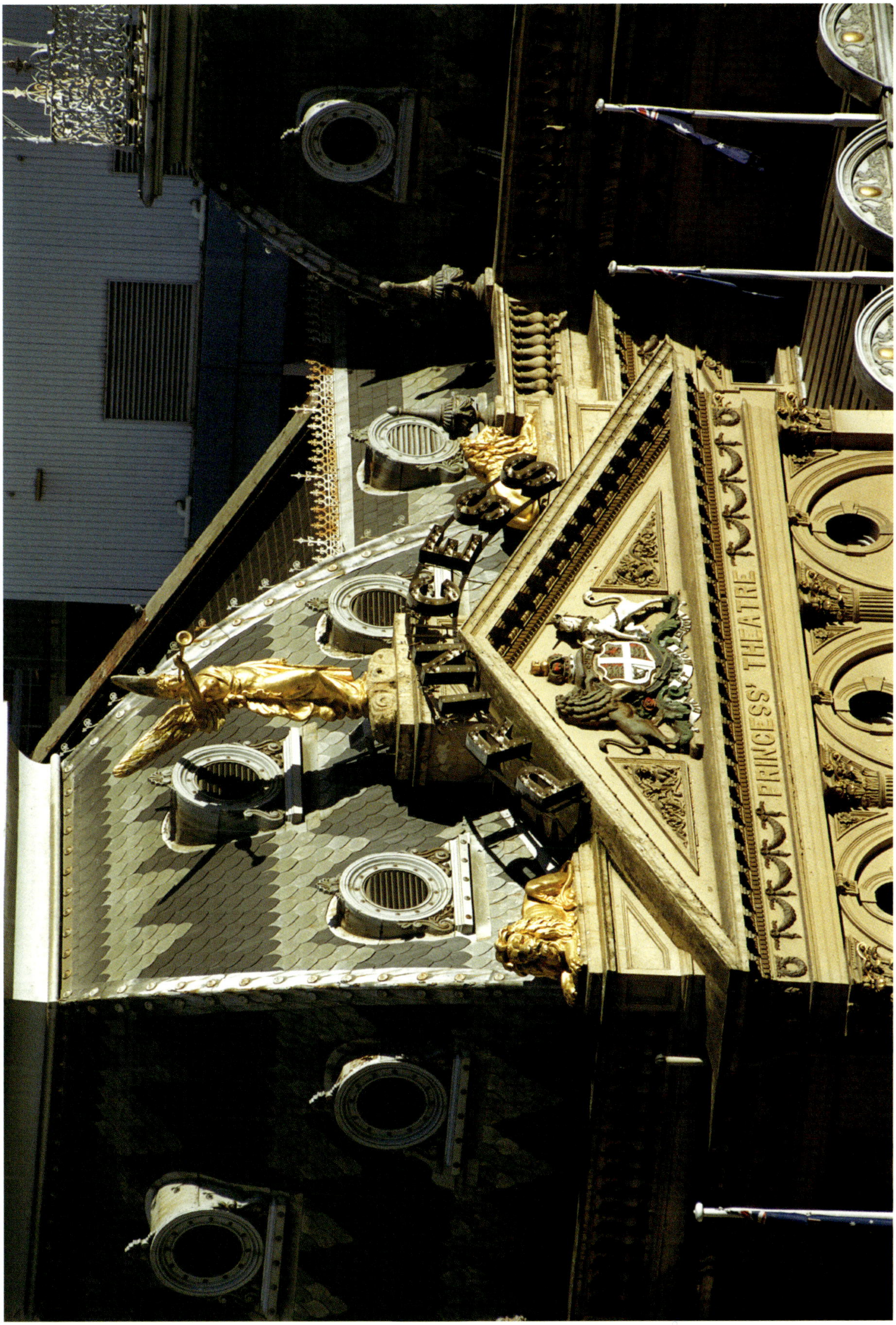

Princess Theatre

Barry Michael

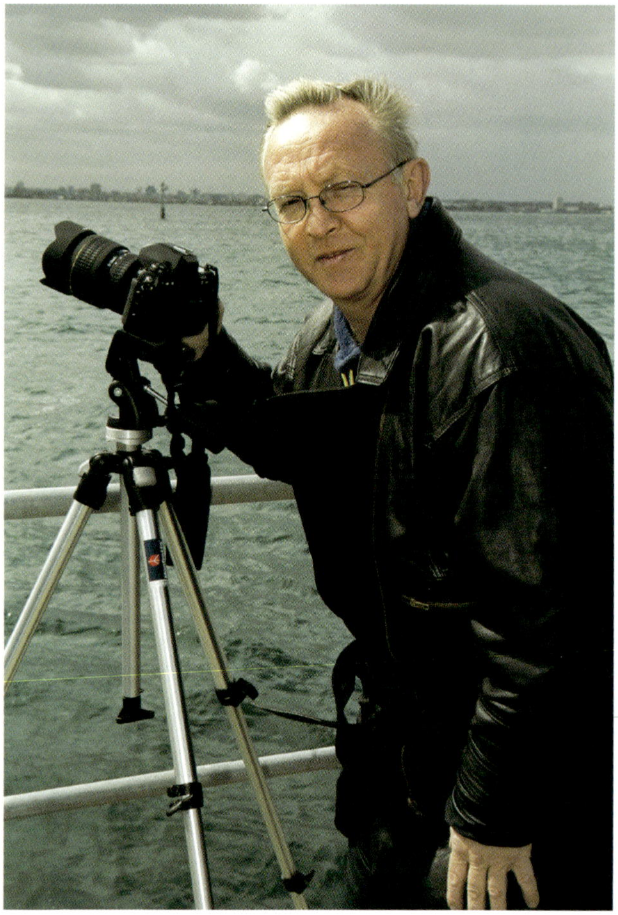

Barry Michael, world champion boxer.

A professional boxing career spanning 60 fights for 48 wins, 9 losses and 3 draws.

Barry's major title wins include: Australian Lightweight title 1978 to 1985 vacated after 9 defences. Commonwealth Lightweight title twice vacated after winning IBF World Super Featherweight title in 1985 held until August 9th 1987. Barry retired after defending his title three times before losing it to American Rocky Lockridge.

Barry's formidable record stands at 60 pro fights. He was never knocked off his feet and never took an eight count.

Breakwater Pier - Williamstown - "When I was a young boy growing up in Williamstown, I received a great deal of pleasure from fishing and I still do now. One of my favourite fishing spots was from the end of Breakwater Pier. The added benefit from fishing at this location was the view of Melbourne. In my opinion it's the best view available!

I also enjoy fishing from beneath the Westgate Bridge. It's an amazing structure and the views change as much as the weather conditions, offering a different perspective almost on a daily basis."

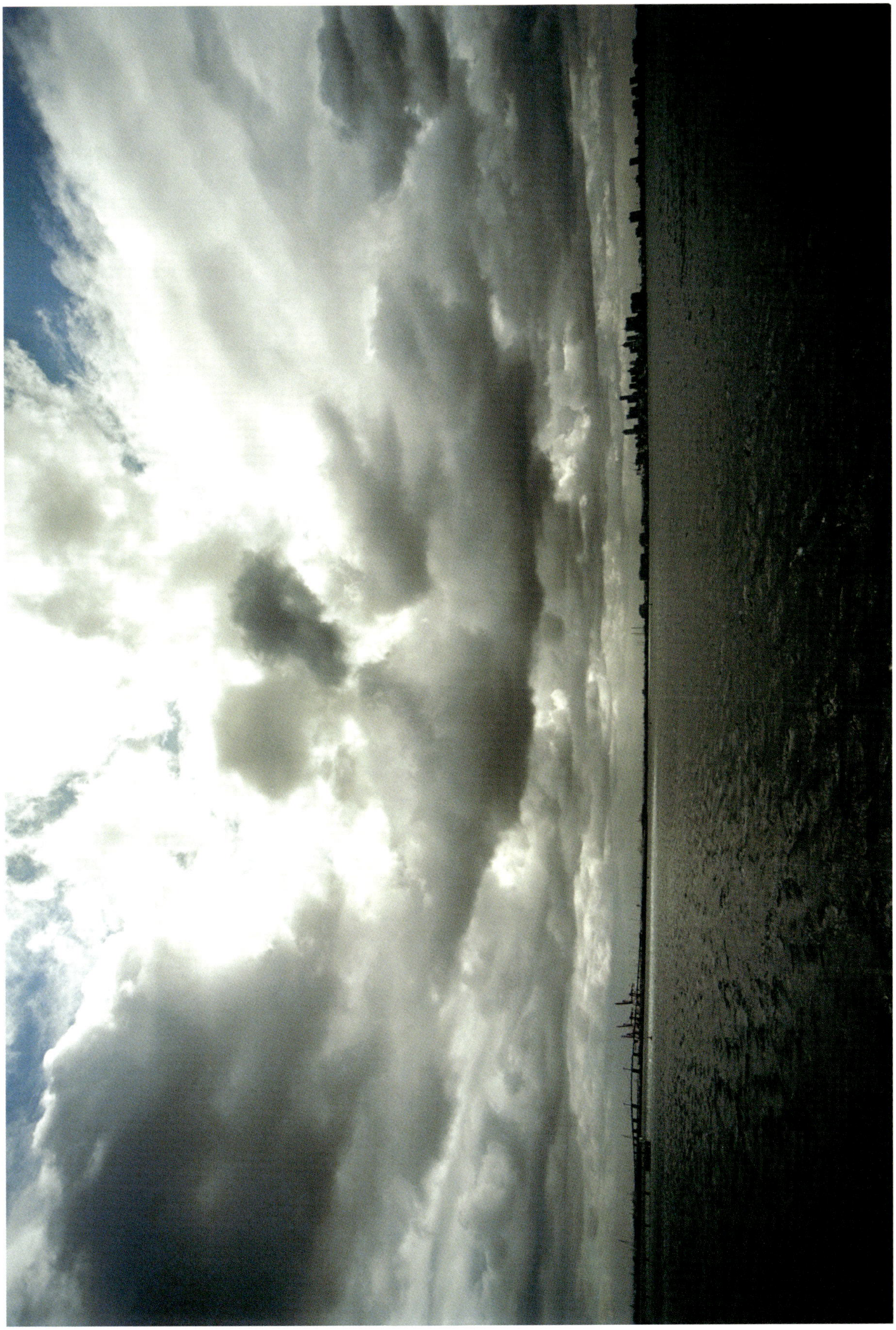

Melbourne from Breakwater Pier - Williamstown

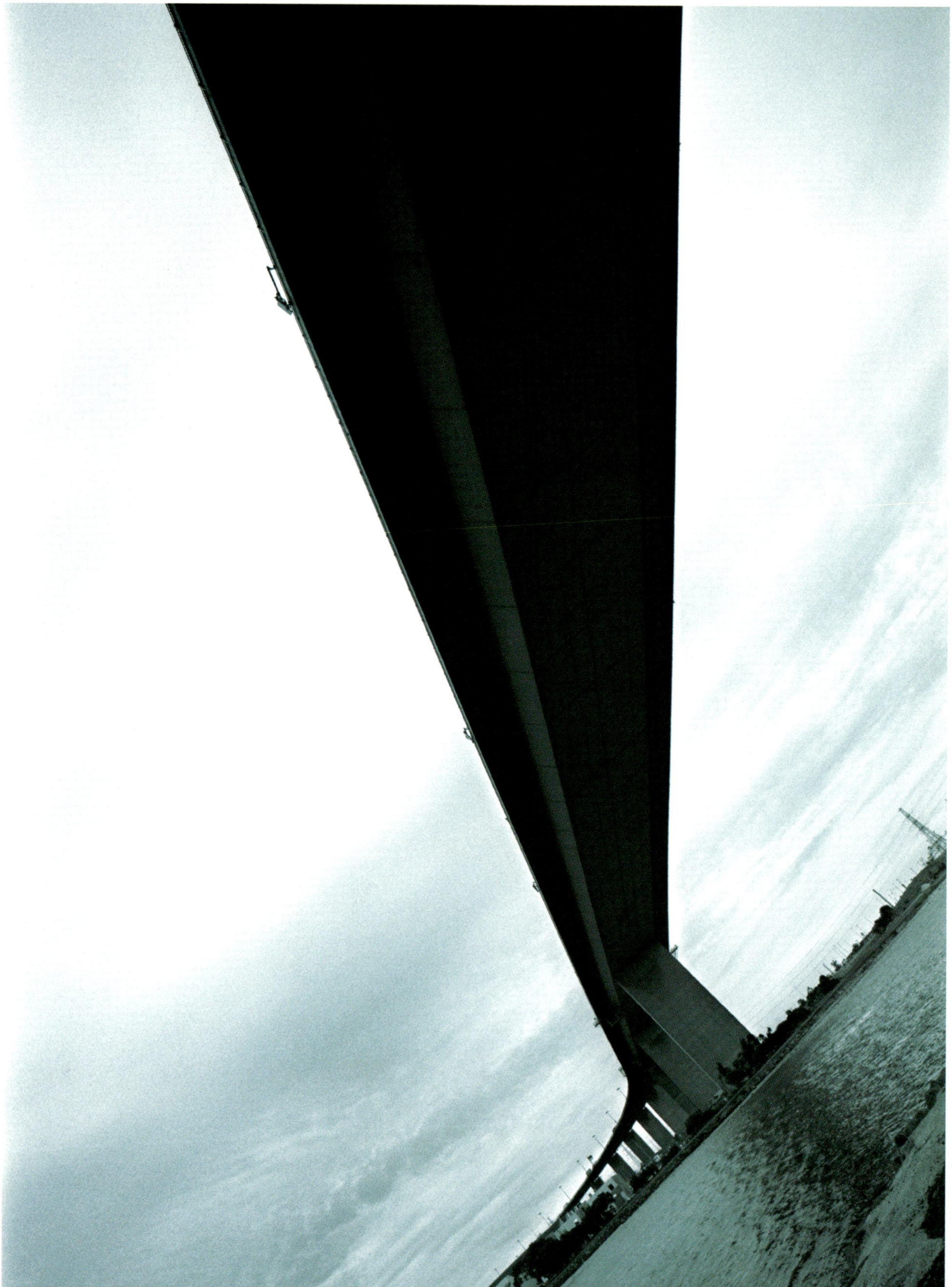

Westgate Bridge

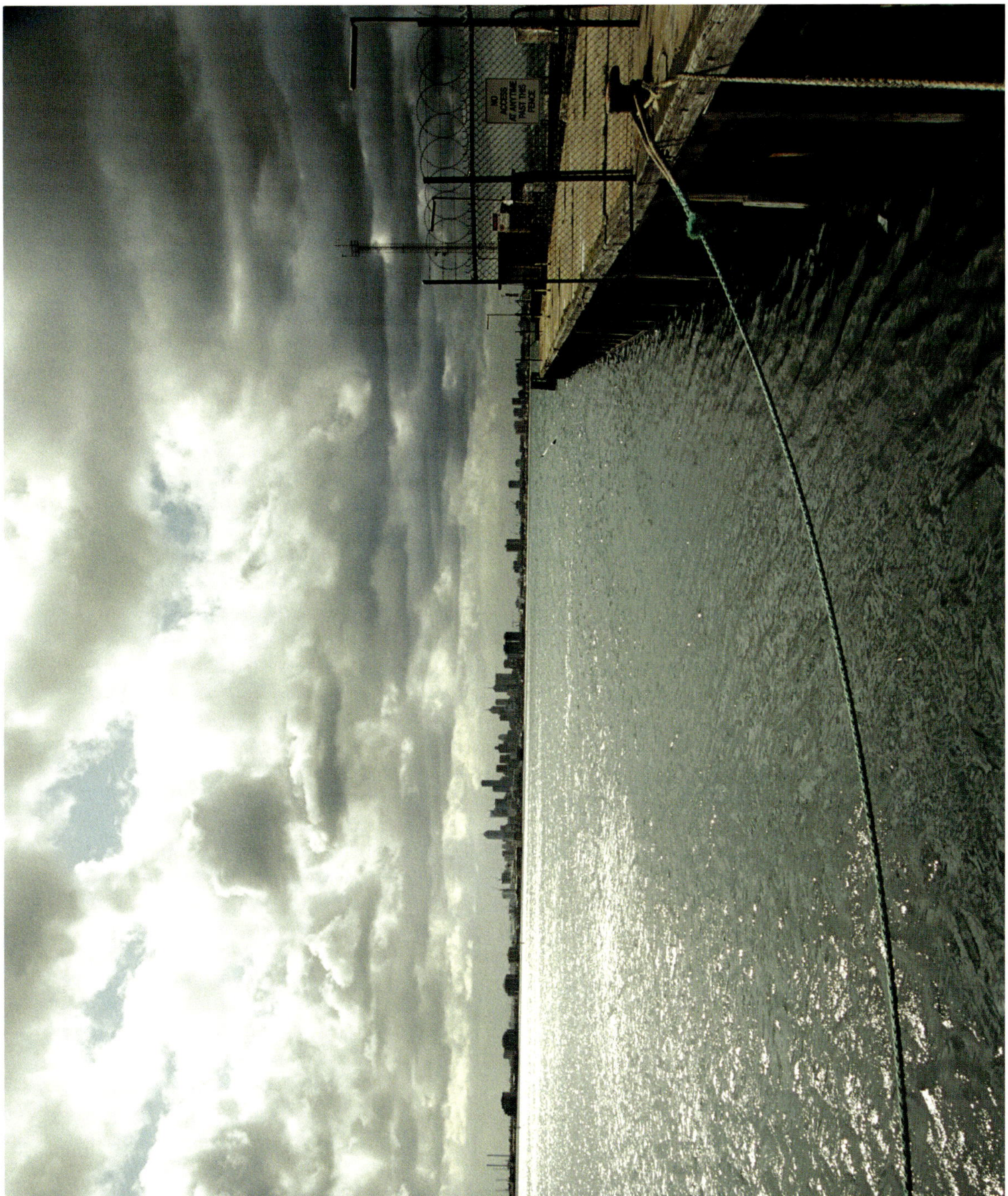

Melbourne from Breakwater Pier - Williamstown

Harry M Miller

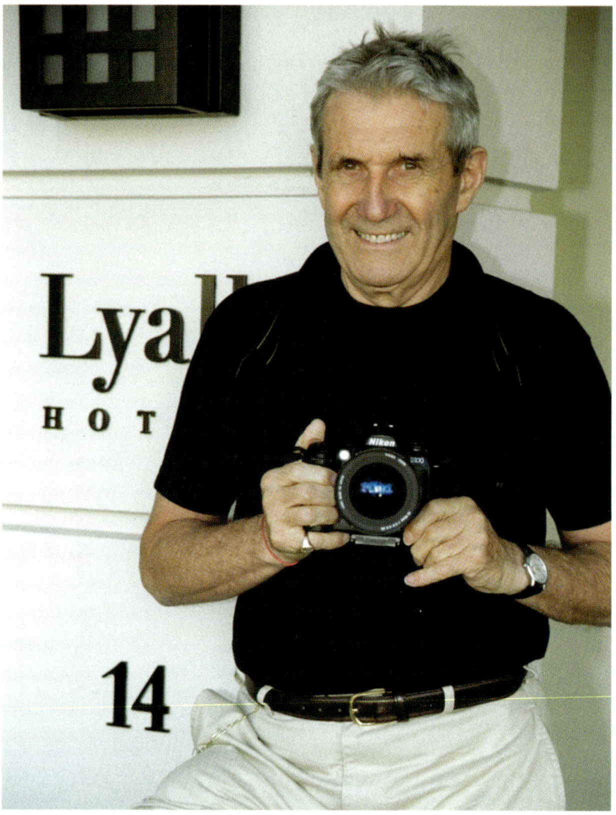

Harry M Miller, moved to Australia from New Zealand in 1963 to commence a career that would influence and shape the Australian and international entertainment scene.

Harry M Miller has an uncanny ability to anticipate public taste. This talent has seen his successful involvement with rock operas 'Hair', 'Grease', 'Jesus Christ Superstar', 'The Rocky Horror Show' and others. Following his successful production of David Williamson's 'The Removalist' in Sydney, he enjoyed the same success in London. As a consultant, his marketing prowess has assisted the Australian Opera, the Australian Ballet, and the Melbourne Theatre Company.

Interludes into journalism and representing Australia as a cultural ambassador for the Australian Bi-Centennial Celebrations and the Australian Expo in France highlight his personal capacity to engage, entertain and influence the Australian and international social fabric. His community contribution to the arts has also seen him reside as Chairman of the Art Gallery Society of New South Wales and as a member of the Board of the National Institute of Dramatic Art. He was also a Director of Qantas Airways.

Harry M Miller's entrepreneurial successes reflect intuition and creativity that has a sound marketing base. His eye for talent in the entertainment industry combined with his management expertise assists him with the ongoing personal management of the country's top media, sporting and entertainment identities.

The Lyall Hotel, South Yarra - Alarmingly, there is no boutique hotel anymore in Sydney or Melbourne. The smallest version of it used to be many years ago, the Sebel Townhouse and Melbourne frankly has never had one.

The magic of The Lyall Hotel is that it is a boutique and very small hotel as evidenced an intimate sitting room, fireplace, etc when sitting there you feel as though you are "at home".

The service is absolutely top flight. They have a great gym, steamroom, massage and bodycare area and the food is excellent. What more could you ask?

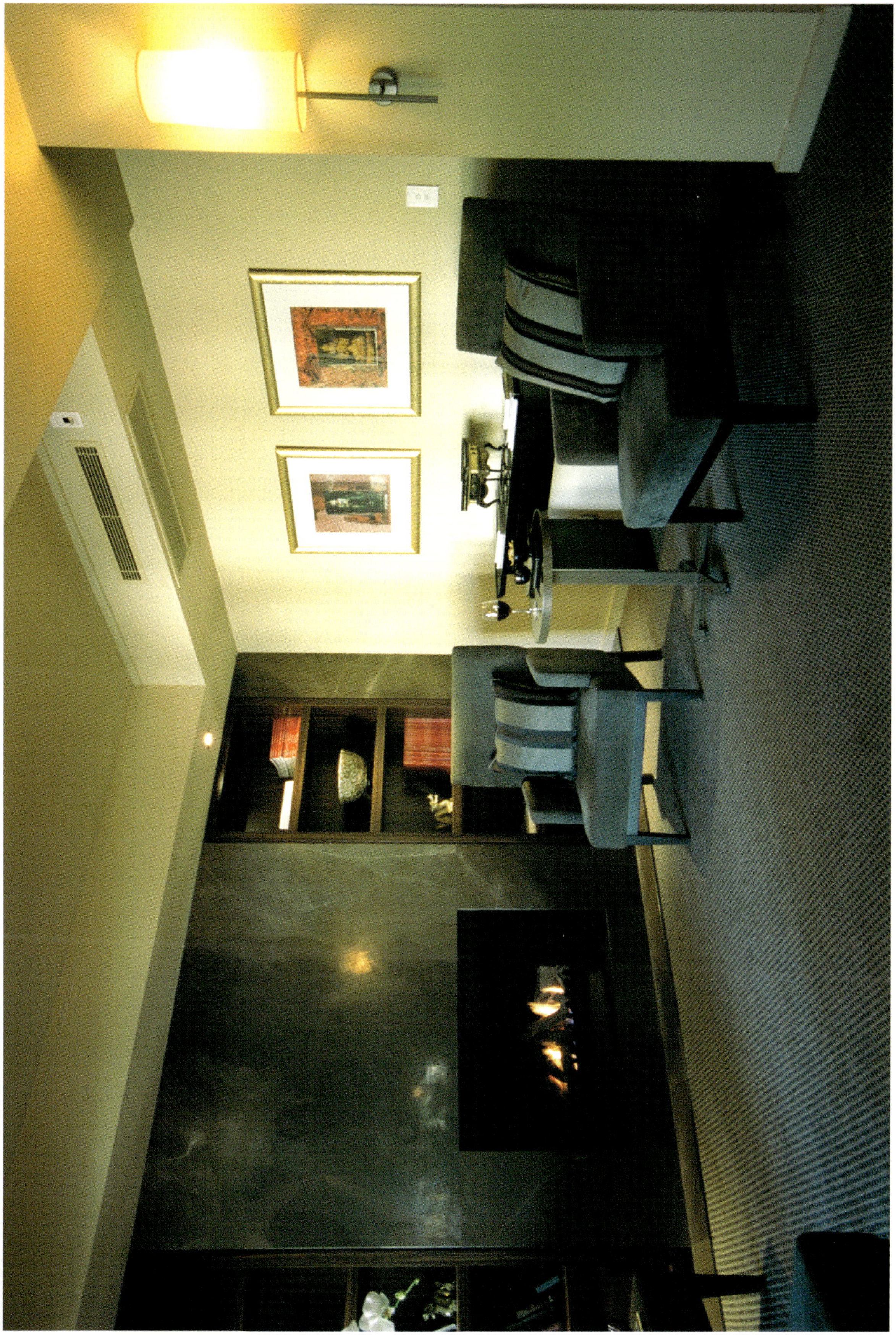

The Lyall Hotel - South Yarra

Dame Elisabeth Murdoch

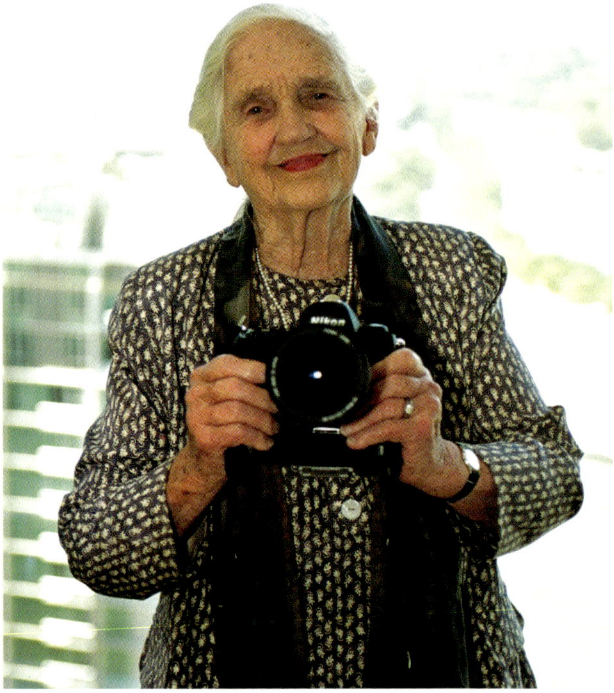

Dame Elisabeth Murdoch AC DBE, philanthropist.

Dame Elisabeth is a highly regarded, revered and loved member of our community. Her vision and drive when coupled with her philanthropy has greatly assisted in strengthening Australian society.

Dame Elisabeth's participation and contribution extends from children's health to medical and scientific research to the performing and visual arts. She is an example of citizenship, an icon of selflessness and a role model for others in the community that she serves.

Royal Botanic Gardens from 101 Collins Street - "I believe that the area of the Royal Botanic Gardens and the Domain is the very heart and soul of Melbourne, it has always been very much part of my life since I was first taken there as a child, nearly 90 years ago and I am very proud to now be the first Patron of the Royal Botanic Gardens."

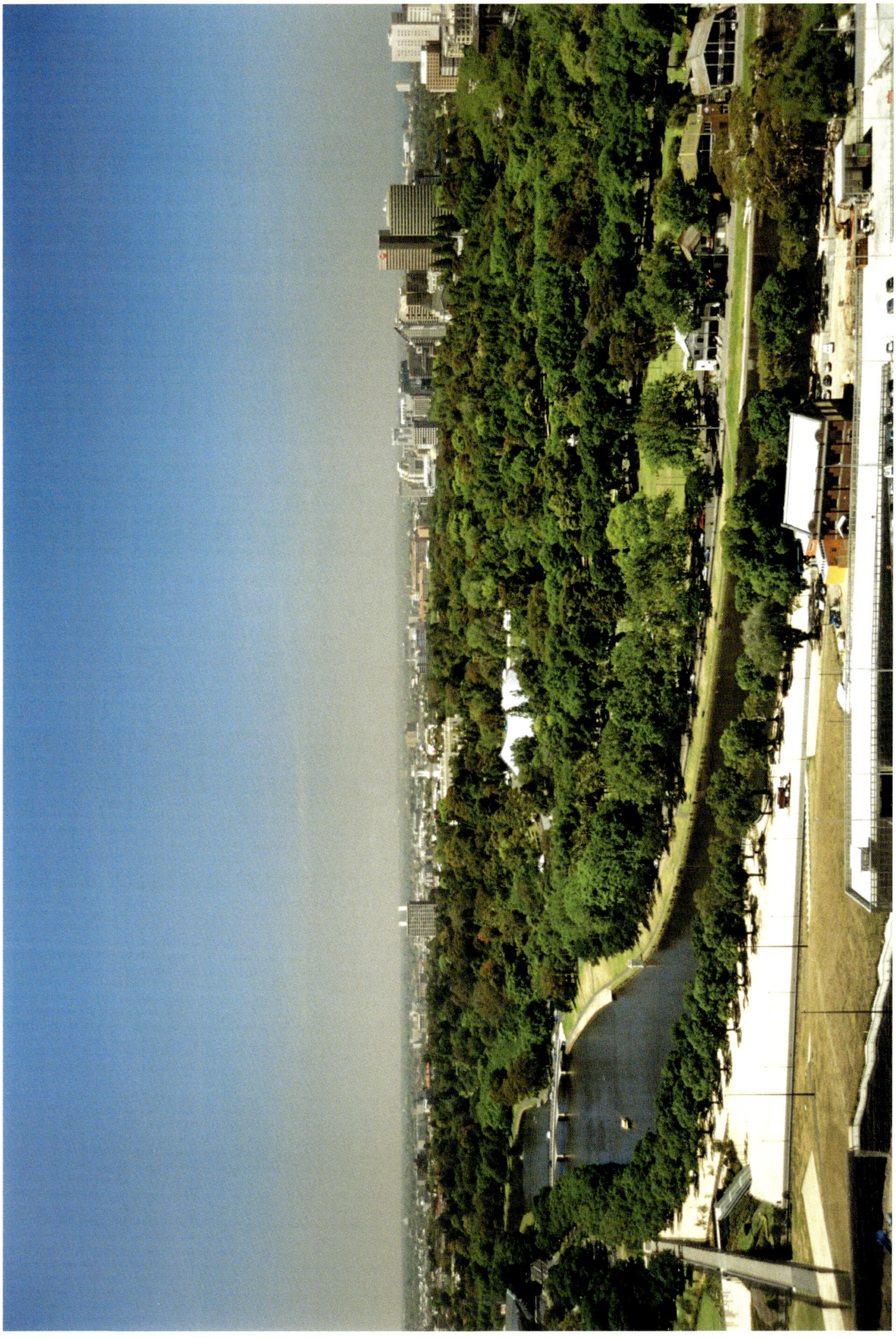

Royal Botanic Gardens from 101 Collins Street

Bert Newton

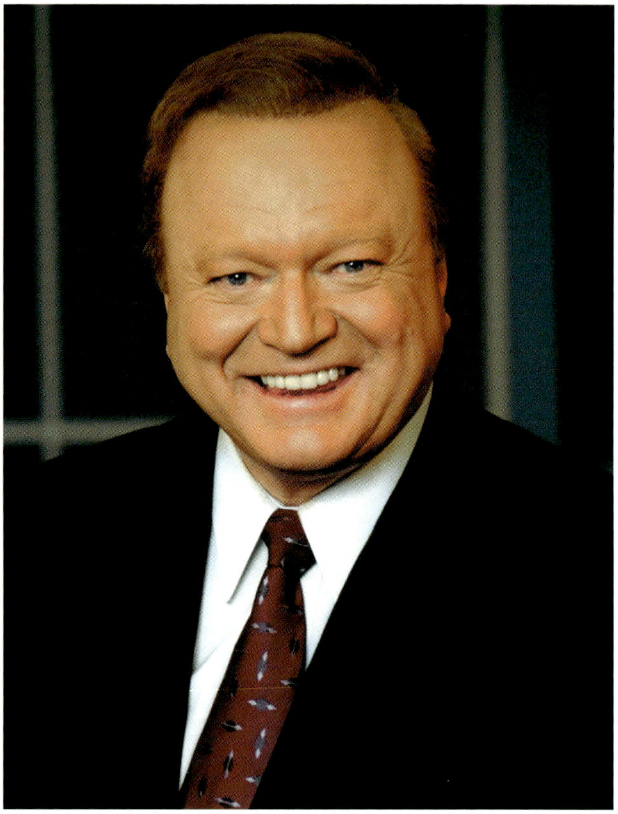

Bert Newton. Since television began in Australia in 1957, Bert Newton, with his twin talents as a natural comedian and sophisticated compere, has been a favourite with the viewing public, visiting celebrities and critics alike. During a visit to Australia in 1983, Bob Hope said of Bert, "Personally, he is a fine man. Professionally, he is one of the best I've ever seen."

His remarkable career has been recognised by an incredible collection of awards including 15 Logies – of which 6 were Gold Logies

Bert has earned a reputation as Australia's premier Master of Ceremonies for special event TV. He has hosted the TV Week Logie Awards for a record 18 times. Other specials Bert has hosted include: The Royal Charity Concert before Her Royal Highness Queen Elizabeth II and His Royal Highness the Duke of Edinburgh, the Royal Gala Concert attended by the Prince and Princess of Wales, three specials celebrating Australian television history and the Sydney Entertainment Centre opening.

Bert's appeal stems from his affable nature and sincerity, and he has been quoted as saying that he thinks he relates more to the average bloke. This could have something to do with being the product of a 'quite traditional' Catholic family. He was born on July 23, 1938 in Fitzroy (a working class suburb in those days), one of six children. He was very close to his mother, Gladys, who died in 1981. His father, Joseph, served in World War II, returning when Bert was seven years old and died when Bert was eleven.

In March 1959, Graham Kennedy and Bert Newton teamed up on Channel Nine in what became the start of an historic partnership that viewers were to love when the inimitable team were *In Melbourne Tonight.* No-one who saw Kennedy and Newton on *IMT* could ever forget their brand of humour and entertainment and Bert became Australia's favourite son with his impeccable sense of timing and his natural warm humour.

1991 saw Bert perform in the $3m dollar theatre production of *Wizard of Oz.* In the title role, he received rave notices right around Australia. It was during this theatrical extravaganza that Network Ten signed Bert for *Good Morning Australia with Bert Newton* right through till 2005.

Bert's real-life partner is his wife, singer-dancer Patti Newton, whom he married on 9 November 1974. They have two children, Matthew and Lauren.

Spring Street – "This is a favourite part of Melbourne for me. My first job was at the radio station 3XY whose offices were housed in The Princess Theatre. The theatre itself is special too because I've done a number of stage shows there. This lovely area of Melbourne was important in my past and continues to be so today."

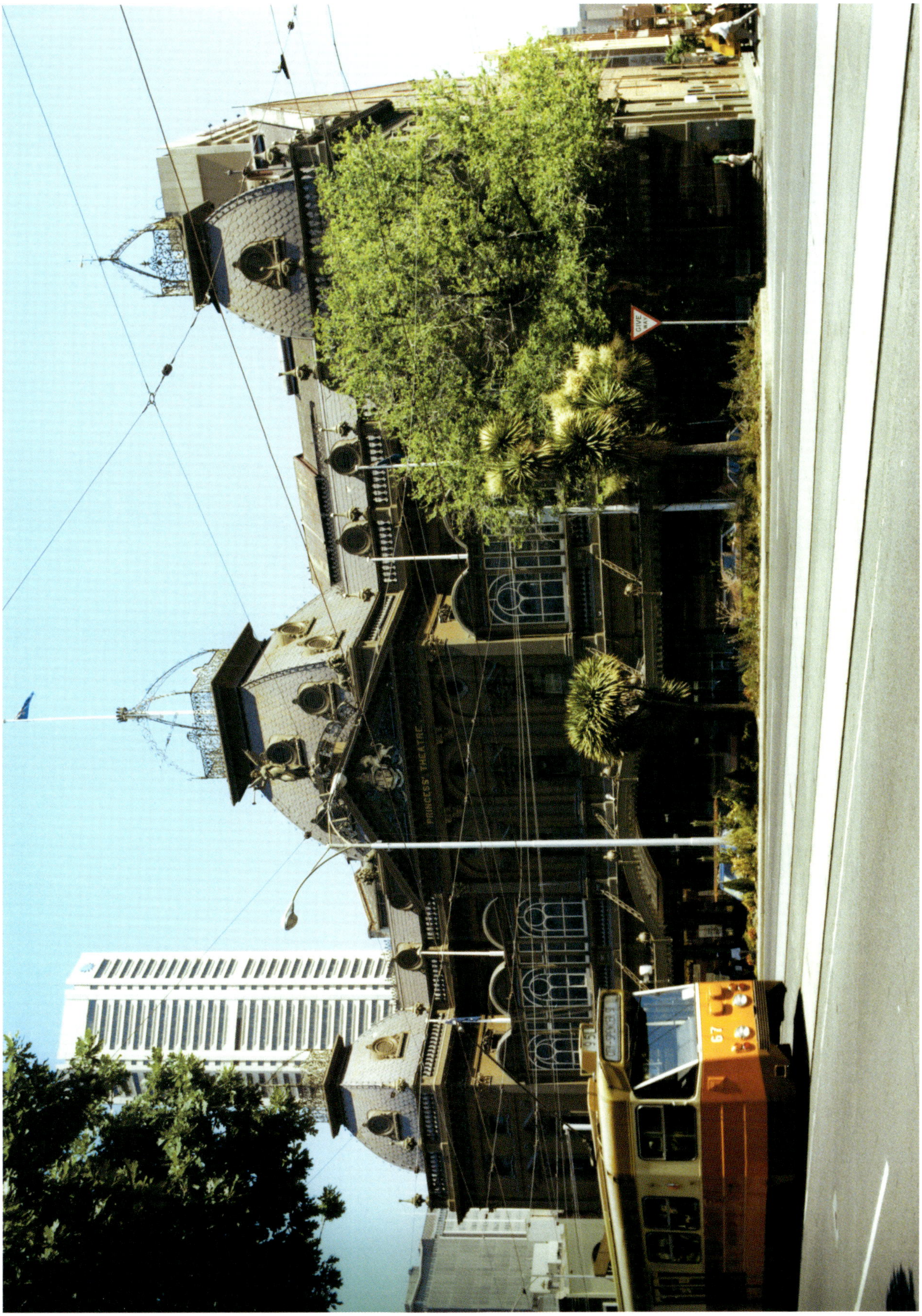

Princess Theatre, Spring Street

Christine Nixon

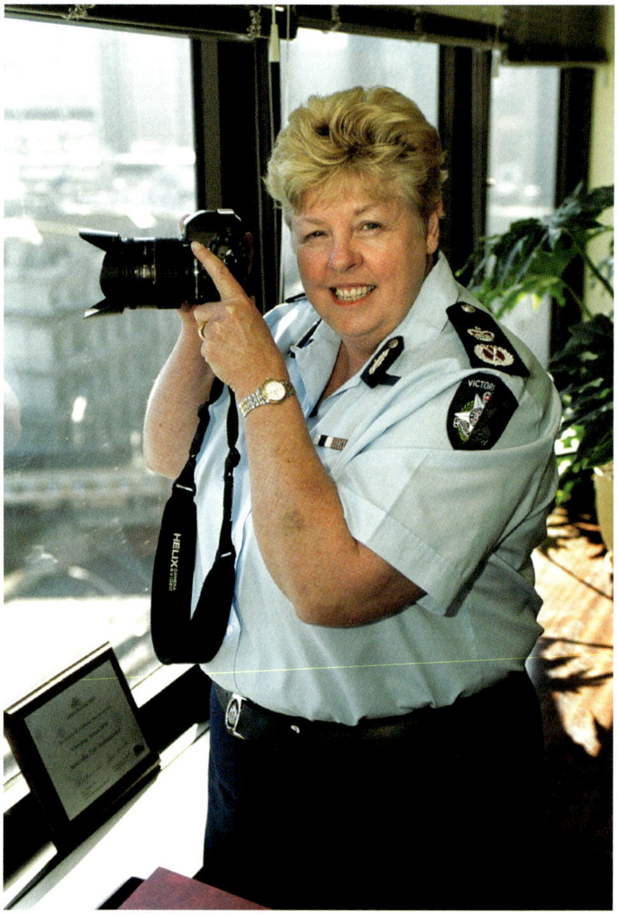

Christine Nixon APM, Chief Commissioner of Police for Victoria.

Ms Nixon commenced duty as Chief Commissioner of Victoria Police on 23rd April 2001, after service with the New South Wales Police Force from 1972.

Ms Nixon is the CEO of Victoria Police, an organisation of 12,800 staff with an annual budget of $1.2 billion operating out of 550 work locations, including 330 police stations throughout the State.

Ms Nixon is the Chair of the Australian Police Professional Standards Council, Co-Chair of the Australian Institute of Police Management and Sponsor of the Australasian Police Multicultural Advisory Bureau.

From my Office - "I decided to take the photographs from my office because it is a wonderful view of such a developing area much like Victoria Police".

"The views encapsulate Port Melbourne, the Yarra River, Victoria Harbour and the Docklands".

"The Docklands precinct is one of my favourite spots in Melbourne and the views from my office are always a focal point for my visitors to admire".

"It seems to be a forever changing landscape full of new developments, construction, waterways, parklands and colour".

"It's always interesting to find out what is going to be built next...."

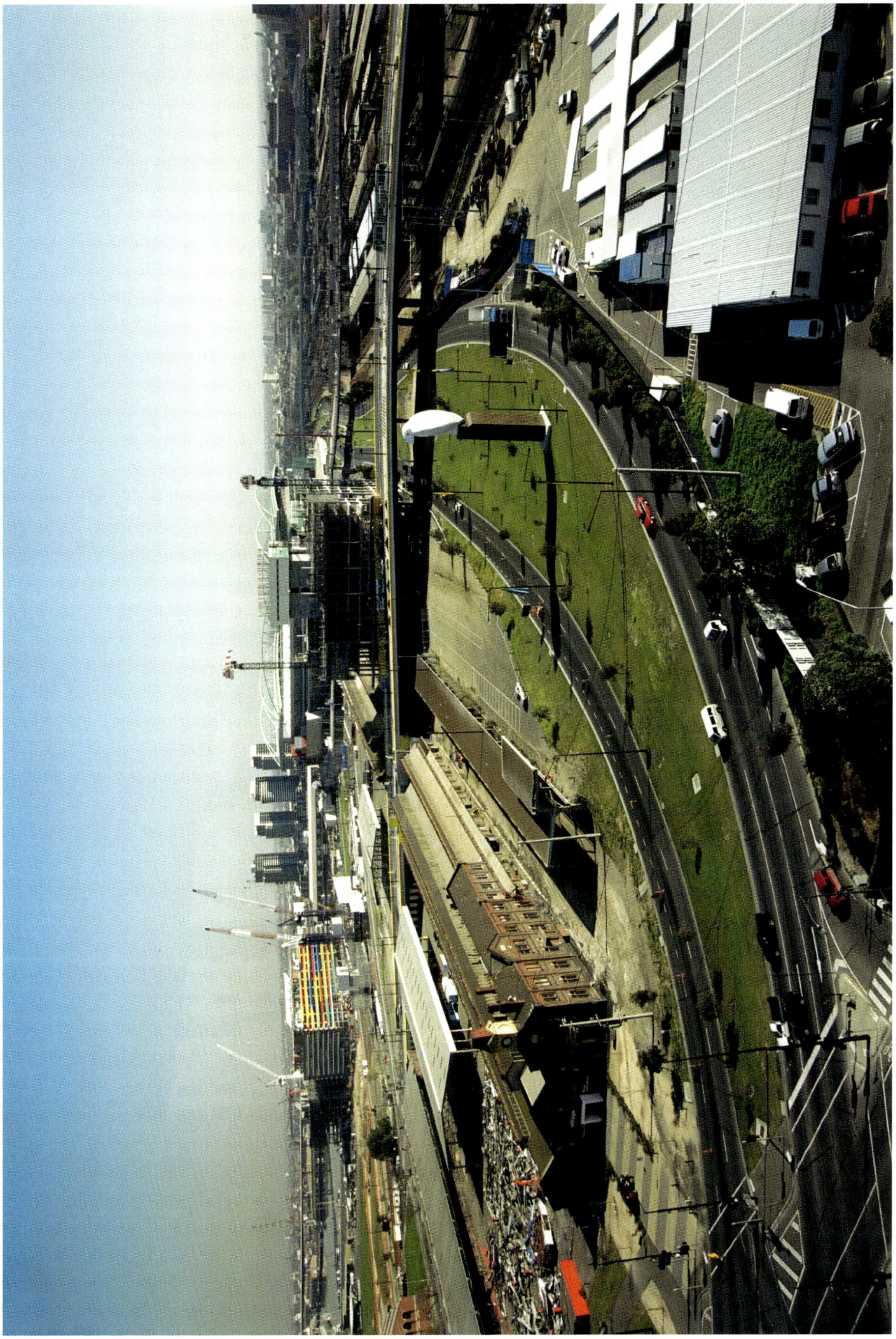

Telstra Dome and the Old Rail Yard

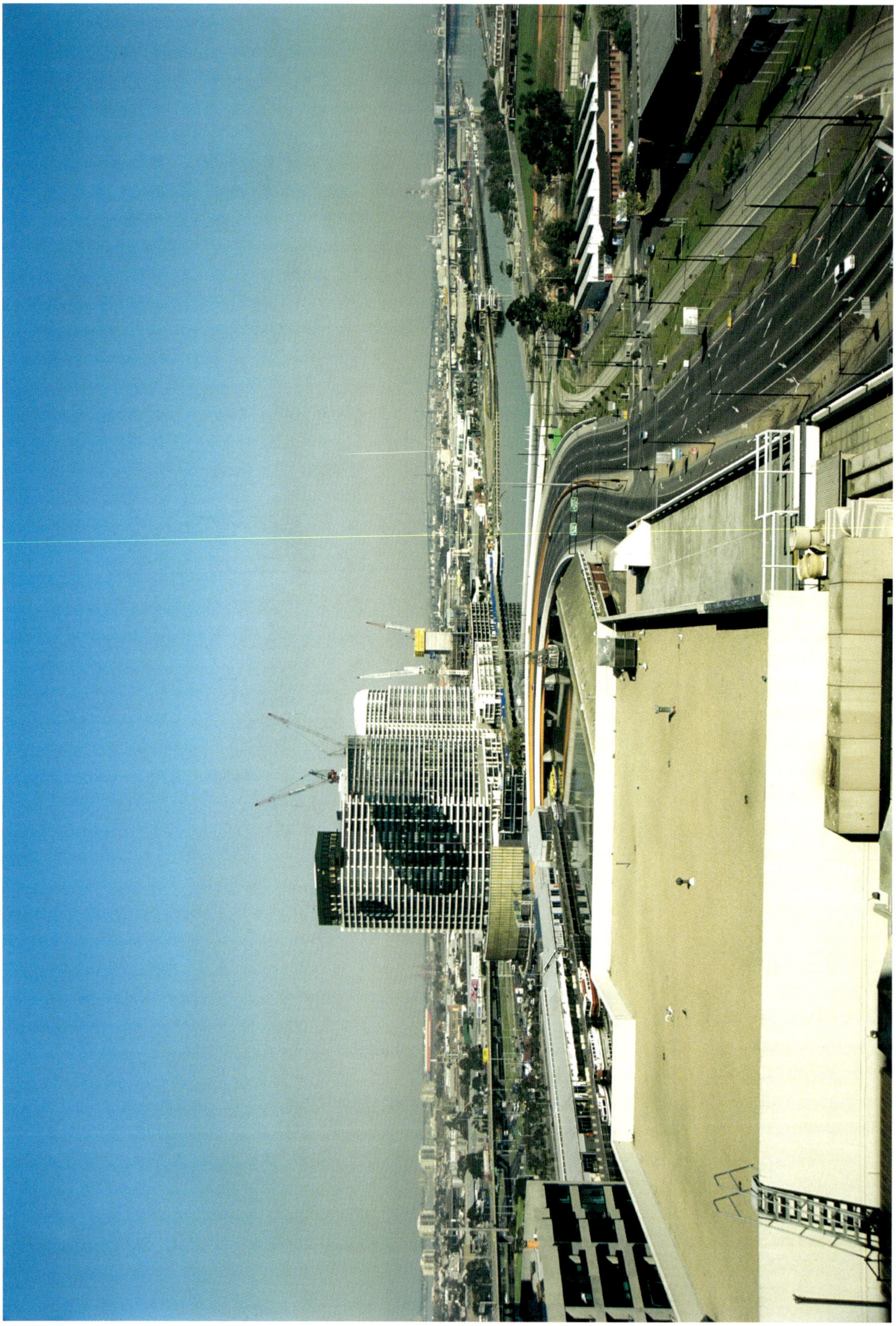

Docklands

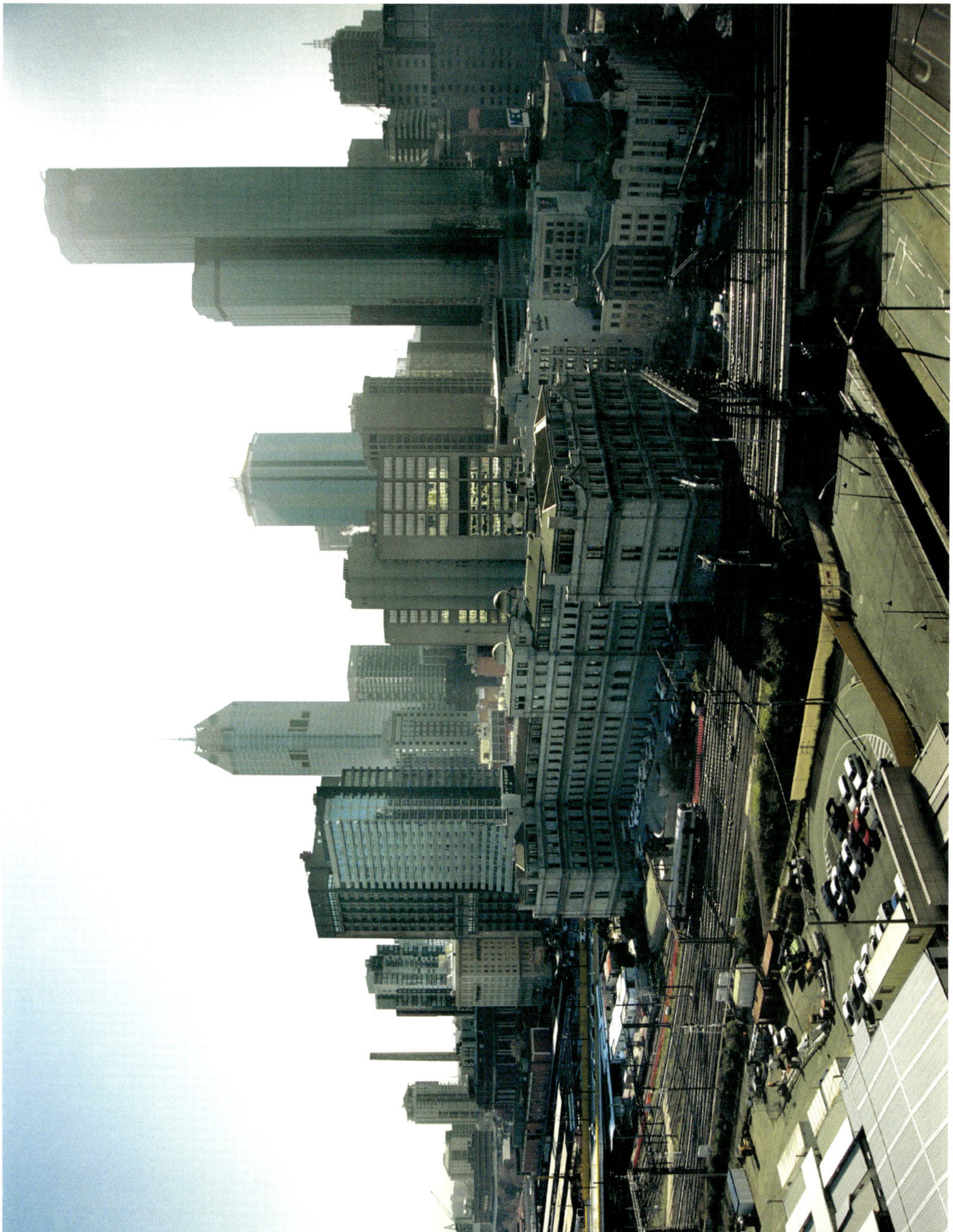

Melbourne from "My Office"

Ann Peacock

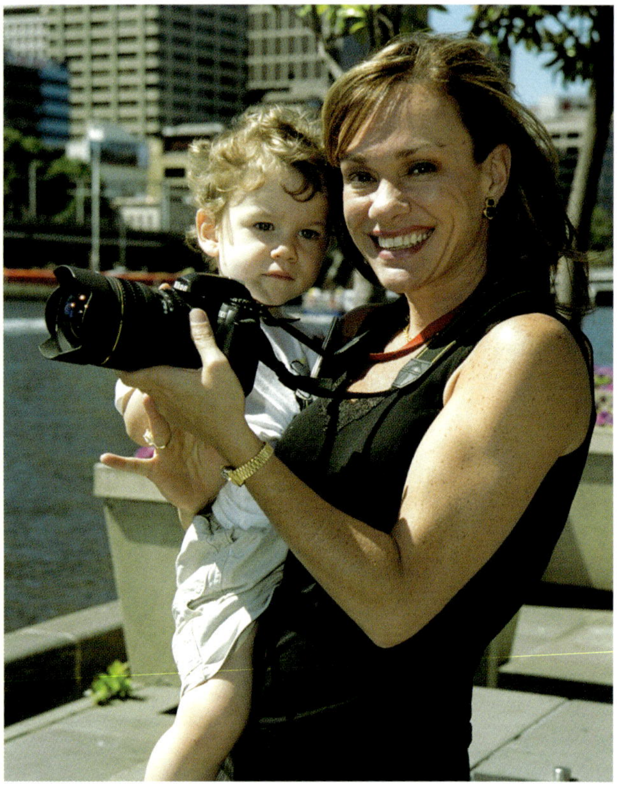

Ann Peacock, General Manager Marketing Communications - Crown.

Ann started work as an Accounts Clerk at radio 3XY. Developing a passion for Public Relations / Publicity, promotions and Media, after 2 years of across the board experience, she was offered a position on-air at radio 3UZ.

She then went on to work at Channel 9 in Melbourne as their evening weather presenter. She has also been a freelance producer for television and contributor for Women's magazines and currently is also Managing Director of Madison Communications as well as writing a weekly page for the Sunday Herald-Sun newspaper.

Ann is married to Michael Kroger and they have 2 children - Andrew 4 and Woody, 20 months.

Promenade outside Crown - "My favourite place anywhere in the world is wherever my children are. I adore being in their company, it is refreshing, relaxing, emotionally fulfilling and we have lots of laughs. At the park, school drop off, drinking / spilling lemonade, in their rooms - in my room at 3am, singing to the Wiggles and trying to control meal times - I love it all. I live to love every day with some time in their company, knowing that an opportunity to be with them which is lost, will never be re-lived and so spending time with them is my greatest and most important reason for everything.

Here we are photographed on the promenade outside Crown, I spend a lot of time at work and really thrive on the days, it truly is Melbourne's most exciting and ever challenging places."

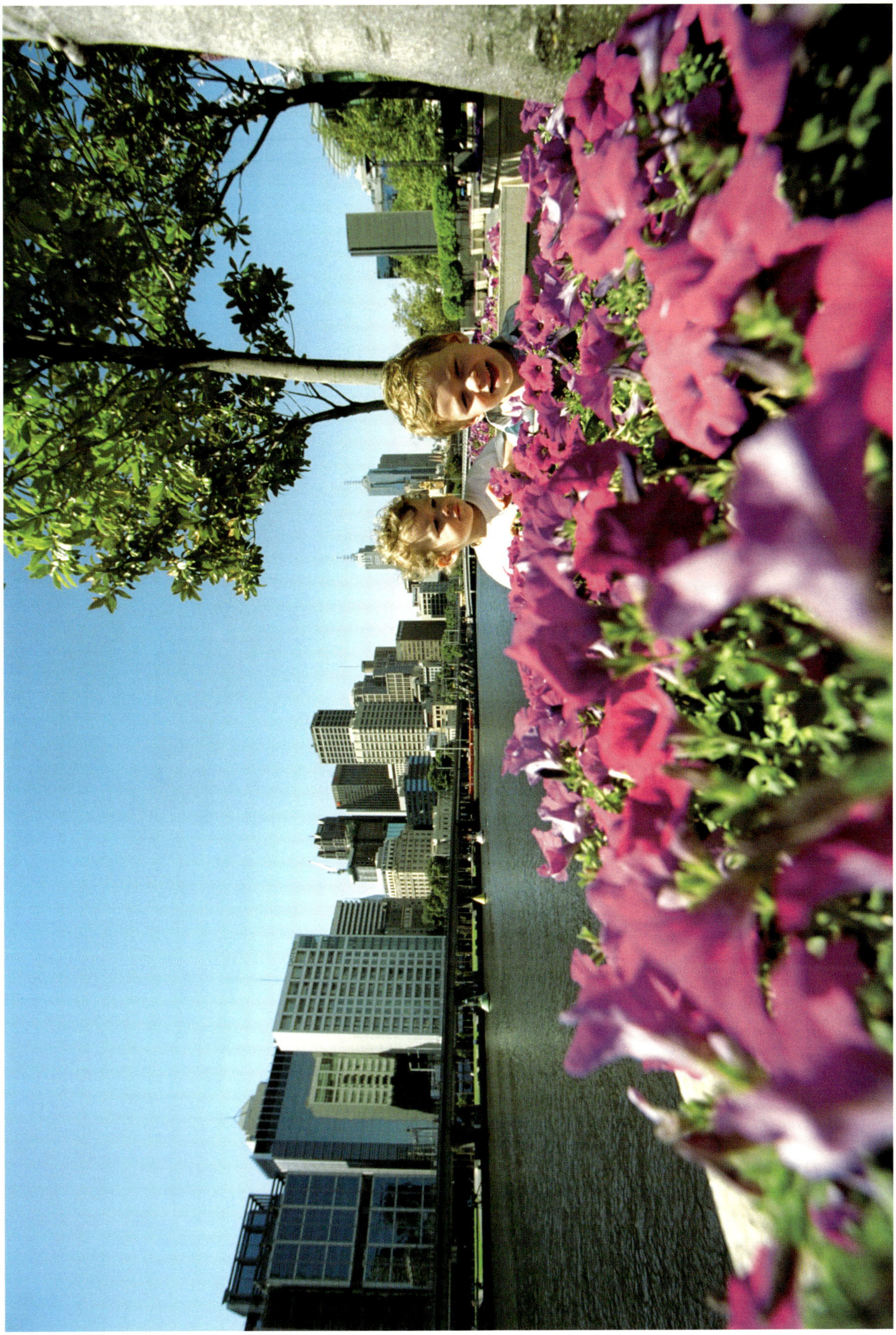

Promenade outside Crown - Yarra Bank

John So

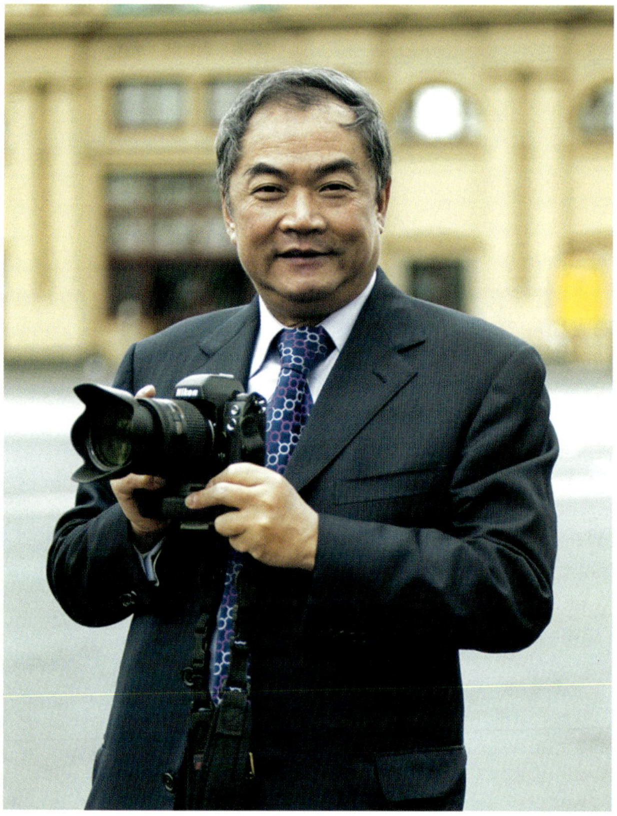

John So, Melbourne's first popularly-elected Lord Mayor. Born in Hong Kong, Lord Mayor John So moved to Melbourne as a 17-year-old and soon earned his Science Degree and Diploma of Education from Melbourne University. He taught science at Fitzroy High School, before opening his first restaurant in Flinders Lane in 1976.

One of Melbourne's longest serving councillors, before his election as Lord Mayor, John So served three terms on the Melbourne City Council from 1991 when he was first elected as a Central Ward Councillor.

John So is passionate about promoting the City of Melbourne and works tirelessly to facilitate business opportunities in the city, and to stimulate tourism, culture and investment in Melbourne.

His vision for Melbourne includes creating closer links between the city and the water, whether that is the Yarra River or Melbourne's Docklands. He celebrates Melbourne's waterfront opportunities and since first elected to Council has worked to shift part of the city's focus to the water.

Always active in community affairs, John So is particularly focused on projects for youth and the older sections of the community. He is a Justice of the Peace, a former director of the Melbourne Water Corporation, Patron of the Victorian Arts Centre and Chairman of the Victorian Chinese Welfare Centre.

His ongoing involvement in various charities includes the Kidney Foundation and the Bone Marrow Donor Institute.
A former Victorian Ethnic Affairs Commissioner, John So is committed to ethnic community welfare issues.

The Lord Mayor is a keen photographer with a large collection of black and white photographs that he took of Melbourne while he was a university student.

Family life for Lord Mayor John So revolves around his partner Wendy Cheng and his children Natalie, Alex, Eva and John junior. Apart from official duties as Lord Mayor and spending time with his family, John enjoys fishing, gardening and the opera.

Victoria Market - The Queen Victoria Market is one of Melbourne's great historic landmarks. I think it represents a great deal about Melbourne, fresh food, cafes, cultural diversity, fashion and entertainment. The market is a great tourist attraction, over 8.5 million visitors a year - it's an iconic institution for Melburnian. I personally love the market atmosphere, and I love the fact that everyone can easily access the market from one of Melbourne's other icons - a tram.

View of Melbourne From Birrarung Marr - Birrarung Marr was Melbourne's first new major parklands in more than 100 years when it opened in January 2002. 'Birrarung' means 'river of mists' in the Woiwurrung language of the Wurundjeri people. It brings the focus back towards the river and has become a space in which people can relax or take part in a variety of activities against a unique and creative backdrop of native flora.

I chose this location to shoot because of the different perspective of the city from Birrarung Marr.

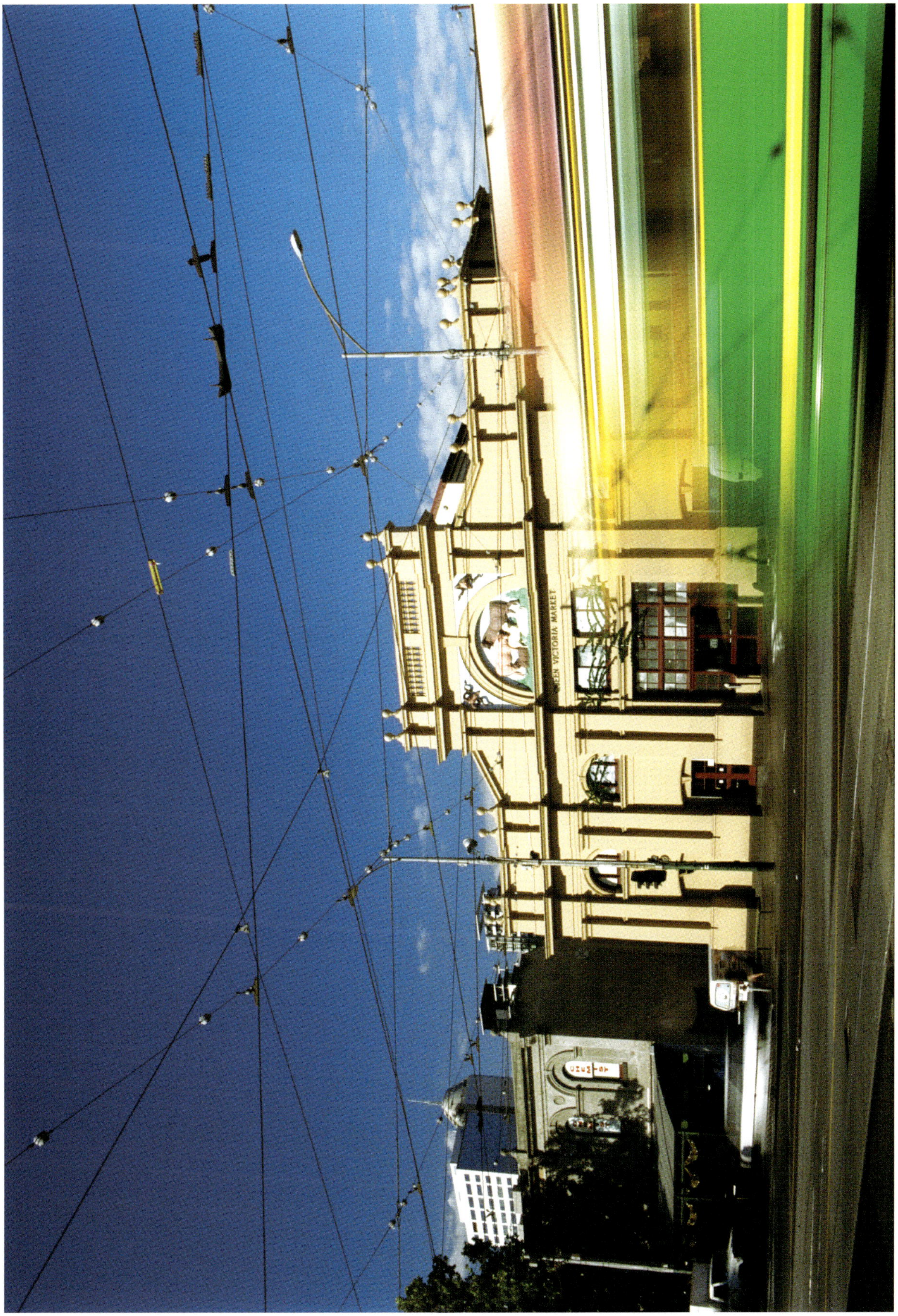

Queen Victoria Market

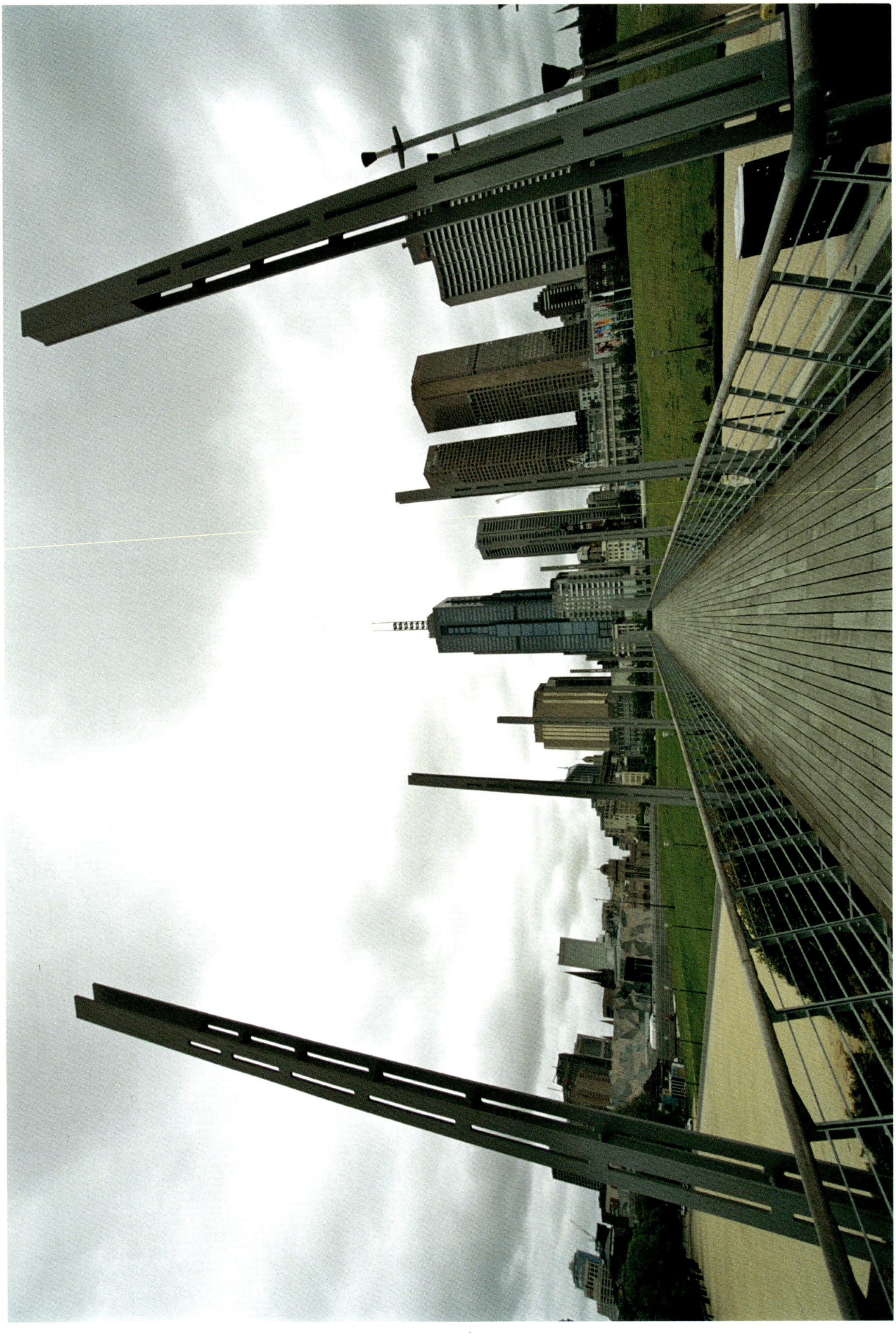

Melbourne from Birrarung Marr

Melbourne - Evolution from a Village to the World's Most Liveable City

Melbourne was founded in 1835, during the reign of King William IV. The City of Melbourne has grown significantly since that time and has developed a rich and varied history. The modern façade and culture of Melbourne has been very much a result of the people that have lived here and the events that have taken place.

John Batman and his party, after entering Port Phillip Bay on 29 May, in a 30-tonne schooner 'Rebecca', anchored their ship a short distance from the heads and made several excursions through the countryside. On 8 June, 1835, Batman and his party rowed up the Yarra River and landed near the site of the former Customs House (now Commonwealth Parliamentary Offices). John Batman recorded in his journal: "about six miles up, found the river all good water and very deep. This will be the place for a village".

A census taken on 2 March, 1841, showed that the total population of the province was 16 671 and that the inhabitants of Melbourne numbered 4479, comprising 2676 males and 1803 females.

The discovery of gold in Victoria in the early 1850s had a remarkable effect on the growth of Melbourne. The Melbourne Morning Herald in October 1851, stated that - "The whole city is gold mad; the city is getting more and more deserted every day". But this trend to leave the city was only temporary, the gold seekers drifting back after a week or two, some successful, some disappointed.

News of the discovery of gold spread all round the world and during 1852, 1853 and 1854 the average number of people arriving in Victoria by sea was 90 000 a year. From 1855 to 1858, the average was still 60 000 with less than 30 000 disappointed people departing each year over this whole period. By 1854, the population of Melbourne was nearly 80 000 but by 1861 had increased to 140 000.

In 1851, Victoria was separated from New South Wales and Melbourne became the capital of the colony. The State Legislation Council, having no other home, sat in St Patrick's Hall in Bourke Street. Building commenced on Parliament House early in 1856 and was sufficiently completed for it to be officially opened on 25 November, 1856, by the Acting Governor General, Sir Edward Macarthur (a son of John Macarthur of Camden, New South Wales, who pioneered the wool industry in Australia).

The State Parliament met in that building until the Federation of the States in 1901, when Australia became a nation. The building then became the seat of Federal Parliament, and the State Parliament transferred to the Exhibition Building (which opened in 1880), where it continued to meet until 1927. In that year, Canberra became the official capital of Australia, and the departure for Canberra of the Federal Parliament left the way open for the State Parliament again to take up residence in Parliament House.

The period between 1880 and 1890 was the time of the land booms, with surpluses in government revenue and buoyant optimism creating great progress for the metropolis of Melbourne. Where previously in the city three or four storey office blocks had been the highest buildings, virtually overnight eight and nine storey buildings were erected as a result of private enterprise. The foundation stone of St. Paul's Cathedral at the corner of Flinders and Swanston Streets was laid in 1880 and the building consecrated at the beginning of 1891.

Following the worldwide depression of the 1930s, the Second World War together with postwar building restrictions and material shortages, building development in Melbourne remained fairly static until the early 1950s.

The late 1950s and 1960s saw enormous changes to the Central Business District. Between 1956 and 1958 Melbourne witnessed the construction of what was to be its first skyscraper. ICI House. In the lead up to the 1956 Olympic Games the removal of verandahs further contributed to the radical changes taking place in the city fabric. The 1960s saw the opening of the first stage of the Victorian arts centre complex, the National Gallery of Victoria.

In the early 1970s digging commenced on the first tunnels for the Melbourne Underground Rail Loop line and this project was completed in 1986. The installation of light towers at the Melbourne Cricket Ground in Yarra Park in 1985 and the construction of the National Tennis Centre in Melbourne Park , saw major alterations to the landscape of one of Melbourne's principal assets, namely its parks and gardens.

The modern Melbourne Museum development in the Carlton Gardens continued this trend, while Federation Square is one of the most recent and different additions to the city skyline.

The world's Most Liveable City has developed in prominence as one of the international Special Events Capitals. Since hosting the XVI Olympiad in 1956, Melbourne has maintained itself as the focus of Australian Rules Football and has become the home of the Formula One Australian Grand Prix and the Australian 500cc Motorcycle Grand Prix. The staging of the XVIII Commonwealth Games in 2006 is further testimony that the lure of Melbourne is undeniable.

Sir Ninian Stephen

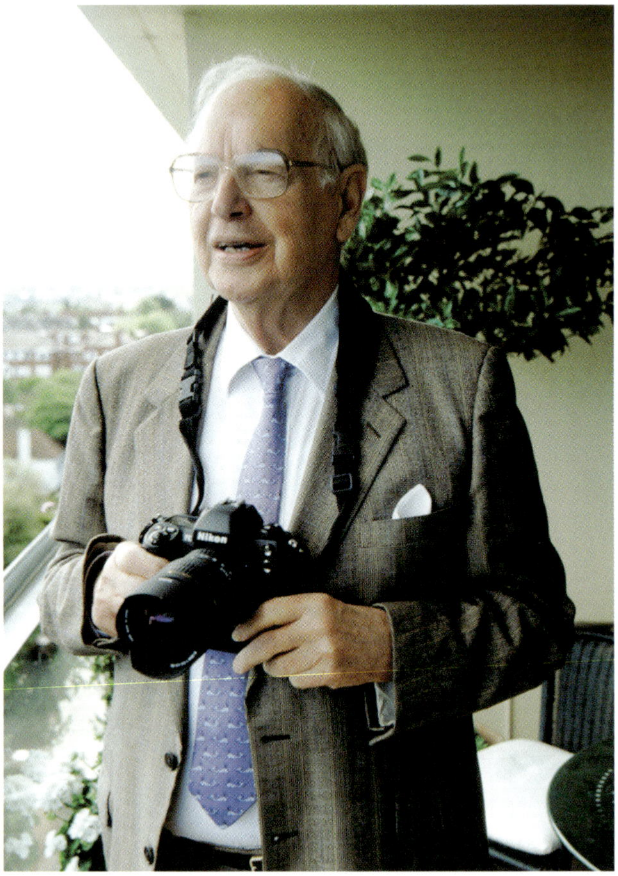

Rt Hon Sir Ninian Stephen KG AK GCMG GCVO KBE

Born in the United Kingdom, educated in the UK, Switzerland and Australia. Sir Ninian was admitted to practise in Victoria as a Barrister and Solicitor in 1949. He was appointed as Queen's Counsel in 1966, to the Victorian Supreme Court bench in 1970 and in 1972 was appointed a Justice of the High Court of Australia.

Sir Ninian served as Governor-General of Australia from 1982 through to 1989. In the time since, he has Chaired various Australian governmental and other bodies.

Melbourne's Parks - "These views are not only my favourites but also my most familiar: the view from our front balcony, overlooking Melbourne's Royal Botanic Gardens, and also the second, a glimpse of the small park which is just across the road from the front door of our block of flats."

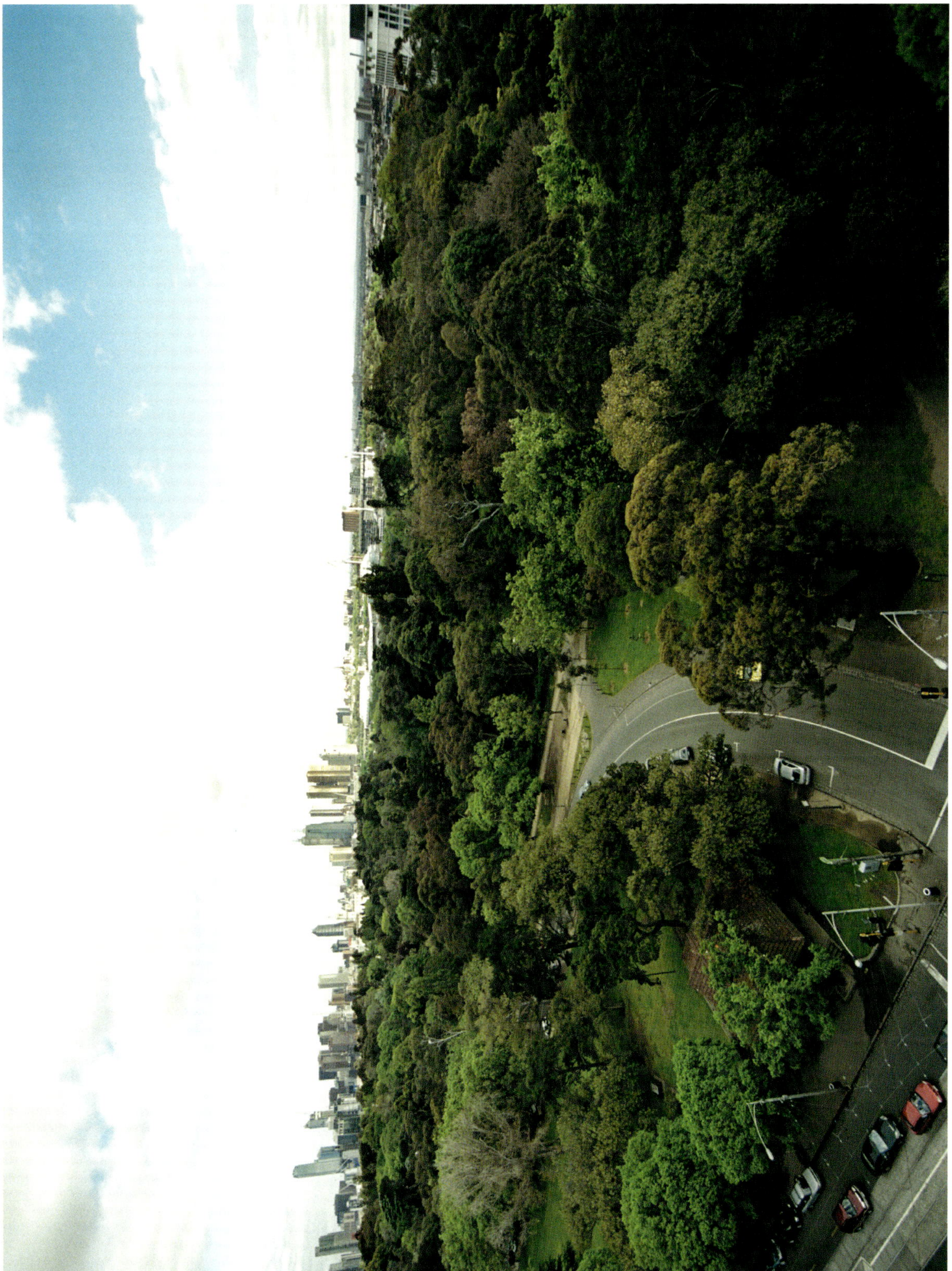

Melbourne and its Parks

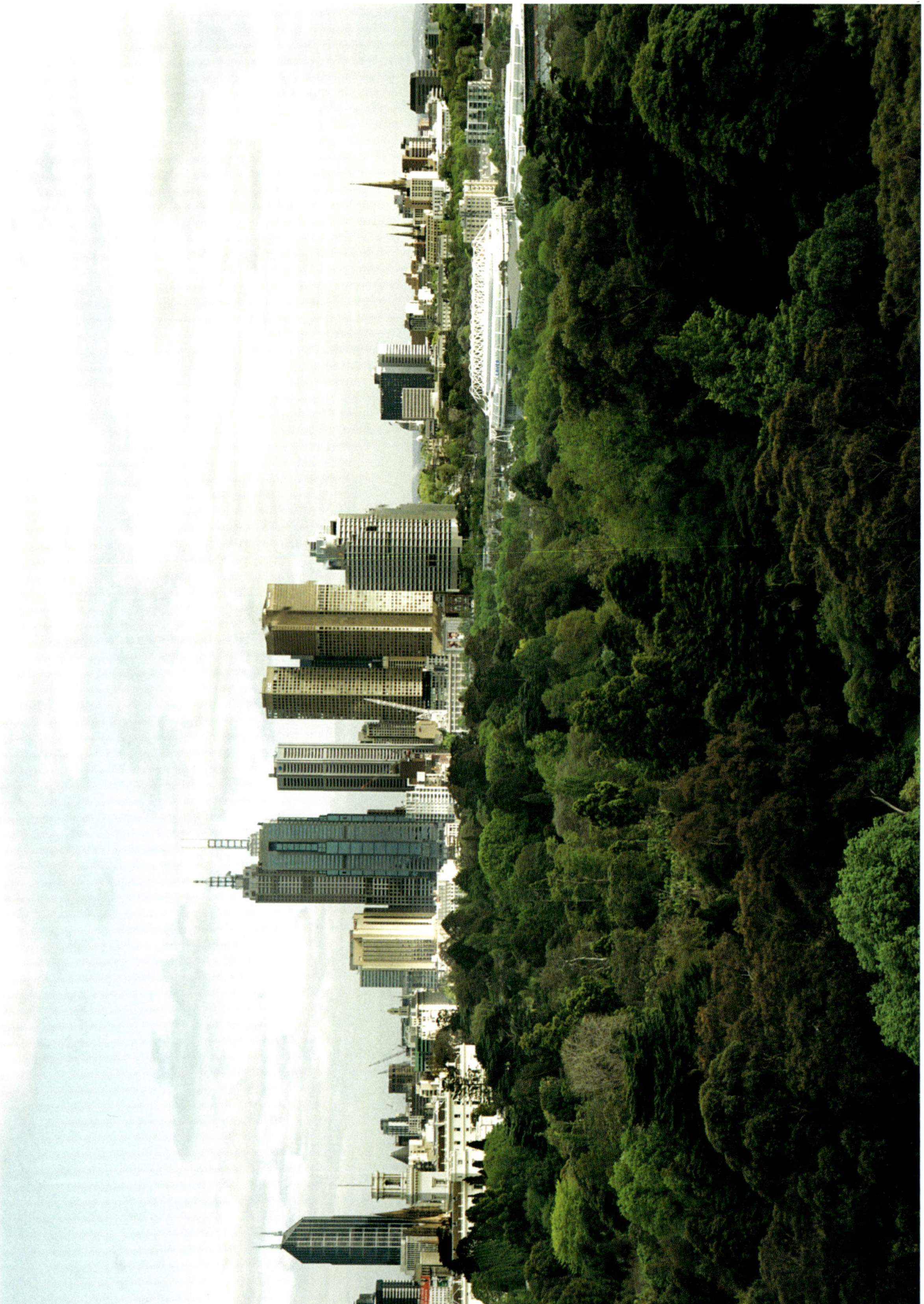

Melbourne with Government House in the foreground

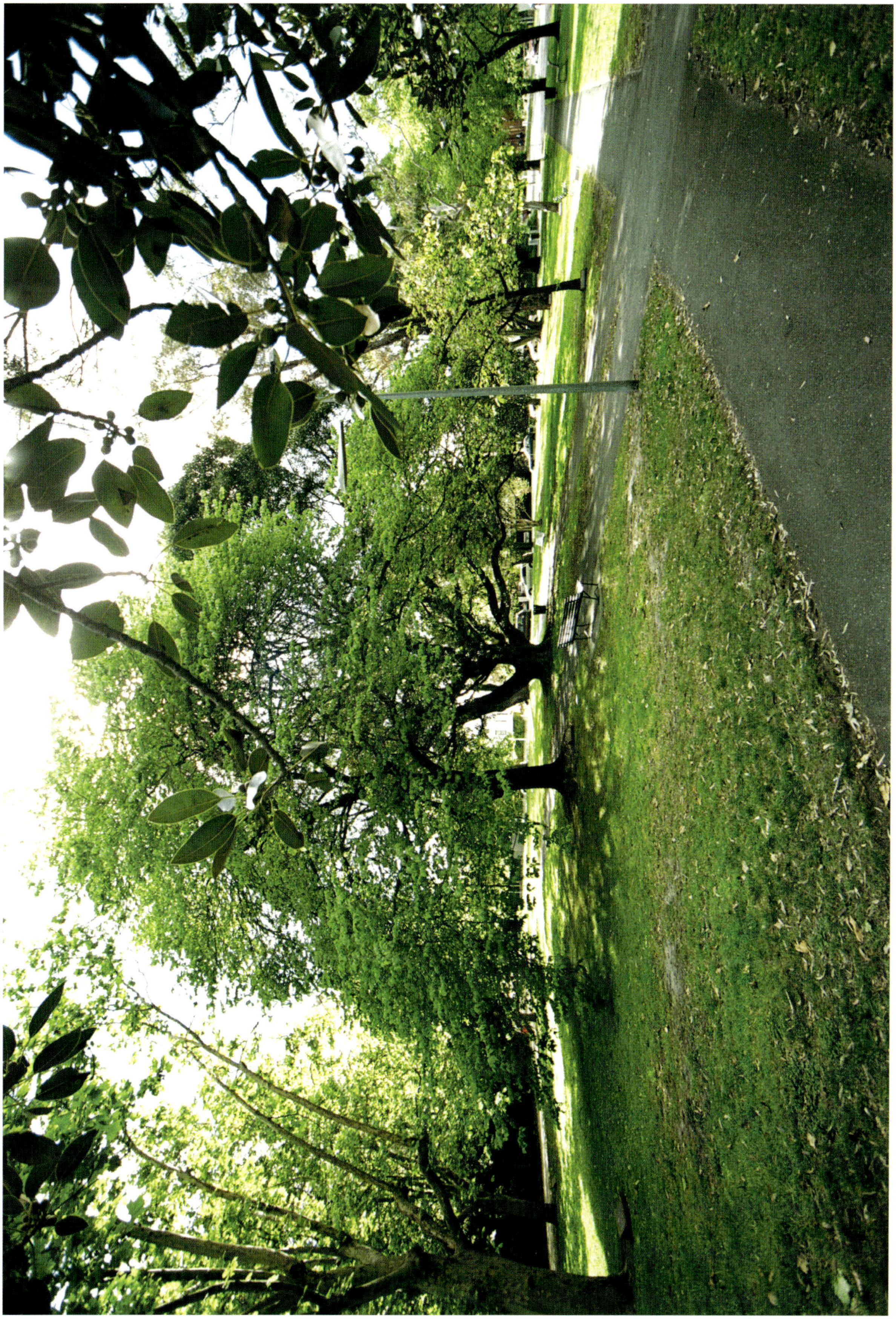

Rotary Memorial Park

Boris M Struk

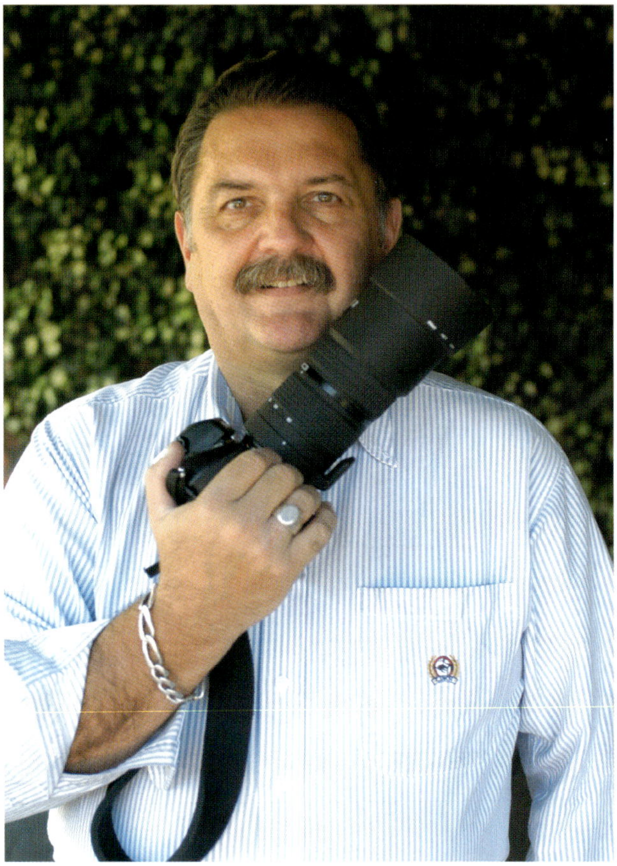

Boris M Struk, Executive Director, Muscular Dystrophy Association.

Following a successful period in Sales and Marketing, Boris established his own consultancy, Business Marketing Service, where he provided services to several major national and international corporations.

Shortly after the birth of Business Marketing Service, Boris' youngest son Ryan, then 3 and a half, was diagnosed to be affected by Duchenne Muscular Dystrophy. Making a commitment to secure sufficient resources to influence the inevitable outcome that Muscular Dystrophy presented, Boris embarked on that journey... initially as a volunteer for the then fledgling MDA, and now as the Executive Director.

In the time since his involvement, Boris' efforts have centered on developing a profile for Muscular Dystrophy and guiding the MDA in the establishment of a wide range of support services for the MD Community, based on his own family circumstance. In 1995, he saw the potential that the "web" had to offer and together with Ryan, established "*The Home of MDA*"... the first MD site on the Internet. To date, this site has received over 7.5 million hits and been cited by many credible institutions and publications.

Boris' reputation for "getting things done", coupled with his strong support for research saw him play a pivotal role in the establishment of the *Melbourne Neuromuscular Research Institute* (MNRI). And more recently, strengthening the position of the Institute by guiding it through the amalgamation with the *Howard Florey Institute,* creating the *National Muscular Dystrophy Research Centre* (NMDRC). His appointment as Board Member of the *Howard Florey Institute* and Director of the NMDRC, further solidifies his commitment to sponsoring and facilitating research.

His passion for photography lay latent for many years while MD took prime carriage for his available time. His concept of *Melbourne's Delights* also lay dormant for several years, with the fear that "someone else would beat me to it"... until now. The *Melbourne's Delights Exhibition* and publication of this book is testimony to the fact that he get things done!

Boris is a Fellow Australian Institute of Company Directors and an Associate Fellow Australian Institute of Management.

Boris is married to Ineke and they have two sons, Leon and Ryan.

Melbourne at Dusk - There are so many beautiful cities in the world, but few have the many different faces that are Melbourne...the streets, lanes and waterways. They all have something to offer, and sometimes from the one place you can witness natures tapestry, peppered with buildings, structures and the Sun playing upon it, reinforcing in one's mind that this is "the world's most liveable city!"

The Maribyrnong River - Originally named the "Saltwater", wends its way through the valleys of the west, formed by volcanic activity eons ago, to near the mouth of the Yarra in Port Phillip Bay. During its course, it passes many of Melbourne's landmarks and bridges. One of these is the Afton Street Bridge, built not so long ago and finally completing a magnificent circuit, from Maribyrnong Road, that one can now complete while walking along both banks of the Maribyrnong River .

Bolte Bridge - It's imposing, it's unique and it is visible from many parts of Melbourne. The view that one gets of Melbourne while driving south is sensational... and ever changing. And the daylight plays such an important role in illuminating the Bolte Bridge with its subtleties of colour, changing from daylight to dusk to dark.

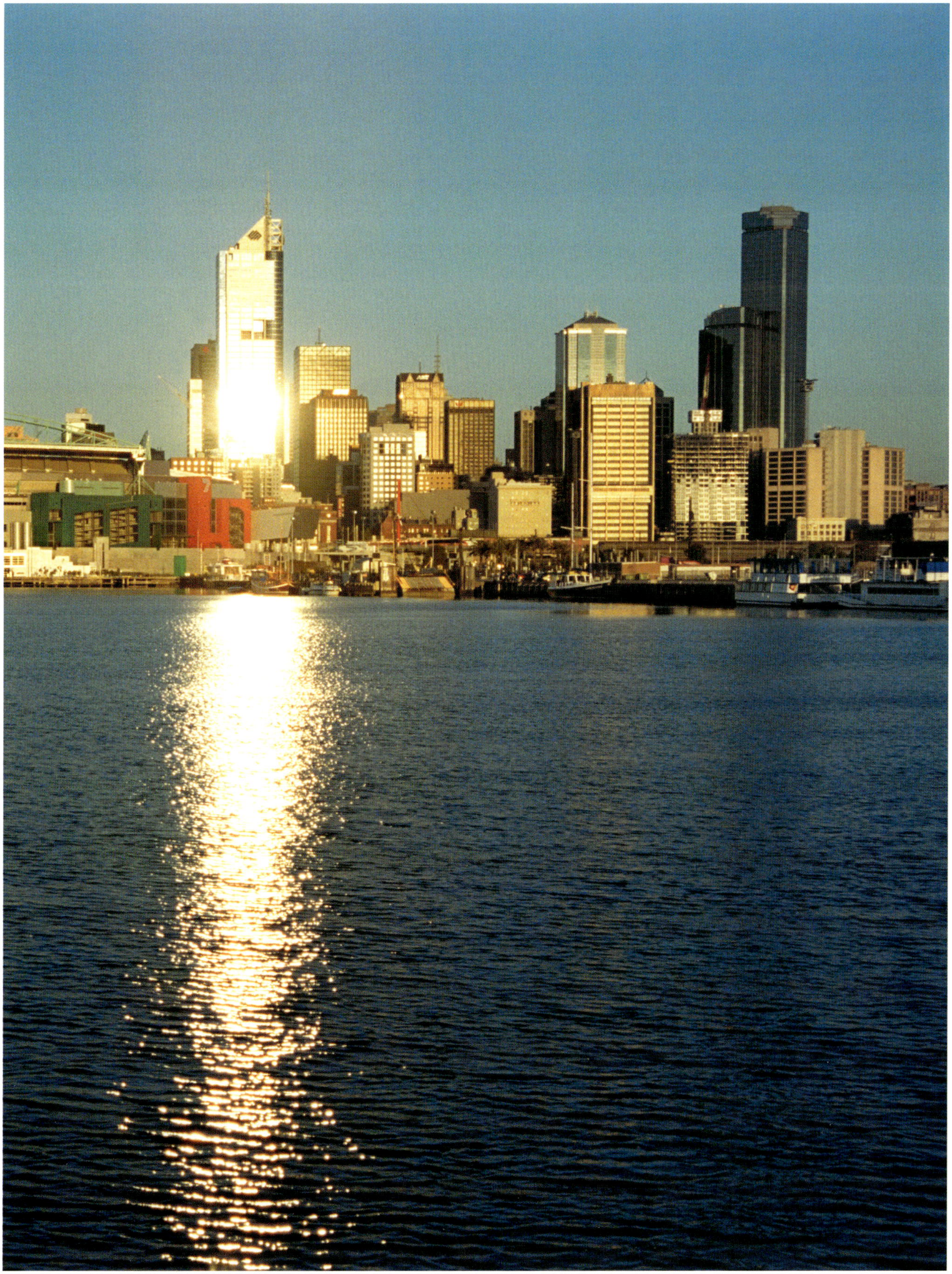

Downtown Melbourne at Dusk

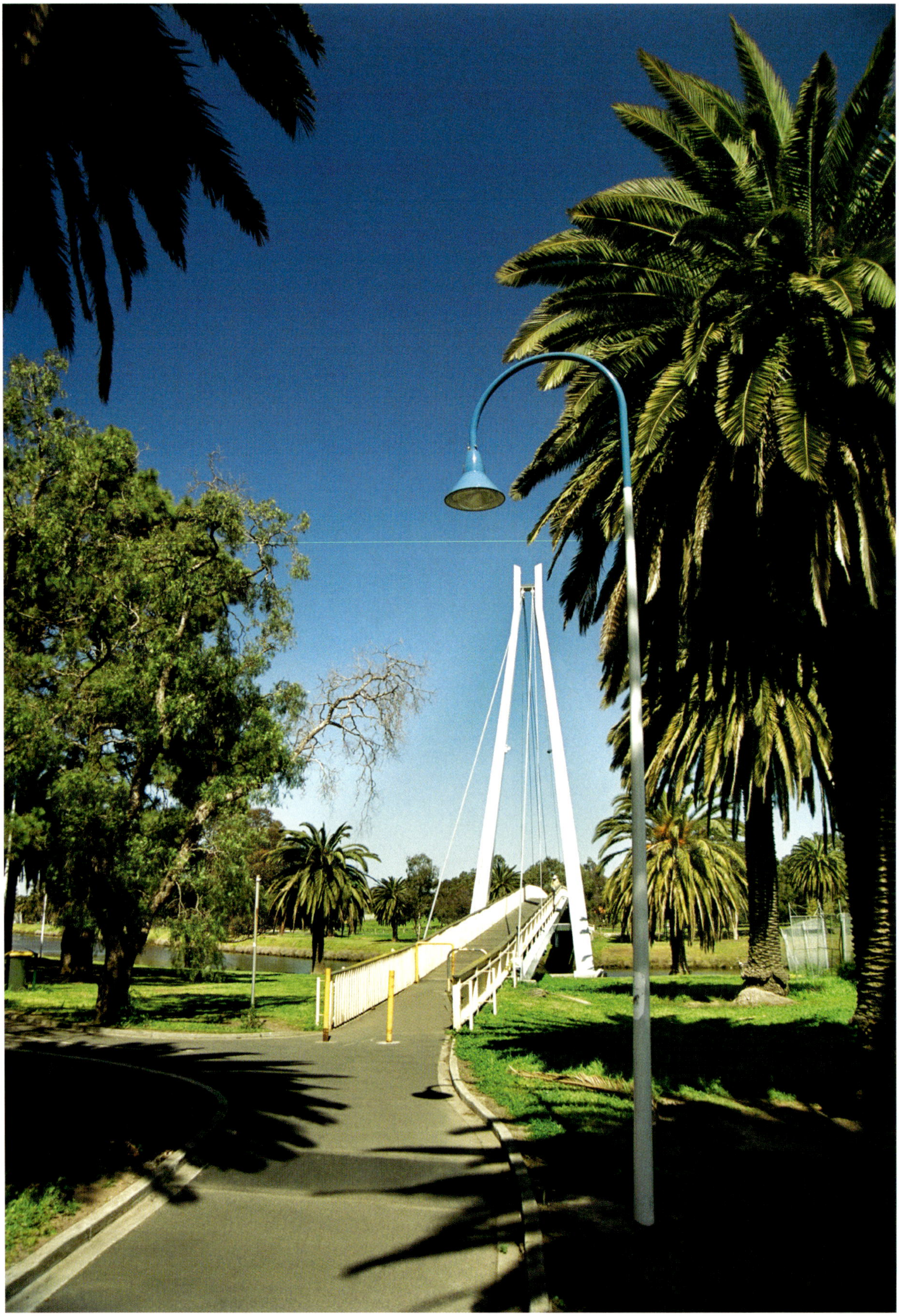

Footbridge over the Maribyrnong River

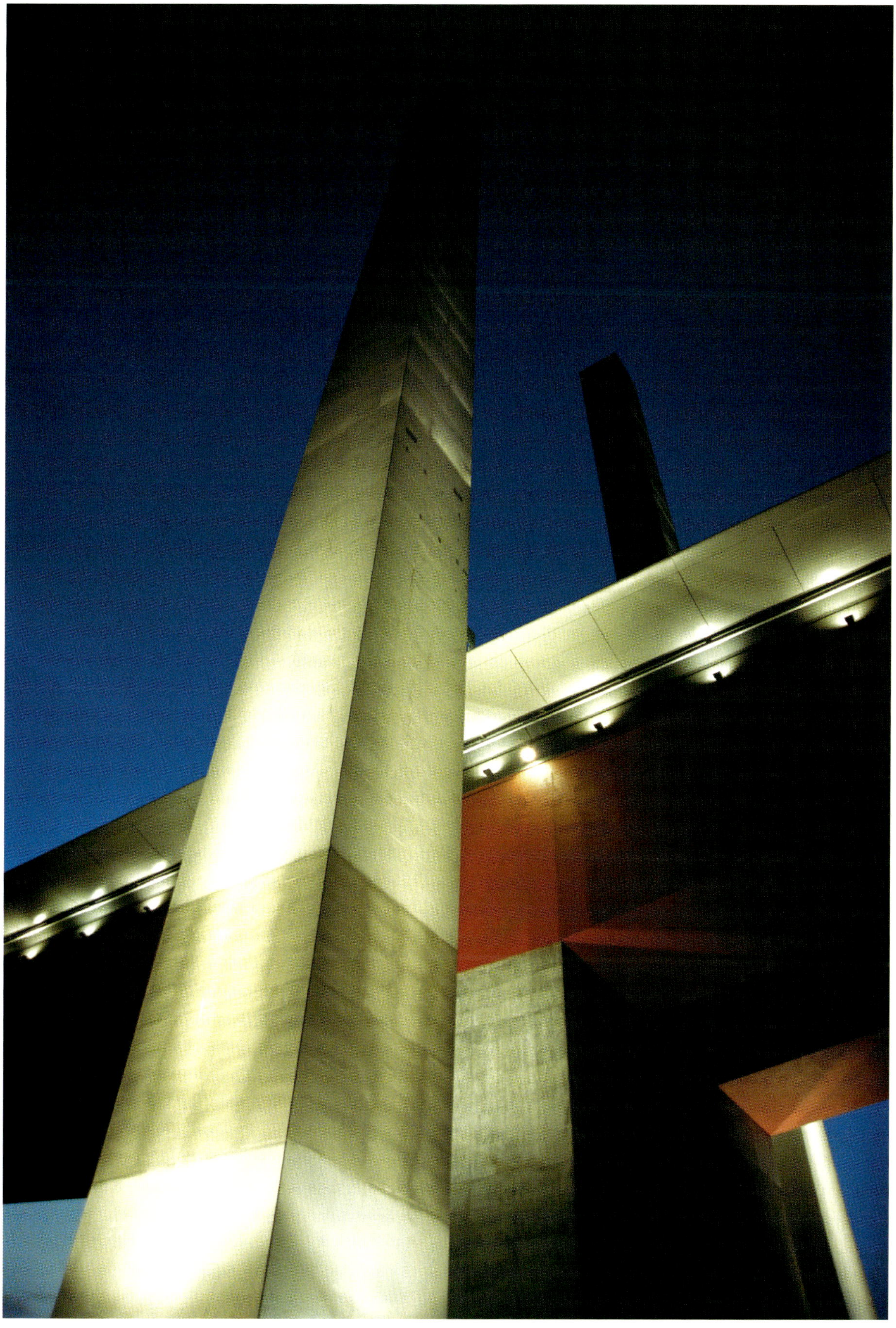

Bolte Bridge

Peter "Grubby" Stubbs

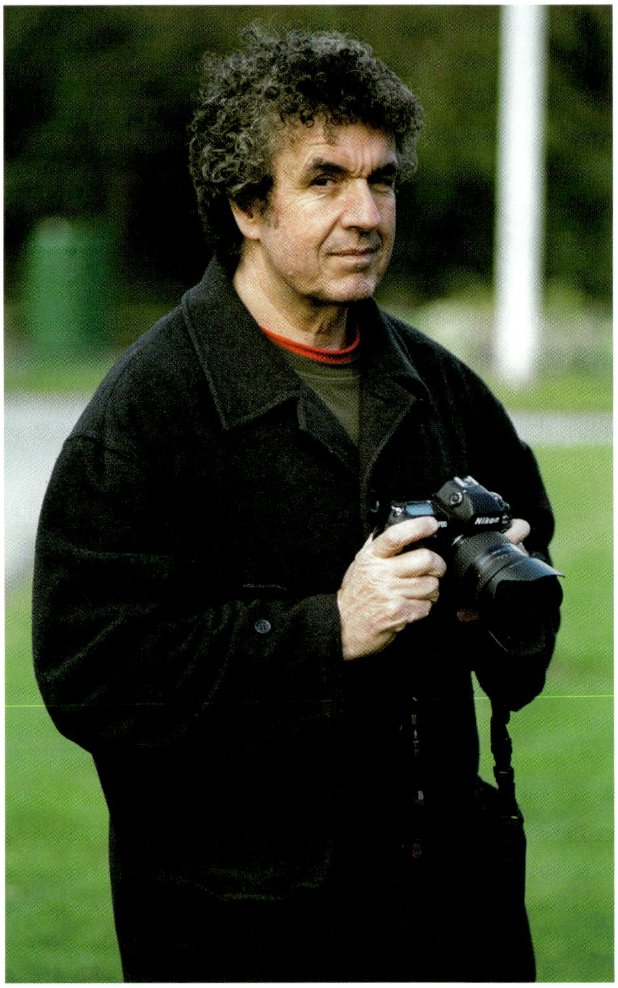

Peter "Grubby" Stubbs, co-host of Melbourne's popular "Grubby and Dee Dee" Breakfast Show on GOLD 104.

He started his working life in the rag trade before kicking off an 18 year career in radio with 3XY's *XY Zoo* in 1985.

Grubby lives with his wife, Jenny, and children Emma, 22 and James, 19, in East Malvern.

He's a lifelong Sydney Swans Football Club supporter, an accomplished bass player, and an avid gym-goer.

Grubby enjoys working on his extensive model railway layout, and spends his spare time at his holiday home on Victoria's south-west coast.

Hedgeley Dene Gardens - "I love the Hedgeley Dene Gardens. Nobody knows that they're here. You go round a corner, go down a lane and all of a sudden... there you are!

I love the lake, the little bridges and the open spaces, the Collins Street lamps and the magnificent trees.

It still causes me great amusement that while attending nearby Korowa Anglican Girls School, my wife did cross-country running here. Pretty tough on the girls!

We walk our dogs here every day."

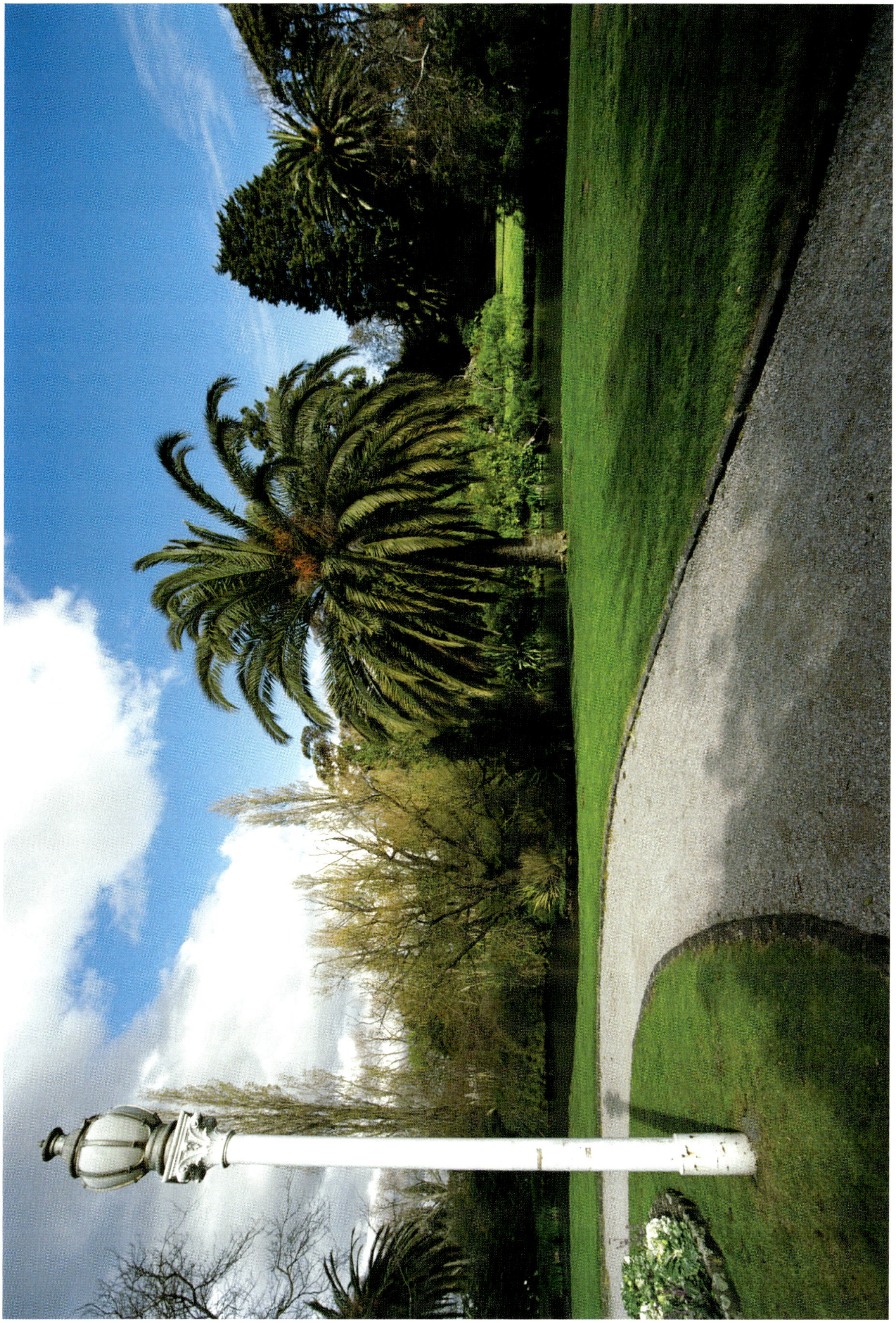

Hedgeley Dene Gardens

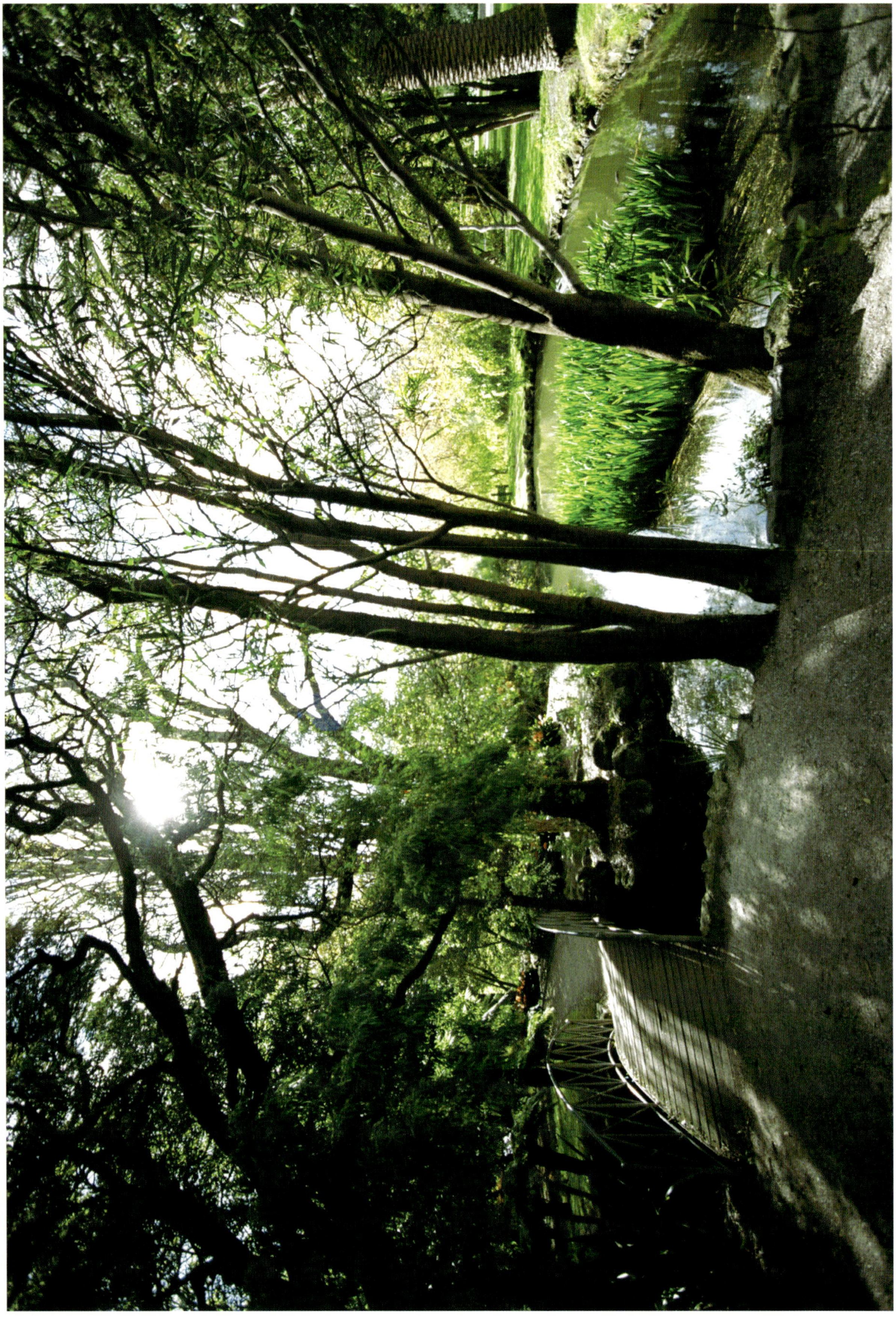

Hedgeley Dene Gardens

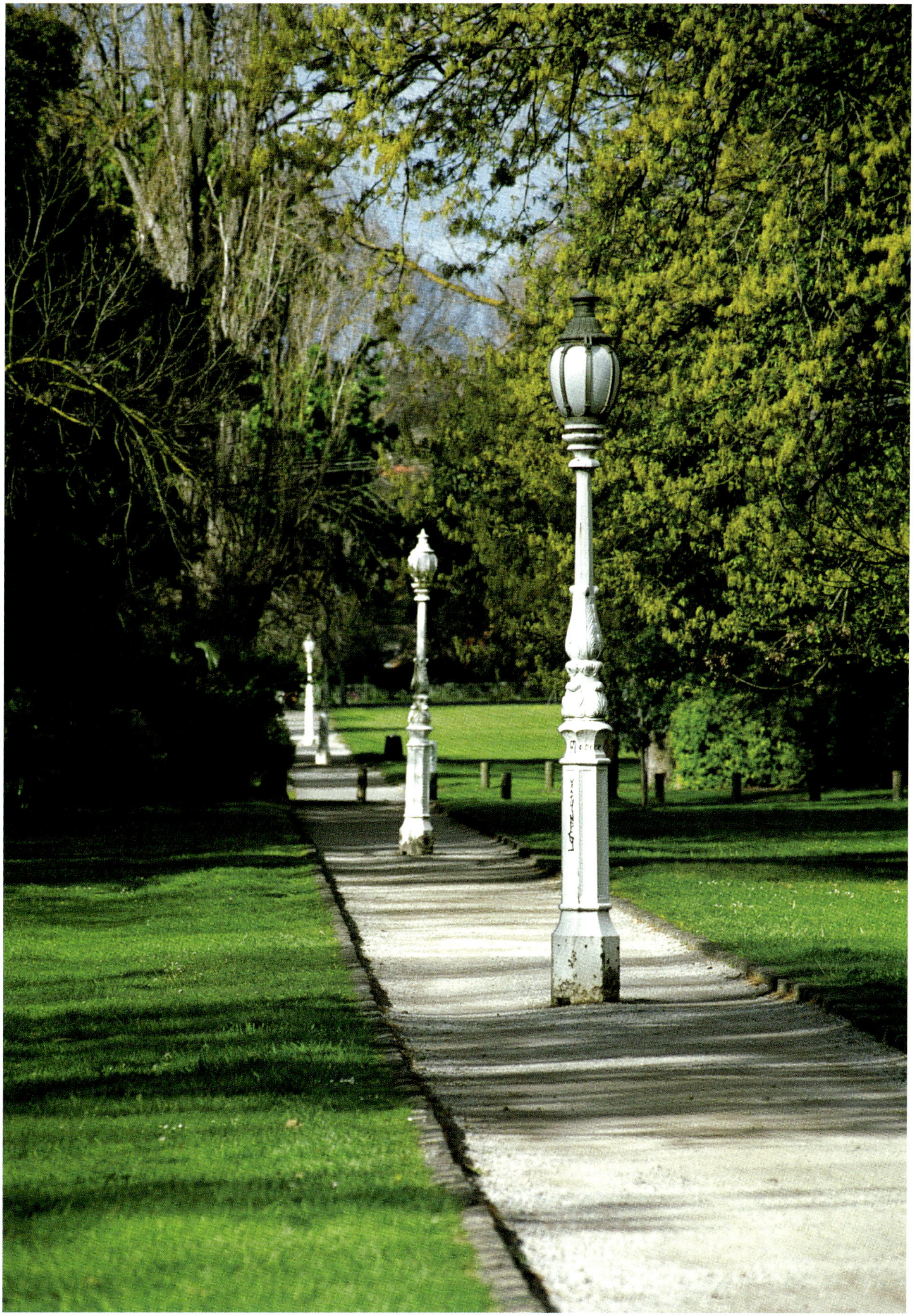

Hedgeley Dene Gardens

Glenn Wheatley

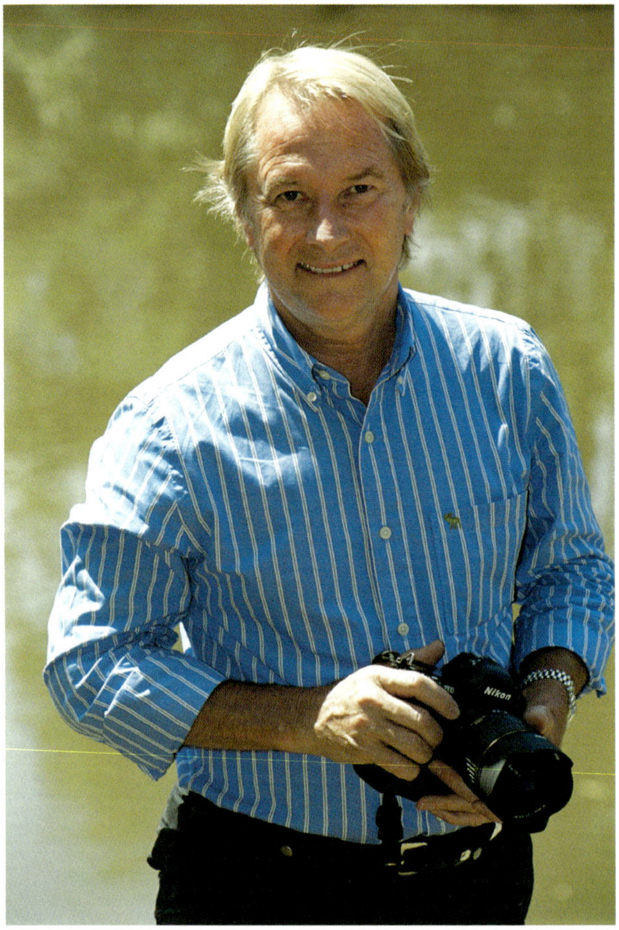

Glenn Wheatley. Glenn's colourful career has centred predominantly around the music industry but has expanded over the years to encompass sport, film, television and radio. From the band, Masters Apprentices' flamboyant bass guitarist, Wheatley went on to play a pivotal role in the Australian contemporary music business managing and promoting Australian artists locally and overseas including Little River Band, Australian Crawl, John Farnham and Delta Goodrem. Glenn's major business involvement now centres on the merged activities of TalentWorks, which allows him to focus his expertise in artist and sports management, music recording and publishing, tour promotion and event management.

Yarra River, Abbotsford - "I am not a native of Melbourne. I was born and raised in Brisbane and used to make jokes about Melbourne's Yarra River. But now that Melbourne has become home, I have grown to love the Yarra.
This is the view I get every day now from my office. I now spend a lot of my day on the phone by the banks of the Yarra, and consider myself a lucky man to be able to work in these surroundings. It is my favourite part of Melbourne and I get to do this every day."

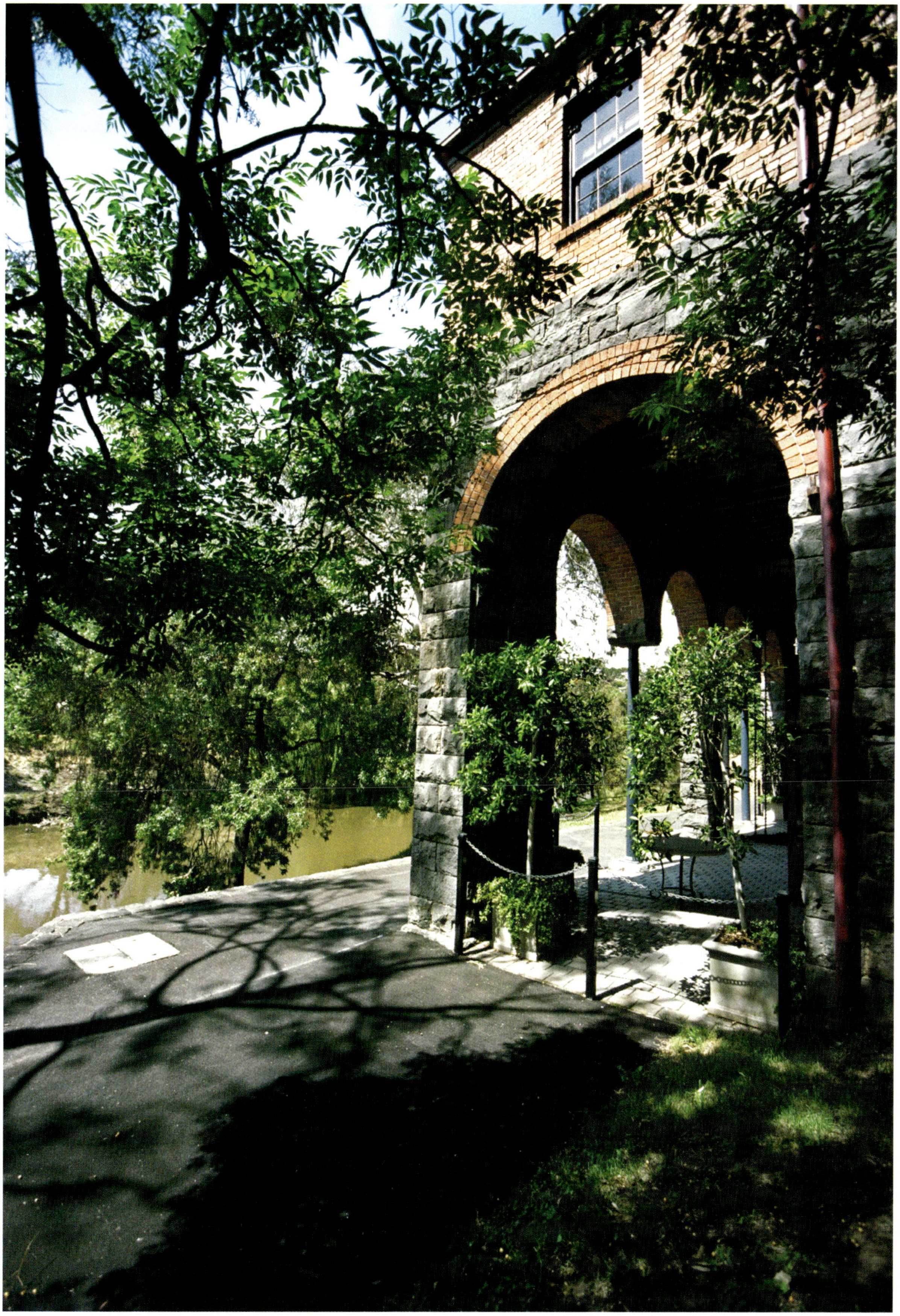
TalentWorks on the Yarra at Abbotsford (The old Abbots Brewery site)

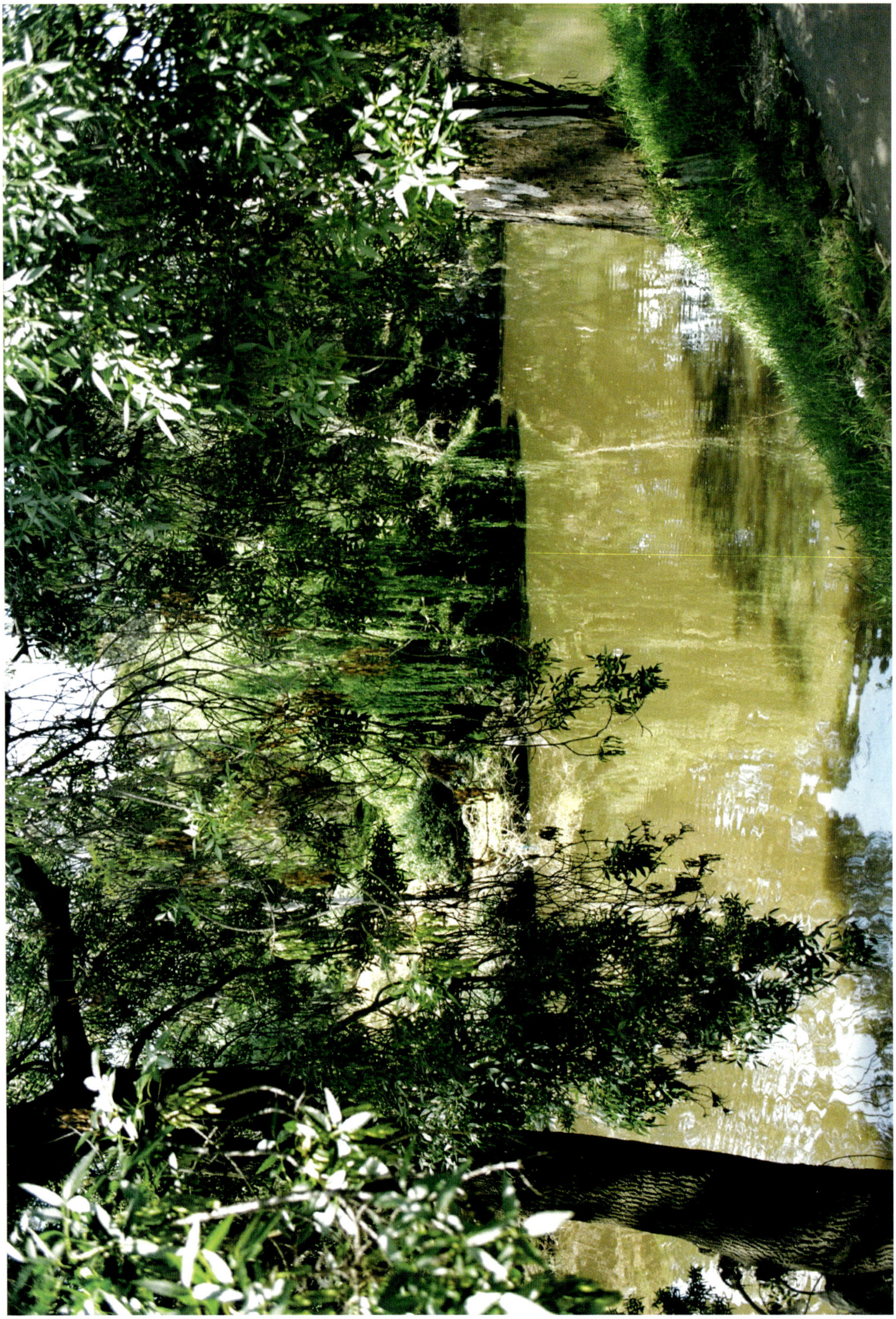

The Yarra from "My office"

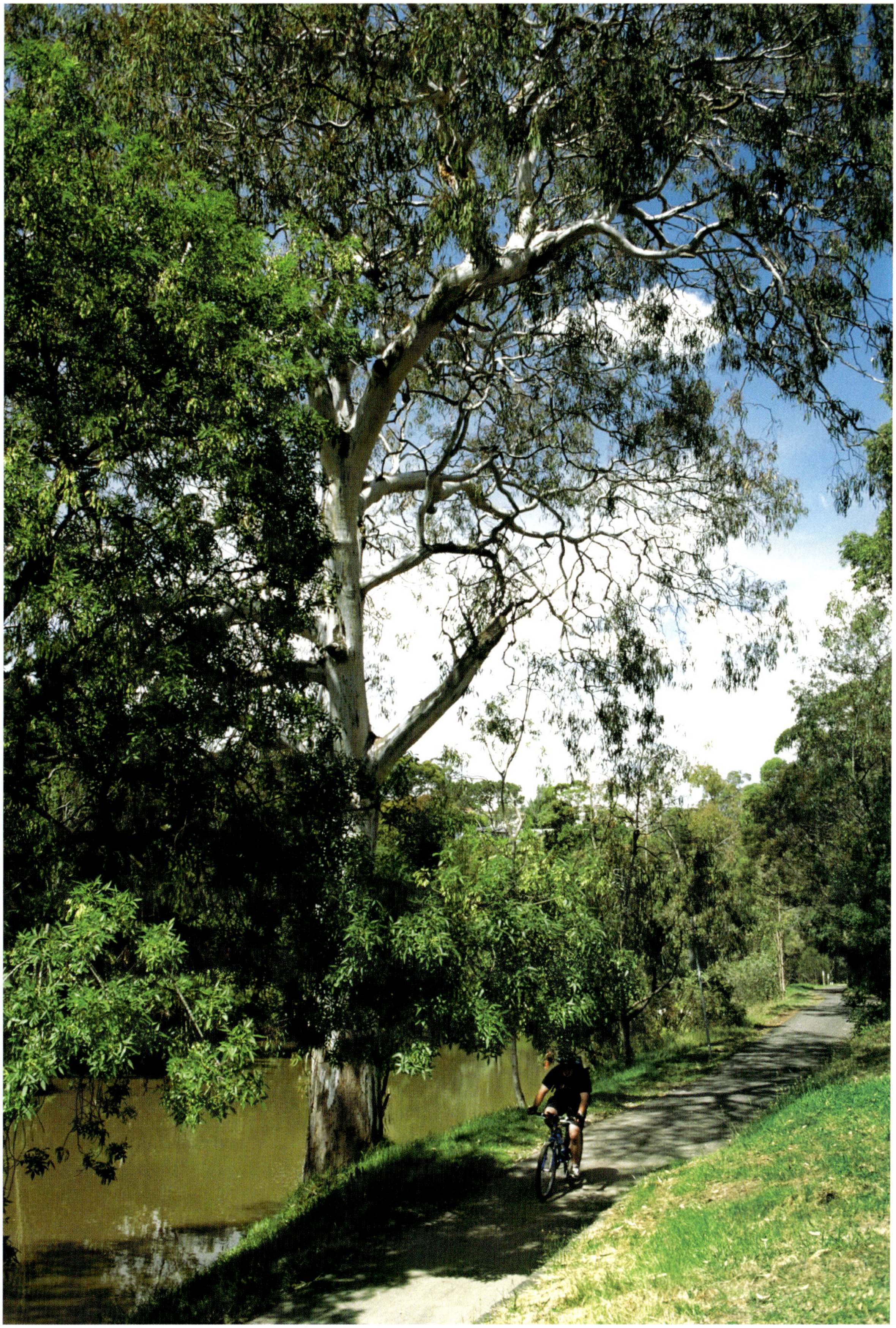

Michael Wooldridge

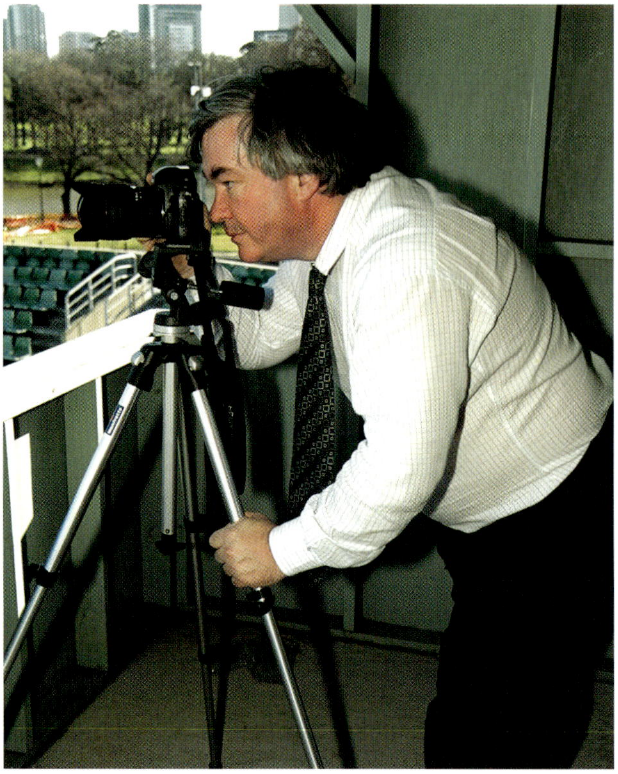

Hon Dr Michael Wooldridge, was Australia's Federal Health Minister from 1996 to 2001. He is currently Chairman of Neurosciences Australia and has a strong and passionate commitment to research in the neuroscience area.

Prior to entering politics he worked as a medical practitioner, with his basic training being in science.

National Tennis Centre - I grew up in a tennis environment, with my parents having met on the international tennis circuit, their circle of friends including many well known personalities in tennis in the 1950s. Much to my parents' disappointment, the talent didn't pass to any of their four children, so an avalanche of tennis memorabilia is waiting to descend on the first grandchild with any aptitude!

Melbourne is the home of Australian tennis and, over nearly 100 years, more Davis Cup finals have been held here than in any other city on the globe.

The National Tennis Centre is a sensational facility, so close to town and so brilliantly suited to the game.

I chose the Margaret Court arena as I remember very well watching Margaret Smith (as she was then known) at Grace Park and Kooyong, and her signature was the first entry in an autograph book I received for my eighth birthday. She was a sensational ambassador for tennis, towards the end of an era that produced so many great players.

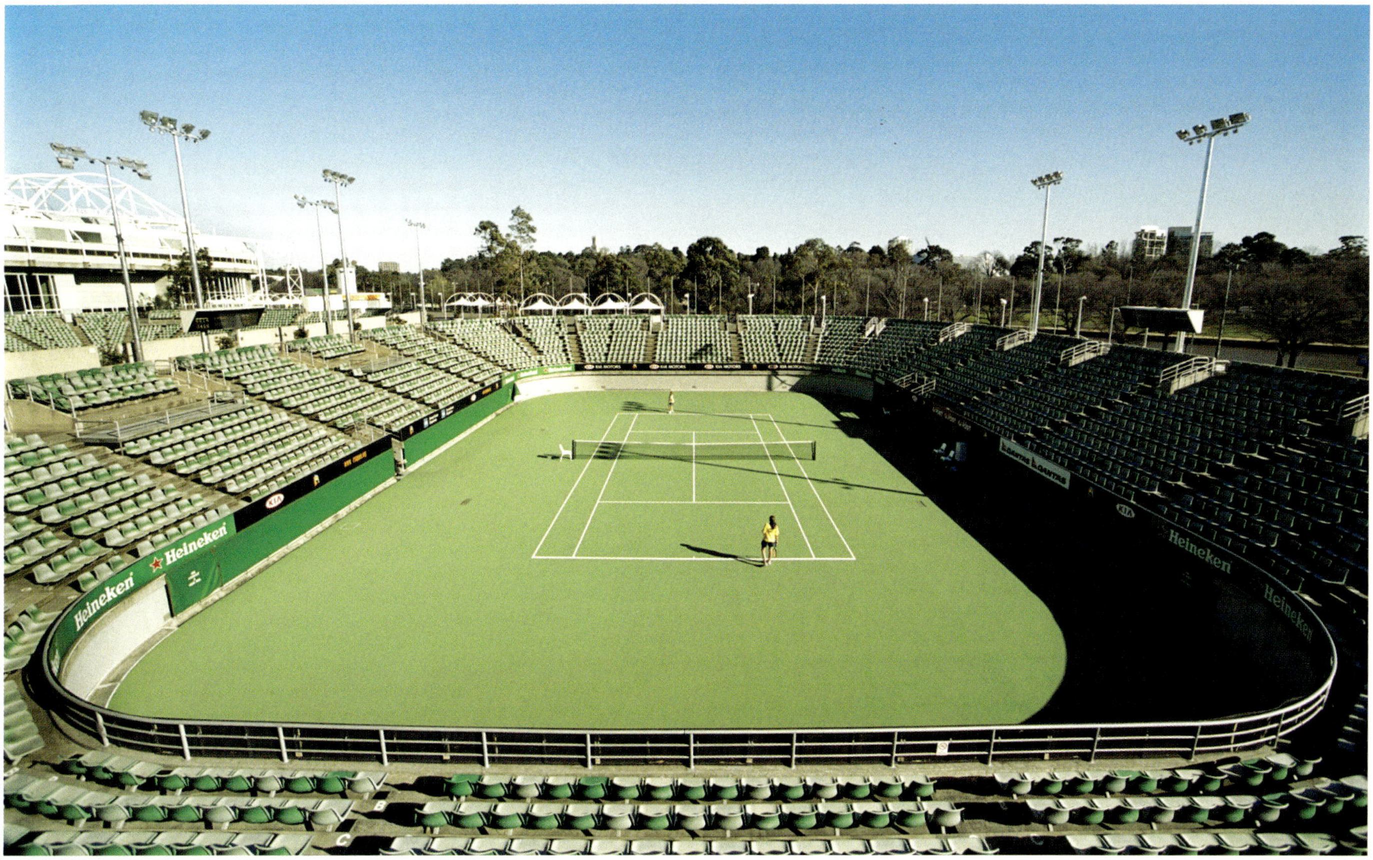

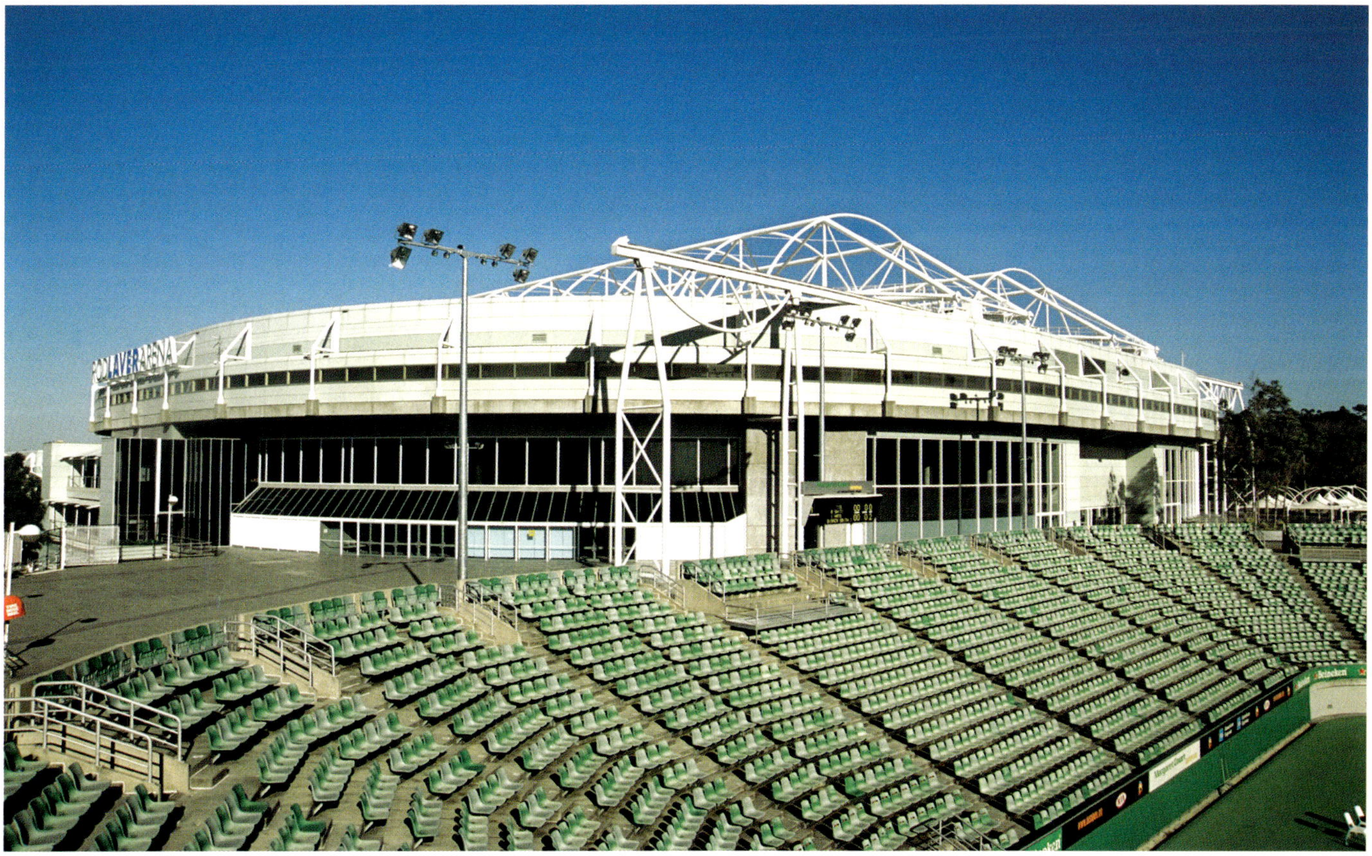

National Tennis Centre

Melbourne's Delights

Acknowledgements

The **M**elbourne's **D**elights project turned into reality with the support of the contributing photographers, who were willing to give of their time and to share that "special place." They made it happen!

Major sponsors also contributed to the realisation of this complex project.

Finally, technical assistance and the portrait photography of most of the contributing celebrity photographers was provided by Leon Struk of **www.LMS-Images.com**.

For more than 100 years, Kodak has been at the forefront of the photographic industry in Australia, and the Asia Pacific. Kodak manufactures and markets photographic and multimedia products and services, supplying both commercial and imaging needs of customers.

Bond Imaging is a proud sponsor of the *Melbourne's Delights Exhibition.* Bond Imaging was responsible for the high resolution scanning, photographic prepress and Lambda digital photographic printing of Exhibition images. All images were printed onto Kodak Professional sheen N-surface digital paper up to 20x30" in size.

Bond Imaging has spent over thirty years cementing our position as one of Australia's leading photographic, display and signage companies. Bond Imaging operates a sophisticated digital services division, adopting the most advanced systems for high resolution scanning, retouching and prepress.

MANFROTTO, who is proud to support the Muscular Dystrophy Association, is an international leader in design and manufacture of camera and lighting support systems. Our products range from camera tripods and heads for still photography, video and film, through lighting stands, clamps, Autopole®, booms, ceiling light rigs, motorised background supports and camera remote-control units, and much more besides.
Manfrotto - the only support your creativity needs

Images for the Melbourne's Delights Exhibition and this book were captured using: Nikon F5, F100 and D100 cameras. The following Nikkor lenses were used: 15-30, 24-85, 35-70, ED 80-200 2.8, VR 80-400.

FOSTER'S GROUP

FED. SQ.

adams print

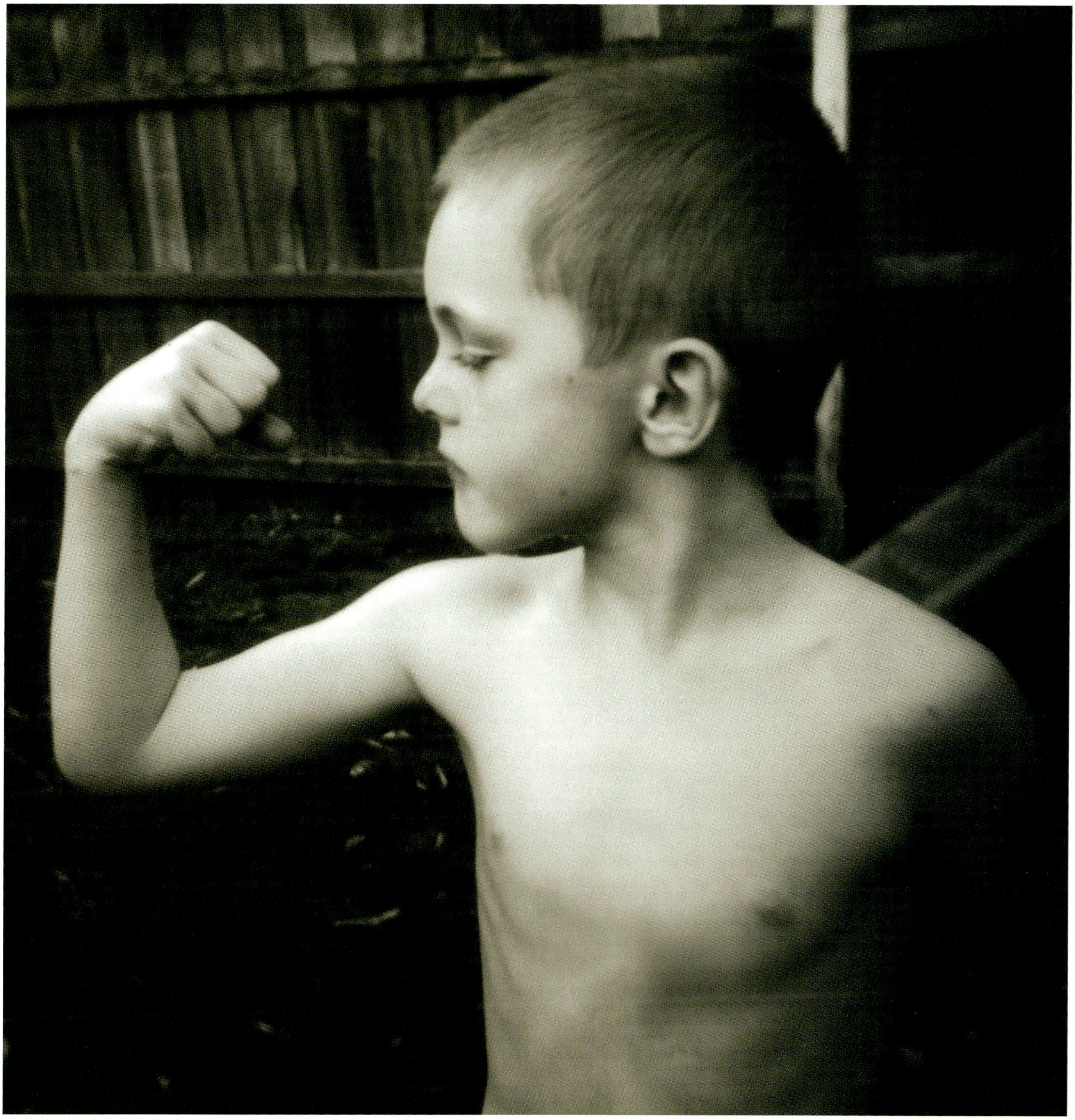